Dedication

To my Quartet: Aneika, Koveil, Kyric, and Vicia

MINORITY TECH

MINORITY TECH

Journaling Through Blackness and Technology

ANJUAN SIMMONS

Jannua Media
a division of Jannua Multiverse LLC | Houston, TX

Copyright

Why I Wrote This Book

I began blogging in 2007 for the sole purpose of documenting my thoughts. It became a way for me to chronicle my perspectives and ideas about life. Over time, it became a living document of my mind. As an African-American technologist, I have experienced the highs of flying around the world implementing amazing software solutions, staying in great hotels, and eating at fine restaurants. I have also experienced the lows of being questioned simply because of the color of my skin. This book (and the blog from which it came) chronicles my life between those two extremes.

My blog runs on a server that I hope is regularly backed up and maintained. However, what if some catastrophic event like a massive solar flare or an EMP attack erased the digital bits that make up my blog? As an engineer, I'm trained to consider redundant systems so I thought that turning my blog into a book would at least protect it from digital harm. Now, I just have to hope that my house doesn't burn down . . .

I also wanted to preserve my thoughts for my children. Many of the concepts I cover in my blog like advanced technology, racism, sexuality, and political activism are too advanced for their young minds (at least at the time I'm writing this). However, they will grow up one day and perhaps wonder, "How did Dad react to the events of his time?" After all, I have wondered the same thing about my own father.

Also, I wanted to create a source book for people with technology questions. I've always enjoyed technology Q&A columns and books, and I've covered some great topics over the years.

Finally, I was recently approached for my permission to allow one of my blog posts to be included in a printed book. This gave me a greater appreciation for the value that others may place on my blog content. I thought, "If there's a book that wants to use my blog's content, why don't I turn my blog into a book?" So, I have done just that. I've curated, organized, and edited the best posts from my blog, and I'm delighted to share with you the book that has resulted from that effort.

How to Read This Book

Keep in mind that this book is a series of articles I wrote on my blog over a period of several years. I had no idea that I would turn those blog posts into a book at the time, but I have structured the content around the major themes of my life. Those themes are the African-American male experience, technology, and diversity.

The majority of the posts in this book are ordered in chronological order with the earlier posts appearing first. However, I did group a few posts by subject when I thought it was necessary.

I used the titles from my blog for each entry in this book, and I preserved the date and time they were published beneath the title of each post.

I tried to keep the body of the posts in their original form, but I did edit as many mistakes as I could find. Also, I put an "Author's Note" in italics before any post that I thought needed further explanation or context.

I did not edit any comments left on my blog because I wanted to preserve the words left by others exactly as they wrote them. However, I did remove the email addresses of the people who left comments in order to protect their privacy. Keep in mind that, like Twitter and Facebook feeds, the comments are listed in the order they were made with the latest ones at the top. However, there are a few posts that list the comments in reverse order due to changes in the blogging software I used.

Since hyperlinks don't work in the print version of this book, I added footnotes to the target addresses for each URL.

Table of Contents

PART 1 – EMBRACING MY BLACKNESS

Like many African-Americans, I understood the nature of my blackness at an early age. Growing up in Texas, I vividly remember certain kids who hurled racial slurs at me (even before they got to know me). This section covers the blog posts I wrote about my experiences as an African-American and how I reacted to various events that happened between 2007 and 2013.

Being Black in America, particularly a Black male, is a reality that is difficult to understand unless it is experienced. Most famous Black men are known for physical qualities like the athleticism of Michael Jordan or the fighting skills of Floyd Mayweather. While physical qualities are great to have, they are difficult to possess as the defining quality of the ethnic group to which one belongs. First, unless a Black man is in the top .01% of people who are physically gifted enough to be a professional athlete, it is difficult to have a career based on athleticism or strength. Second, true power, at least in the modern world, is gained through mental and intellectual strength. There are far more opportunities for those who know how to use their brains than those who simply have strong bodies.

The focus on the physical qualities of Black men must also be examined against the backdrop of how we're portrayed in the media. Those portrayals are often stereotypical characters like the streetwise thug or the inarticulate man of the ghetto. The media doesn't go much deeper than portraying Black men as Pimps or as Pootie Tang.

I've always been an intellectual so sports and the media provided no help for understanding who I was as a Black man. I had to find that out through thought, experience, and observation.

These posts covered my desire to understand the word "nigger" (despite the horribleness of the word), lessons I picked up travelling around the world, a code of conduct for Black Men (to save us from our circumstances and from ourselves), explaining affirmative action (since so many people don't understand it), how African-Americans can work to solve our problems, what I learned from Trayvon Martin (the Emmett Till of our time), and the realization that I will have to teach my children, as my parents taught me, how to embrace their own blackness in a culture that often fears it.

1

A Nigger Primer*

11/04/2007 08:15:06 PM

AUTHOR'S NOTE: Yes, one of the first blog posts I wrote was about the word nigger. It's a word that I've been called, and it's a word I've heard other people, of all skin colors, say. Very few people have taken the time to understand its origins. The word nigger, unfortunately, is a key part of the Black experience in America, and this post is my attempt to understand it.

The use of the term nigger has brought down yet another public figure. Duane "Dog" Chapman[1] effectively ended his career when he was recorded using the word nigger in reference to his son's girlfriend. He joins comedian Michael Richards (Seinfeld's Kramer)[2], professional celebrity Paris Hilton[3], comedian Andy Dick[4], and Larimer County Republican Party Chairman Ed Haynes[5], in the group of famous (or at least public) people whose use of the word nigger in the past year has been discovered and broadcast by the media. Also, while he did not use the word nigger, shock jock Don Imus[6] called female college basketball players "nappy headed ho's" which has the same negative racial connotation as nigger. Some of these famous people experienced little or no repercussions. For example, few even know about Paris Hilton's or Andy Dick's use of the term. However, others, such as Michael Richards, suffered immediate and severe negative news coverage. Imus and Haynes either resigned or lost their jobs which will probably be the fate of Chapman.

------

[1] http://www.reuters.com/article/mediaNews/idUSN0235922720071102

[2] http://www.tmz.com/2006/11/20/kramers-racist-tirade-caught-on-tape/

[3] http://www.eurweb.com/story/eur31208.cfm

[4] http://www.helium.com/tm/358863/quite-often-incident-focussed

[5] http://colorado.mediamatters.org/items/200710250004

[6] http://www.reuters.com/article/mediaNews/idUSWEN229420071101

These incidents lead me to believe two things. First, quite a few white people use the word nigger when referring to black people in private conversation. Now, I am sure that MANY white people NEVER use the word. I know a large number of good decent white people who I greatly respect and trust. However, the number of high profile white people being caught using the term suggests that at least a significant percentage do use the word. Second, a guide needs to be produced to help white people avoid the potentially severe penalties for being outed as a user of the term. While I cannot do anything about the former, I am attempting to provide the latter through this blog post.

What makes me qualified to write such a guide? First, for those who do not know me personally, I am an African-American man. That puts me in the demographic that is most harmed by the racist thinking that often accompanies the use of nigger by non-blacks. It also puts me in the group that most often claims the right to use in word in a non-negative (and even positive way). Second, I do not use the word nigger in conversation. Let me re-emphasize that. I NEVER use the word nigger because I was raised to consider it a bad word, if not the worst of words. So, although I can potentially be most harmed by the word, I do not assert a special right to "reclaim the word" which is what many targets of racial slurs do (more on that later). Therefore, I think that I can be objective in discussing the use of nigger in ways that many cannot.

The etymological origin of nigger can be traced to the Spanish word *negro* and the French word *nègre* which both ultimately descend from the Latin word *nigrum*. Both of these words translate to the English word "black" which is, of course, a color. Just as dark skinned people are called "black people" today without offense, nigger was used inoffensively as a way to refer to black skinned people in the seventeenth and eighteenth centuries. However, the negative connotation of the term began to emerge as the condition of black people began to decline as they progressed through hard centuries of American slavery. By the nineteenth century, the word had become the pejorative most view it as today, especially in the Southern States of America. To be called a nigger communicated all of the stereotypical characteristics of black slaves: lazy, stupid, untrustworthy, licentious, and violent. The word even conveyed the idea that black people were sub-human and not much better than animals. Few can argue against the fact that, in the modern era, nigger is an extremely demeaning and

3

offensive word.

Complicating the understanding of nigger by white people is the use of the word (often pronounced "nigga") by black people when referring to other black people, even going so far as to use it as a term of endearment. This observation is often used by white people caught using the term to defend themselves saying that they thought it was an acceptable way to refer to black people based on its use by black people. This is historically ironic, due to the fact that black slaves were encouraged by their white masters to call each other nigger as a sign of submission. If a black slave referred to another black slave by such a derogatory and hateful term, then that communicated an acceptance of the negative and dehumanizing assessment conveyed by the word by both the slave who used the term as well as the slave to which he was referring. Given the fact that black slaves vastly outnumbered white people on most plantations, it was expedient for slave masters to indoctrinate their "property" with feelings of inferiority and submission. Slave on slave use of the word nigger reinforced this message and put white people at ease. The extent of this brainwashing can be seen today in the mouths of black people and is often found in rap lyrics. In fact, famous rapper Nas[7] plans to soon release an album titled *Nigger*. Obviously, the power of white slave masters continues to reach deep into the psyche of the descendants of black slaves. Rappers like Nas and many members of black celebrity culture defend the use of nigger by claiming that they want to take power away from the word by using it themselves. I question this for historical and contemporary reasons. First, black people calling each other nigger caters to the historical desire of some white people to keep black people in oppression and slavery. Second, it plays into the desire of many modern white people to see black people struggle against each other. If we are too busy demeaning each other, than less effort is needed to hinder the progress of black people which is often played out via psychological methods since laws prohibit open discrimination.

So, what is a white person to do? First, I hope this post has provided historical insight into the use of a word that I believe many white people probably use but never bother to research. Second, white people should understand that black use of nigger when referring to other blacks is usually

---

[7] http://www.mtv.com/news/articles/1573280/20071101/nas.jhtml

based on similar ignorance of the origin of the term. In light of this, I ask that white people realize that nigger is not a term that any respectable person should use and excise it and other racial slurs from their vocabulary. If you never use the word, you don't have to worry about losing your job or being exposed on TMZ.com[8] as a closet racist. Finally, I request that the use of nigger within the black community be seen as one of many issues that African-Americans have to work out as we continue to recover from brutal centuries of slavery in this country. The Emancipation Proclamation (which, actually, did not free any slaves since it only applied to rebel states) may be been issued in 1862, but mental and social freedom from slavery is not so easily obtained.

*Primer (textbook) A textbook formerly used in primary education (often pronounced "primmer" in General American) to teach the alphabet and other basic concepts (definition taken from Wikipedia[9])

Comments

AUTHOR: Nelson Webber
URL: http://wnelweb.blogspot.com/
DATE: 11/05/2007 02:41:33 PM

Thank-you for this thoughtful, historical and insightful post.

There are several points (maybe not points actually, more like observations and personal revelations) I'd like to make concerning this topic.

I grew up in central Virginia. When I was born, segregation was still the order of the day. I do not recall encountering another child of a different color from my own until about 5th or sixth grade, when enforced busing was introduced in my city. By that time, my prejudices, such as they were, were pretty much in place. I was not raised to believe that blacks were inferior to whites, just that they were 'different' from whites. I believe my

---

[8] http://www.tmz.com/

[9] http://en.wikipedia.org/wiki/Main_Page

parents at that time would not have considered themselves to be racists. In retrospect, many of theirs views (which were passed on to me) were racist. Still, as a child, I had no real animosity towards blacks that I recall. One of my fondest childhood memories is of a lovely woman who worked for my parents as a maid. She also helped raise me and I loved her dearly. I could no more have associated the word nigger with her than I could have with my own mother.

I was also raised to believe that nigger was a bad word and was not to be used in polite or any other kind of conversation.

Of course, I heard it.

Desegregation went relatively smoothly in my city. I recall no race riots or armed enforcements or anything along those lines. Of course, there were individual conflicts as might be expected with any culture clash, but even they were no more than schoolyard scuffles.

It wasn't until high school that I became a conscious, practicing racist. And when I did so, it was because I wanted to fit in with my friends. That is not an excuse, just a fact. In retrospect, I wish I had had the courage to stand up to them and tell them that what we were doing and thinking and saying was wrong (as I knew it to be), but I did not. Peer pressure is what it is. My attitudes, prejudices and actions at that time are still some of my deepest regrets.

Back to topic: nigger is not a word to be used. I don't think it should be forgotten, because the historical facts from which it derived should not be forgotten, but I don't think it should be feared either. We all must learn from the past, lest we repeat our mistakes. Through knowledge may come understanding. From understanding may come a dispersal of fear. I believe fear is what underlies and drives forward prejudice. Continued use of 'nigger' or any other racial terms in any but an historical perspective does nothing but drive fear and push people apart.

My son is in a daycare program with children of different races. As far as I know, he has no concept of that difference in a negative light. I hope he never does, but I know that is probably an unrealistic hope. When the time comes when I must teach my children about words like nigger, cracker, spic, chink, etc., I plan to teach them the history behind the words and exactly why should not be used when referring to other people. I'm going to do my best not to perpetuate racism in my children, even as I continue to expunge it from myself. I look forward to the day when we can all look back at our prejudices and the times when we identified ourselves by race or ethnic background and know that we never need do that again. I look forward to the day when tolerance and acceptance no longer need to be practiced in terms of race (or faith, for that matter) because the need for them no longer exists. I doubt I will see that day in my lifetime, but I continue to hope and work towards it anyway.

For now and for the record, I'm an English Scottish Germanic Cherokee American. Well, actually, I was born in The United States of America, so I'm an American of English, Scottish, Germanic, Cherokee descent. Oh, and I'm Caucasian and my skin shade varies with the amount of sun to which I am exposed.

Nigger: remember, do not fear.

Pax,
Nelson

p.s. If you do not mind, I would like to use this response to your posting in my own blog, referencing your blog, of course. You have my email address. Please let me know.
Thanks,
N.

The New Negro Problem

06/11/2008 05:45:07 AM

In 1944, Swedish economist Gunnar Myrdal published a study called *An American Dilemma: The Negro Problem and Modern Democracy*[10]. In this study, Myrdal claimed that white people, in general, want to see black people (then called 'Negros', although this term is usually inappropriate to use today) disappear from America. This is due to the perception by whites that blacks are inferior in every way. Without earning the benefits of having them as slaves, white people saw no use for black people in America.

However, Myrdal believed that the "the Negro problem" was a "white man's problem". This is due to the fact that white people, through enslavement and institutionalized racism, were responsible for the low estate of black people. Only by using the privileges that the social and economic structure of America gave to whites could blacks be elevated. Once blacks were able to improve their situation, then white people could look at them favorably and cease to see them as inferiors, thus leading to improved racial harmony. Of course, such a solution requires Whites to accept that the racist systems that maintain their superior position in America are responsible for the vast majority of the problems that plague Blacks. Therein lies the paradox of Myrdal's Negro Problem: white supremacist systems put Blacks in an inferior position which causes Whites to see them as lost causes and unworthy of assistance.

I suggest that there is a "new" Negro problem. As black people have improved their situation, white people see fewer and fewer reasons to accept the problems (social, economic, health, etc.) that have historically plagued the African-American population of this country. Furthermore, black people who have been successful, such as athletes, actors, politicians, etc., give the impression to other races that there is no longer a need to pay special attention to racism. Since many blacks have "made it", then the struggle for racial equality must be over.

---

[10]

http://en.wikipedia.org/wiki/An_American_Dilemma:_The_Negro_Problem_and_Modern_Democracy

This unprecedented level of success in the African-American community, particularly in the ascension of Barack Obama[11], is a potential problem because there are many black people who still struggle with the many damaging legacies of slavery. Without a focus on their needs, then a large segment of the African-American population will continue to suffer from racist attitudes directed at them from blacks as well as whites. While struggling in darkness, their problems are ironically hidden by the blinding light of black luminaries such as Oprah Winfrey[12] and Dick Parsons[13].

The solution to this problem is for successful black people to be ever vigilant in the defense of those African-Americans who still have not found success due to racism, ignorance, or simply bad luck. Also, white people need to understand that the crippling effects of centuries of racism cannot be reversed by the relative new phenomena of equality and inclusion. Only then can the appropriate assistance (educational, economic, and social) be extended by those who have often been denied the American Dream[14]. I am not calling for eternal welfare for African-Americans, but I am calling for help for black people who have a desire to improve their situation but simply cannot due to the realities of our nation's history. As Myrdal postulated, the improvement of the state of African-Americans will help all Americans free themselves of the historical negative view of blacks.

Comments

AUTHOR: Antuan Simmons
URL: http://www.myspace.com/antuanlive
DATE: 07/01/2008 05:43:31 AM

---

[11] http://www.barackobama.com/

[12] http://www2.oprah.com/index.jhtml

[13] http://en.wikipedia.org/wiki/Dick_Parsons

[14] http://en.wikipedia.org/wiki/American_dream

Embracing My Blackness

Uh got to get back wit ya on that. but uh I'll try to give an answer

but blacks being the white man's problem or burden (uh one of these) Is this given to all blacks that are huuuh under the social ecomomic/ or financial line, that is a burden on society because of A crime, because they cannot support themsellves properly on meager salaries, drug use behavior because of course if your meager salary cannot sustain you, people usually sell dope to make money, hey got to have a roof over your head, and money used to house and clothe brothers who have been incarcerated. been going on for years,
but to educate, and empower, and motivate, a a large majority of a race takes time, and do we actually have the humaity and love to do it. I agree on what you said about black should take the reins and help out our fellow black man, but how many blacks will turn the white man's burden into the upper to middle class black man's burder or black womens burden. and who will fund these great educators and teachers to help out those who have lost their way, maybe in a perfect world, but hey I would like for that to come true to. I feel it is not to late.

AUTHOR: Anjuan
URL: http://www.anjuansimmons.com
DATE: 06/16/2008 03:00:07 PM

Joe,
Thanks for leaving a comment on my blog.

I would like to better understand your position. You say that you don't know any blacks that have interest or concern for their families. How many black people do you know? I know many black people that have a great amount of interest and concern for their families. Conversely, I also know several white people who have very little interest or concern for their families. This is not a matter of skin color. It is a matter of who the person is.

Are you denying that centuries of slavery have had a tremendously crippling effect on those who descended from slaves? Are you descended from slaves?

What African states have education, employment, criminal, and IQ levels similar to African-Americans?

What is your explanation for what you call low black achievement?

AUTHOR: Joe
DATE: 06/16/2008 02:33:24 AM

Blacks I know don't have anything like the interest or concern for their families that whites and especially asians do, so the idea they are 'held back' by psychic trauma 'cos of injustices suffered by ancestors is crazy.... Then there's every other ethnic group who's overcame historic injustice without requiring the special favors blacks need.... Then there's EVERY other country in the world where the special racial history of America doesn't apply - yet the racial profiles in education , employment, criminality and IQ match America's patterns - even majority black African states.

You're dismissing the most obvious, parsimonious explanation for low black achievement in measures in civility. If you want to blame stereotypes - show the stereotypes aren't true.

America and The Loss of the Black Genius

07/24/2009 04:30:15 PM

AUTHOR'S NOTE: Despite the blatant racism I have seen used against me and against others, I have always been encouraged by Blacks who have transcended racism and enriched America through their gifts. Many of these Black intellectuals were either born in slavery or soon after the abolition of slavery in America. They give me hope that perhaps I can transcend the intellectual, legal, and economic slavery that still shackles too many of my fellow African-Americans to this day.

Our world is marked by the contributions of those who used their vast mental capacity, creativity, and near limitless dedication to give the world the push necessary to advance society to previously unknown levels. The word we use to describe people like this is genius. These are individuals like Leonardo da Vinci, Isaac Newton, Thomas Edison, and Albert Einstein who used their genius to propel humanity forward via the leaps made possible by their work. While others may have contributed to the innovations they created, it is unlikely that our world would be as advanced had they never lived.

While true genius is rare, most people who study human intelligence believe that it is evenly distributed throughout the world. In other words, no one geographic area has a genetic monopoly on human genius. However, the political, social, and economic conditions of the various societies around the world do have an impact on creating environments were genius can thrive. This is important because genius is not born; it is cultivated.

Open societies that allow freedom of expression, accept new ideas, and allow people to pursue their desires with relatively few restrictions tend to produce geniuses. That is probably why many of the great minds of history come from the Enlightenment period of Europe and the United States. History also shows that intellectuals can move from an oppressive society to an open one resulting in a "genius transfer". This was demonstrated during World War II when Jewish scientists fled Germany and went to the United States finding a place at universities and research institutes. A few of them became involved in the Manhattan project and were instrumental in creating the atomic bomb which would eventually be used to end the war.

12

However, what if an open society imports a large group of people but deprives them of the freedom needed to cultivate the characteristics needed to develop a genius mind? Over half a million slaves were shipped from Africa to the United States between the 16th and 19th century. This number reflects those who survived because thousands died during the trip from the African interior to the western coast of Africa as well as during the trip across the Atlantic. By the time of the 1860 census, the number of slaves in America had grown to four million people.

Let's suppose that genius is so rare that it occurs in only one out of a million people. That means that in 1860 there were possibly four black slaves who had the same level of intellect and creativity held by Einstein, Newton, and Edison. That may sound like a small number, but geniuses often make paradigm shifting changes to society and culture. However, robbed of their freedom, these individuals were unable to make contributions to America outside of the menial labor black people were forced to do. No other racial group living in America was prevented from contributing to the intellectual and artistic advancement of America more than the black slave.

We can see glimmers of what might have been by the work of those who were able to transcend slavery and display their mental prowess. George Washington Carver[15] was born as a slave, but he patched together an education and become one of the leading botanists of his day. Benjamin Bradley[16] was also born into slavery, but his skill at mathematics allowed him to gain access to scientific equipment. He created one of the original designs and prototypes for a steam engine, but, as a slave, he was denied from obtaining a patent for his invention.

Who knows what America would be like of it had allowed the millions of black slaves who lived in its borders access to education and the mental stimulation needed to nourish strong minds? Countless inventions and advancements may have been created. However, the suppression of the black mind did not end with the abolition of slavery in America. There are untold thousands of black people who live in poor neighborhoods who are

---

[15] http://en.wikipedia.org/wiki/George_Washington_Carver

[16] http://en.wikipedia.org/wiki/Benjamin_Bradley

also denied the ability to basic education. How many Newtons or Einsteins are in the ghettos of America?

I'm an African-American who owes a great deal of my success to my education. I graduated with an electrical engineering degree from the University of Texas at Austin, and I'm now in the process of finishing my MBA at Texas A&M. I hope you will join me in finding and taking part in ways to help people of all colors to obtain access to education even if it has to be patched together like the one created by George Washington Carver. We have to go into impoverished neighborhoods with the intention of helping everyone we can, but with a special intent to look for those signs of exceptional intelligence. Whether it's a worn mathematics book hidden in a backpack or an intricate mural drawn by a young student, we should help nurture burgeoning geniuses trapped in circumstances that are often beyond their control. Perhaps we'll find the intellectual who will help guide us to the next quantum leap.

What I've Learned from Visiting Five Continents

04/26/2010 03:33:31 AM

AUTHOR'S NOTE: I originally wrote this for one of my good friends, Kiratiana Freelon (KirtianaTravels.com). While I don't specifically mention race in this post, international travel has been a key part of helping me understand my place in the world as a person of color.

Also, my wife and I visited Peru a couple of years ago, so I have now been to six continents!

International travel is one of my guilty pleasures. I've flown through almost every time zone on the planet, sampled food as common as bratwurst[17] in Germany and as exotic as kangaroo[18] in Australia, and have engaged in fun activities like snorkeling off the Great Barrier Reef[19]. However, I almost made a decision early in my career that may have resulted in me never leaving the United States, and I learned the first of many lessons derived from visiting five of the seven continents[20]:

Lesson 1: Travel is a Risk Well Worth Taking

Early in my career as a technology consultant, I was given the opportunity to travel on an international deployment team. When my supervisor approached me about serving as the technical resource on the team, I said, "No, thanks." I spent almost my entire life in my home state of Texas[21], and my international travel had primarily involved things like one or two

---

[17] http://en.wikipedia.org/wiki/Bratwurst

[18] http://www.kangaroo-industry.asn.au/recipes/recipe_frame.htm

[19] http://www.cairnsgreatbarrierreef.org.au/

[20] http://en.wikipedia.org/wiki/Continent

[21] http://en.wikipedia.org/wiki/Texas

trips to border towns in Mexico[22]. I had no interest in traveling outside the United States during the time. First, there was a girl I had a romantic interest in and being outside of the country would undermine the progress of our relationship. Second, the team would be gone for long weeks at a time to places on the other side of the world. Third, I would have to fill out a lot of paper work for things like a passport and visas, and I would have to get a battery of vaccinations to protect me from third world diseases. I felt that there were too many risks and not enough rewards.

Thankfully, my supervisor gave me another chance to join the team, and, for reasons I don't quite remember, I said, "Yes". Yes, there was a ton of paperwork to fill out. Yes, I had to get three shots in each shoulder for things like malaria and polio which made me sick to my stomach for days. Yes, a few days before I was to fly to our first deployment site (Cairo[23], Egypt) a group of American tourists were killed in Luxor[24], Egypt, which resulted in travel advisories warning against travelling to the region. Yes, there were many risks, but the experience was more than worth it. The following pictures show adventures that I would have never had if I had not accepted the offer to take my first overseas trip.

---

[22] http://en.wikipedia.org/wiki/Mexico

[23] http://en.wikipedia.org/wiki/Cairo

[24] http://en.wikipedia.org/wiki/Luxor

This is me standing in front of the Great Sphinx.

Here I am standing with the Mohammed Ali Mosque[25] behind me.

Embracing My Blackness

The pictures on the previous page are of me:
° *Floating down the Nile river in a dinner boat*
° *Killing the locals in a game of dominoes*

As I explored the sights and sounds of Cairo, I realized that I almost turned down the experience of a lifetime. I was extremely grateful that I had decided to face my fears and go on this trip. I felt a growing sense of confidence that emboldened me to make another risky decision.

After the team wrapped up our deployment in Cairo, I had three choices. First, I could return to the United States and have more down time before the next trip. Second, I could join my colleagues who were taking a side trip to the Red Sea in order to do some sailing and diving. Third, I could go somewhere else in the general region. Looking at a map of the possibilities, I decided that I would go to Israel[26]. My supervisor warned against my decision to make the trip since Iraq had just launched missiles over the border into Israel. He stopped just shy of forbidding me to go and urged me to wait for a safer time to visit the Holy Land. However, I decided to go despite his protests because I had grasped the second lesson of my travels:

Lesson 2: There is Never a Safe Time to Visit Israel

Israel constantly faces the threat of violence either in the form of suicide bomb attacks or armed conflicts between Israeli and Palestinian military forces. After realizing that I had almost missed out on the fantastic time I had in Cairo, I didn't want to pass on the chance to visit the Holy Land[27]. Therefore, I boarded my flight from Cairo and soon found myself at Ben Gurion[28] airport.

---

[26] http://en.wikipedia.org/wiki/Israel

[27] http://en.wikipedia.org/wiki/Holy_land

[28] http://www.iaa.gov.il/RASHAT/en-US/Rashot

20

The pictures on the previous page are of me:
° *Kneeling beside the Stone of Anointing in* <u>*The Church of the Holy*</u>
<u>*Sepulcher*</u>[29] *(one of the* <u>*Stations of the Cross*</u>[30]*).*
° *Standing in Jerusalem with the* <u>*Mount of Olives*</u>[31] *behind me.*

I soon found myself exploring Tel Aviv and taking in my first experience in Israel. After spending the night in <u>Tel Aviv</u>[32], I boarded a bus and soon found myself in <u>Jerusalem</u>[33].

Walking in the city that was the birthplace of my faith was an amazing experience. Not only was I able to visit the places shown in the pictures above, but I was able to also do things like place a written prayer in the <u>Wailing Wall</u>[34]. In the years that have passed since I visited Israel, I have never read about a time when the region would have been a safer place to visit. I'm glad I took the chance I had to make the trip.

My next lesson in international travel would be learned at the next location my team visited: Lagos, Nigeria.

---

[29] http://en.wikipedia.org/wiki/Church_of_the_Holy_Sepulchre

[30] http://en.wikipedia.org/wiki/Stations_of_the_Cross

[31] http://en.wikipedia.org/wiki/Mount_of_olives

[32] http://en.wikipedia.org/wiki/Tel_aviv

[33] http://en.wikipedia.org/wiki/Jerusalem

[34] http://en.wikipedia.org/wiki/Wailing_wall

Lesson 3: Leaving Your Country is Often the Best Way to Understand Your Roots

Although Cairo is on the African continent, it is very Middle Eastern in its culture. It was in Lagos[35], Nigeria, that I obtained a true understanding of African culture. Although Nigeria is a country steeped in corruption[36], I found the people to be extremely open, loving, and hopeful. I was there right before the election of Obasanjo[37] to his first term as President of Nigeria.

---

[35] http://en.wikipedia.org/wiki/Lagos

[36] http://www.africaeconomicanalysis.org/articles/gen/corruptiondikehtm.html

[37] http://en.wikipedia.org/wiki/Obasanjo

Embracing My Blackness

The picture on the previous page is one of me hanging with some of the office ladies who took me in as one of their own – while keeping me out of "wahala".

As an African-American, I am the descendent of slaves. While I have not yet traced my ancestry far enough back to determine exactly what part of Africa my ancestors came from, I know that they were from the west part of Africa in the same general area as Nigeria.

I remember arriving from the airport and seeing oceans of black people. I had never experienced anything like that! It was early in the morning, and I can distinctly recall seeing beautiful black children walking to school in their uniforms, dancing, singing, and playing as they went on their way.

Despite the fact that my heritage differed in many ways from theirs, I was embraced by the people I met in Lagos. While my white colleagues stayed within the security of the hotel after hours, I toured the city and learned about the local history. Sensing my curiosity and respect for their culture, Nneka, one of the ladies from the office who befriended me, gave me a nickname: "Nnamdi[38]".

---

[38] http://www.behindthename.com/name/nnamdi

I attended a church service in Lagos where the women wore hats similar to the hats worn by African-American women in American churches.

Going to Nigeria gave me a better understanding of who I was as an African-American. I saw many similarities between the generosity of the people of Nigeria and that of the predominately black neighborhood in which I spent most of my childhood. The experience allowed me to see the linkages between the African and the African-American way of life.

Lesson 4: Big Cities are Pretty Much The Same Around the World

My next international destination was Berlin[39], Germany. By this point, I had visited enough large cities at different locations around the world to realize that, on the macro level, almost all large cities around the world are pretty much the same. This was made apparent to me by the near ubiquitous presence of McDonalds[40] around the world. Those golden arches were, at

---

[39] http://en.wikipedia.org/wiki/Berlin

[40] http://www.mcdonalds.com/us/en/home.html

least in my mind, a concrete example of how much "Americana[41]" had spread around the world. Additionally, almost every major city had concrete jungles of buildings with congested streets and large numbers of people milling about.

The distinctions and truly unique aspects of international travel are found in places of worship and small towns. The churches in Berlin uniquely contained the history of Germany in the same way I learned about Cairo in its mosques and Coptic churches. Similarly, when I visited Celle[42], Germany, I felt that I received a much better understanding of Germany than in the much larger city of Berlin. I resolved at that point that, if at all possible, any time I visited a foreign country, I would make time to go into the country towns and not just stay in large cities.

Lesson 5: America's Sex Saturated Culture is Actually Prudish Regarding Nudity

As American entertainment spreads across the world, we see more countries fight against the perceived sex saturated culture of the United States. Recently, Beyoncé was banned from performing in Malaysia[43] due to the suggestive nature of her lyrics and clothing.

However, one hidden truth that I learned from traveling around the world is that Americans are really prudes. I was sitting in a steam room in the gym of the hotel I lived in while I was in Celle when several German men and women entered. I smiled and waved my hand in greeting. They smiled and waved back. They then proceeded to take off their robes, and sit down and continue their conversation – totally in the nude. I sat there in my towel trying to understand the situation. As an American, such open nudity was something that I had never before encountered. I sat for a few minutes thinking about the proper protocol. Am I being offensive by being the only

---

[41] http://en.wikipedia.org/wiki/Americana

[42] http://en.wikipedia.org/wiki/Celle

[43] http://news.bbc.co.uk/2/hi/entertainment/8315829.stm

non-nude person in the steam room? Should I take off my towel? I
eventually decided to stretch, stand up, say *auf wiedersehen*, and exit the
steam room.

As I walked back to my room, I was thought about a similar insight I
gained in Cairo. I was touring around Cairo and had stopped at a corner to
consult my map to determine the best route to my next destination. While I
was standing there, a woman, who I assumed was a native of Cairo, sat
down on the curb next to me with her baby. She was covered from head to
toe in a burqa[44], and her face was hidden behind a metal mask.

She then proceeded to partially disrobe, take out one of her breasts, and
nurse her child. This was in broad daylight in the early afternoon, and the
woman was doing what would have probably gotten her arrested in many
parts of the United States. As she sat there, her conservative clothing and
her public nudity served as a living example of a paradox I was hard
pressed to reconcile. Many Americans would have also shared the
incredulous look I'm sure I had on my face, but I'm sure she and the other
people walking by simply saw a woman taking care of her child.

Lesson 6: Having Friends Around the World is Awesome!

As I continued my travels, I learned the benefits of having friends in
international locations. When I decided to visit East Asia, I added the
Philippines to my travel itinerary because I became friends with co-workers
who were from Manila[45]. Prior to my East Asia expedition, I had never
"met up" with friends at an international destination.

---

[44] http://en.wikipedia.org/wiki/Burqa

[45] http://en.wikipedia.org/wiki/Manila

I'm standing with some of my Philippine friends in front of the White House. In exchange for travelling with them in Washington, DC, they showed me around Manila.

During this trip, I visited Tokyo[46], Hong Kong[47], and Bangkok[48] in addition to Manila. However, the experience I had touring around with my friends in Manila made it a much more intimate experience. They took me off the beaten path (see Lesson 4) and allowed me to truly experience the history and culture of the Philippines. The only thing better than travelling abroad with friends is travelling with your spouse. Which brings me to my next lesson:

---

[46] http://en.wikipedia.org/wiki/Tokyo

[47] http://en.wikipedia.org/wiki/Hong_kong

[48] http://en.wikipedia.org/wiki/Bangkok

Lesson 7: Travelling with Your Spouse Makes Travel Sweeter

After I toured around East Asia, I took a couple of years off from travel due to my need to be more focused on my career. I also had another reason to take some time off from the international road. The girl who I was so concerned about before my trip to Cairo and I continued to work on our relationship. We eventually got engaged and were married on March 9th, 2002.

I was fortunate to marry someone who also loved traveling around the world. When planning our honeymoon, we knew we wanted to go somewhere outside of the United States. We finally agreed to spend our honeymoon in Belize[49].

Here's my wife and I after tubing in Belize.

---

[49] http://en.wikipedia.org/wiki/Belize

Embracing My Blackness

Sharing the joy of international travel with my wife allowed us to both experience something we both love doing. We were able to build memories that we still talk about to this day. It is an amazing experience to explore foreign destinations with someone you deeply love and always want to be by your side.

Lesson 8: It Pays to Upgrade for Special Events

I often enjoy "roughing it" when travelling outside of the United States. I do things like take long hikes, rent all-terrain vehicles and drive over undeveloped landscapes, snorkel, etc. I feel that I haven't truly experienced a foreign land if I haven't "gotten my hands dirty".

However, there are times when it pays to spend a little extra money to upgrade an experience. I found this out when my wife and I visited Sydney[50], Australia.

---

[50] http://en.wikipedia.org/wiki/Sydney

Here's my wife and I in Sydney with the famous Sydney Harbour Bridge[51] behind us.

Of course, no trip to Sydney is complete without a visit to the iconic Sydney Opera House[52]. My wife and I went to see Don Giovanni[53] performed there. Thinking that any seat in the Opera House had to be a good seat, we selected some of the cheapest tickets. We excitedly exited our taxi and entered the building. It was when we got to our seats that we realized our mistake. The seats were stacked very close together and had hard backs with almost no leg room. I'm a fairly tall guy (6' 2") so I felt like my knees were in my chest while we watched the play. While the

---

51 http://en.wikipedia.org/wiki/Sydney_Harbour_Bridge

52 http://en.wikipedia.org/wiki/Sydney_Opera_House

53 http://en.wikipedia.org/wiki/Don_Giovanni

show was good, I could think of little more than the discomfort I felt sitting in those chairs! I resolved then to always pay a little extra to make sure that a once in a lifetime experience is not marred by being a little too frugal.

Lesson 9: Travel While You're Young if Possible

Travelling around the world is expensive. I have been fortunate to have a large amount of my travel expenses paid for by my employer because I was travelling to do a job. Also, I used the airline and hotel points I earned travelling for work to subsidize the cost of the travel I did purely for pleasure. So, I have not had to spend an excessive amount of my own personal money to see the world.

However, not everyone is as fortunate. This was made clear to me when my wife and I booked a cruise with Royal Caribbean[54] to visit the Southern Caribbean. We visited several islands over a seven night trip. We noticed that several people on the ship were in their 60s, 70s, and even 80s. While talking with them, we learned that many of them had saved money for decades to take the cruise. I was saddened that many of these elderly passengers were getting their first taste of life outside of the United States while using canes, walking chairs, and wheel chairs to get around. I was immediately aware of the blessing of travelling while young as my wife and I bounded off the ship and rushed around island towns in the small time frames we had to explore while the ship was docked.

If at all possible, I encourage everyone to travel while young if at all possible. It makes the experience so much more enjoyable.

Lesson 10: International Travel is a Hobby that Constantly Provides Future Adventures

---

[54]

http://www.royalcaribbean.com/findacruise/destinations/home.do;jsessionid=000013
V7D7l7nvHzRb_xTLDdiXw:12hbiocus?dest=CARIB

The more I travel, the more I want to travel. I've been to all of the continents except for South America[55] and Antarctica[56]. I also want to go back to Israel and Africa and take my wife and our three children. There are hundreds of places around the world that I want to explore and truly integrate with the local culture. I am a lifelong international traveler, and it is a passion that I know will give me many years of enjoyment and fun . . . and provide even more lessons!

Comments

AUTHOR: Anjuan Simmons
URL: http://www.AnjuanSimmons.com
DATE: 04/28/2010 08:51:49 PM

Hi Kiratiana,

Thank you for the kind comment! Sure, I can add a lesson learned about travelling internationally as a black man. I'll add it and make a few more edits.

When would you like to publish this on your blog? I think the best way to proceed would be to create a user ('Anjuan Simmons') on your blog with the Contributor role. This will allow me to login and write the post, but I won't be able to publish it. You can then publish whenever you want.

Does that work for you?

Anjuan

AUTHOR: cherub
DATE: 04/28/2010 08:11:25 PM

---

[55] http://en.wikipedia.org/wiki/South_america

[56] http://en.wikipedia.org/wiki/Antarctica

Embracing My Blackness

Wow! THis is incredible! Actually I think it is better than anything I have written on my own blog. I've definitely been leaning toward the quick articles with practical information. Stuff like this is the kind of stuff that makes you wanna keep going back to a blog.

I think this is definitely one of those inspiring articles....Could you add a bit on how it is to travel as a black man? Maybe a lesson learned? I know so many black men who have the money to travel internationally, but just don't!

Whew! INCREDIBLE!!!

A Code of Conduct for Black Men

04/27/2010 07:30:24 AM

In general, I dislike reading or hearing the phrase "disproportionally represented". That is due to the fact that this phrase usually is preceded or followed by a negative statistic about black men. However, I try to be a person who engages problems rather than avoid them, so I did a Google search of this phrase. This report[57] from The Henry J. Kaiser Family Foundation summarizes many of the themes I found in my search results:

- The unemployment rate for young African-American men is over twice the rate for young white, Hispanic and Asian men.
- African-American men are disproportionately represented in the criminal justice system. The percentage of young African-American men in prison is nearly three times that of Hispanic men and nearly seven times that of white men.
- While African-American men represent 14% of the population of young men in the U.S., they represent over 40% of the prison population.
- Young African-American men die at a rate that is at least 1.5 times the rate of young white and Hispanic men, and almost three times the rate of young Asian men. While the death rate drops for men ages 25 to 29 for most groups, it continues to rise among African-Americans.
- For young African-American men, more deaths are caused by homicide than any other cause.
- The homicide death rate for young African-American men is three times the rate for Hispanics, the population group with the next highest homicide mortality rate.

---

[57] http://docs.google.com/viewer?a=v&q=cache:IsUYm0MgW-8J:www.kff.org/minorityhealth/upload/7541.pdf+%22disproportionately+represented%22+%22african+american+men%22&hl=en&gl=ca&pid=bl&srcid=ADGEESiXhl2 1mtGB8-_hArTiOc-KGm55dH1722ktJMl80dDqeLXo2ILpUH7eiCh6SqWEga-sHRRlfweJ0INBcFUxoQGQgsxS32vVYmTgJajGgwICAKrtFUB5aEeKrVjgbJMlrJ74i 9vD&sig=AHIEtbTmPCBJSacAL0jcR09i6Gy-lNEgjA

- HIV is the sixth leading cause of death for young African-American and Hispanic men, yet for other racial groups, HIV is not among the top 10 causes of death.

A paper[58] published by a researcher at Syracuse University titled **Barriers to Marriage and Parenthood for African-American Men and Women** yielded these additional tidbits: The absence of African-American fathers in the home is seen as a primary factor of the insidious deterioration of African-American families. "Positive male role models are virtually non-existent within many inner city communities. Many young African-American men have had limited or no personal experience with a stable father figure and have little to model themselves on." Another research paper[59] which was published by the National Institute of Diabetes and Kidney and Digestive Diseases stated, "The prevalence of extreme obesity in African-American men is higher than in any other minority group. Among African-American men, the prevalence of obesity increased from 27.5% in 1999-2000 to 31% in 2003-2004. Poor dietary patterns together with physical inactivity are highly prevalent in minority males and are major contributors to the high obesity prevalence rates."

These statistics point a sobering picture. In almost every category of life, African-American men are at the top of every negative descriptor and at the bottom of every positive one. As a naturally curious person, I have put a lot of thought into answering one question: Why?

58

http://docs.google.com/viewer?a=v&q=cache:BuahKaHuqZAJ:www.thrivingcouplest
hrivingkids.syr.edu/Pdfs/0VOConnerresearchpr0jspring05.pdf+%22disproportionatel
y+represented%22+%22african+american+men%22&hl=en&gl=ca&pid=bl&srcid=
ADGEESi1fCJZBwpGe5vqP3ak7_JWDoNv4oFAodcOdDpPujsAUEGVaQoRFwV
NO-
LXWeHN_14SsKHb8qdVPNFzmZlaATiyw36ZE7k_T2LJ_r5MjvWIwpuaHvoMlBnb
CHDK-Jt3jU9AETFF&sig=AHIEtbRCqOTS-reZuhzbVxOsXuLcZQVTTw

59

http://webcache.googleusercontent.com/search?q=cache:PY78AumASL0J:www.natc
om.org/index.asp%3Fdownloadid%3D2067+%22disproportionately+represented%22
+%22african+american+men%22&cd=19&hl=en&ct=clnk&gl=ca&client=firefox-a

Part of the reason for the challenges currently facing black men can be found in our history. A heritage of centuries of slavery, Jim Crow laws, and institutionalized racism is hard on a brother. However, a damaged past does not remove the responsibility to repair our present situation.

My life is disproportionately UNDER-represented by these statistics. I was born into a two parent home and raised by both of my parents (who have now been married to each other for over 35 years). I have an undergraduate degree in electrical engineering and an MBA. My net worth passed the six figure mark years ago. I married a black woman at the age of 27 (neither of us had been previously married), and we have been married for eight years. During the course of our marriage, we have had three children. Neither of us have any side kids[60]. My wife has undergraduate and graduate degrees in business and a PhD in business. While far from perfect, my life is also far from the picture of black men painted by the statistics quoted above.

I also know that I am not alone. I know many black men who have built similar lives. They are educated, often holding advanced degrees. They maintain strong marriages and are actively building their careers either as corporate professionals or as entrepreneurs.

Yet, obviously, a large number of my fellow black men are having trouble taking advantage of the opportunities I have been able to leverage. Why is there such a stark difference between their lives and the lives of almost every black man I personally know?

The difference is certainly not due to any special characteristic I have. Believe me, I have made my share of stupid mistakes. However, I have avoided making most of the mistakes that cause permanent damage to a black man's long term potential. This is not due to anything that I have done. I believe it is due to something that was done to me.

While both of my parents were actively involved in my life, it was my father, Douglas Simmons, who taught me how to be a man. Many aspects of who I am, ranging from how I walk, talk, hold myself, etc., are directly

---

[60] http://www.urbandictionary.com/define.php?term=side+kids

due to his influence. My father shaped me into a man through his constant presence during my childhood. I think a large part of the discipline that he instilled in me came from his experience as a Marine[61] who served in Vietnam[62]. As a Marine, my father learned to live life according to a code of conduct. Many aspects of this code were passed onto me. Having a code of conduct simply means that there are positive behaviors you **always** do, and there are negative behaviors that you **never** do.

Principles, values, standards, or rules of behavior that guide the decisions, procedures and systems of an organization in a way that (a) contributes to the welfare of its key stakeholders, and (b) respects the rights of all constituents affected by its operations.

Definition of Code of Conduct from Wikipedia

Here are various pictures of my Dad during his days as a Marine.

---

[61] http://www.marines.com/

[62] http://en.wikipedia.org/wiki/Vietnam_War

Here's my Dad aboard ship with his fellow Marines. I suppose he could relate to being the only person of color on the team.

Too many black men grow up without a code of conduct. Random forces are allowed to shape them in ways that are often negative. Just like a well-manicured lawn requires constant care and attention, young black men require a diligent hand to guide their growth. While many single mothers and men of other races are working hard to provide this guidance, I think there are few substitutes for a strong black adult man in the life of a young black man.

However, we cannot have strong black adult men if we do not learn to live according to a code of conduct. I am a Christian, but I think that such a code should be broad enough to allow black men of other faiths to embrace it. It should also be general enough to allow black men to implement it in a way that suits their particular needs. This code is a combination of principles instilled in me by my father as well as ideas I've discovered through experience. Here is my proposed Code of Conduct for Black men:

Article 1 - Relationships

- **Section 1 - Informed Consent:** If I am sexually intimate with more than one person, then every person involved should be aware of that fact including the disclosure of any same sex activity.
- **Section 2 - Hands Off:** I will never violently harm a woman.

- **Section 3 - Make One, Raise One:** If a child results from my sexual activity, I will be directly involved in developing that child into a responsible adult.

Article 2 - Fatherhood

- **Section 1 - Presence:** I will be physically and emotionally present in the life of my offspring.
- **Section 2 - Talent Search:** I will help my children understand their talents and provide assistance in developing those talents.
- **Section 3 - Mirror Mirror:** I will strive to be a positive example for my sons to emulate and for my daughters to use when selecting a mate.

Article 3 - Economics

- **Section 1 - Revenue Generation:** I will generate income either as an employee or as an entrepreneur.
- **Section 2 - Par Excellence:** My work will always show a high level of quality.
- **Section 3 - Saving Plan:** I will set a portion of my income aside in order to save for future needs.

Article 4 - Health

- **Section 1 - Eating Habits:** I will maintain a healthy diet.
- **Section 2 - Physical Fitness:** I will engage in regular exercise.
- **Section 3 - Health Checks:** I will regularly seek the counsel of health professionals in order to sustain good health.

As I said, this is meant to be a simple code that is easy to remember and implement. If every African-American man made this code a part of his life, then many of the statistics I cited at the beginning of this article would dramatically reduce or disappear altogether. I challenge every black man reading this to find and apply some standard to your life so that we can achieve our full potential and corporately make a positive contribution to society. We are the generation that can reverse statistical trends and build a brighter future for our sons. As a greater man than me is fond of saying, "We are the ones we have been waiting for"[63].

If you have any comments on my proposed Code of Conduct for Black Men, please leave a comment. Also, let me know if you think any Articles or Sections need to be added, modified, or removed!

Comments

AUTHOR: robinbmurphy
URL: http://twitter.com/robinbmurphy
DATE: 07/17/2010 11:22:05 PM

Great post! Wish I had seen it earlier.

I would add financially present to Article 2, Section 1.

AUTHOR: Anjuan Simmons
URL: http://www.AnjuanSimmons.com
DATE: 05/01/2010 08:14:29 AM

I did receive a fair number of comments to the Facebook version of this post.

Everything you said is valid. However, the Code is meant to be flexible. Just like the Constitution details the high level workings of the federal government without meddling in the decisions of the individual States, the Code can be adapted by all men without forcing them to fit into a particular religion or creed.

AUTHOR: newsaga
DATE: 04/28/2010 09:32:52 PM

No comments? Wow.

---

[63] http://www.youtube.com/watch?v=moIWTfv8TYw

Embracing My Blackness

An informal comment from a man on the other site I posted it on:

Doesn't mention anything regarding relating to women.

Where's the part about loving, honoring, and making a choice to marry a woman before getting her pregnant? So, basically it's incomplete.

I'm surprised you haven't gotten more comments? :-(

AUTHOR: Finally... A Code of Condu
URL: http://i2ameverywoman.wordpress.com/2010/04/28/finally-a-code-of-conduct/
DATE: 04/27/2010 06:22:21 PM

[...] Finally... A Code of Conduct 28 04 2010 I was doing my mid day lunch Facebook check in when I found this amazing post by a great guy that I have had the pleasure of meeting on a few occasions. In "I'm Every Woman", we have written a number of posts about all the things that men we know have not done, and why we think they have not done it. We have often asked what is wrong with these do-wrong men, what is the missing thing? What is the thing that they don't have, that makes them different from these men who seem to be able to manage to sustain a home, a family and some level of stability. Apparently there is a code of conduct, and not everyone got the memo. Anjuan Simmons wrote this in his post "A Code of Conduct for Black Men" [...]

Why Black Men Have Left the Church

12/10/2011 04:24:26 PM

AUTHOR'S NOTE: Despite being a devout Christian, I didn't write a lot of blog posts about my faith. First, I've always wanted to be known for what the Greeks called Arête, or personal excellence. Second, I've found that people often draw incorrect conclusions about me if the first thing they learn about me is my faith. I'd rather have the excellence of my life speak for my beliefs than simply label myself. That being said, I never shy away from questions about Christianity like the one person who inspired this post asked me.

A friend posed this question on Facebook:

Why are Black men between 18 and 40 missing from the church? I pray that more black men come to know Jesus personally and that they will take the spiritual headship that God has called them to.

My answer:

There are a few reasons (though none of them excuse the absence):

1. Arrogance ("I don't need another man to tell me what to do just because he's standing in a pulpit");

2. The Hypocrisy of Church Leadership (what's up, Eddie Long?);

3. Church Greed ("I ain't paying for the pastor's Bentley");

4. The declining role of religion (and growth of atheism) among African-Americans.

As a black man who has his family in church every Sunday, I see the absence and mourn it, but I understand why it exists.

3 Guidelines for Affluent Whites Who Want to Help Poor Black Kids

12/14/2011 03:05:30 AM

It's hard for white people to discuss racism. Most of us can remember those awkward moments in high school history class when we discussed slavery in America and saw several of our fellow fair skin students mopping their brows during the entire discussion. Or, some of us had geography class where there was that one white student who enjoyed mispronouncing Niger (either the African country or the river) just a little too much. By the way, Niger does not rhyme with trigger.

These high school moments of awkwardness often result into an implicit agreement when teen-agers become adults to avoid the subject altogether. So, I was intrigued when a colleague sent me a tweet about an article published on Forbes titled If I Were A Poor Black Kid[64] written by Gene Marks[65]. Marks is a middle aged White man with a CPA who has worked as an executive at Fortune 500 companies like KPMG and, in addition to writing articles and books about technology, runs his own consulting business. In his Forbes piece, Marks distills his advice for how poor black kids can improve themselves, specifically through the use of technology.

As someone who advocates for minorities to enter and succeed in the technology industry, I found myself nodding in agreement with much of what Marks shared in his article. However, while most of the content was sound, it didn't quite sound right. In other words, while I could appreciate Marks' tune, his tone was off, and a few aspects of his piece were pitchy. And, by pitchy, I mean preachy.

However, instead of bashing Marks as several people did in the 487 comments left on the article, I thought he created an opportunity to have a

---

[64] http://www.forbes.com/sites/quickerbettertech/2011/12/12/if-i-was-a-poor-black-kid/

[65] http://www.quickerbetterwiser.com/

constructive conversation. Forbes caters to business leaders (often affluent White males) so, despite the weaknesses in Marks' article, I think it presents a great learning opportunity for those in the publishing company's target demographic who have a genuine interest in helping poor black kids. However, in order for these affluent whites to truly be effective, there are a few guidelines they should follow in order to avoid the mistakes made by Marks in the post.

1 - Be Careful Playing the Obama Card

Marks starts his article by referring to a recent speech by President Obama:

President Obama gave an excellent speech last week in Kansas about inequality in America.

Marks credits this speech with providing the impetus to get him thinking about poor inner city kids. While I think Marks truly liked Obama's speech, referring to it sounds like the old cliché used by whites to fend off charges of racism: "Hey, I can't be racist. I have a black friend". Since President Obama enjoys enormous support in the black community, Marks' reference to him comes off as pandering to a group that would probably be offended by the rest of the article. Yes, we love us some Barack Obama, but we also don't like the appearance of someone trying to make us fall for the okie doke. Most of us are mature enough to have a discussion about race without confirmation from Whites about how good President Obama is at giving speeches.

2 - Poor Black Kids Are Not a Monolith

Throughout the article, Marks refers to the group he is trying to help as "poor black" or "inner city" kids. While there are common experiences that many impoverished black kids share, the reality is that many of them have diverse experiences. I'm sure that if Marks drove the two miles he claims separate his house from the "inner city" he would find kids there that are as unique as his own. I would imagine that Marks, like most affluent Whites, has spent very little time with poor black kids. So, the only inputs to his mental model of their lives are probably news reports (which are probably mostly negative), television and movies (also mostly negative), and perhaps, if Marks is charitable, once or twice a year when he takes part in a

45

clothing or toy drive for underprivileged children. Just as doctors cannot properly prescribe medicine to patients they haven't seen, affluent whites like Marks are poorly positioned to help poor black kids they rarely spend any time around. If they did, then they would understand that the "inner city" also includes intact two-parent homes, law abiding citizens, and even a brilliant child or two. I'm not advising affluent whites to move into the ghetto, but taking time to serve as mentors to poor black kids would be much more effective than writing articles about a subject they don't understand in a publication run by a white male billionaire.

3 - Don't Project Your Reality

Marks references several free or low cost online tools that poor black kids can use to improve their studies. He lists Project Gutenberg[66], Wikipedia[67], Backpack[68], Skype[69], and others. While these technologies can be powerful learning tools, Marks looks at their use from the perspective of a middle class white male who probably grew up in a middle class home in a white neighborhood. I doubt Marks has ever experienced anything close to the reality of black kids living in poverty. He has probably never had to go through a school day on an empty stomach, had to cut class to go to work to help pay household bills, or, while walking home from school, experienced the fear of being stopped by police officers because they are looking for someone who "looked like him". I think Marks looked at the technology tools he mentioned in the article and probably thought, "These really would have helped me as a student when I was a kid" and tried to project that usefulness to poor black kids. As I stated before, Marks and other affluent whites need to truly engage with poor black kids and truly understand their reality instead of project a false one constructed by their experience of growing up in White America.

---

[66] http://www.gutenberg.org/

[67] http://www.wikipedia.org/

[68] http://backpackit.com/

[69] http://www.skype.com/intl/en-us/home

I hope Marks' article is not the last time he writes about using technology to help poor black kids, but I encourage him to try to understand poor black kids if he truly wants to help them. As someone who grew up in a very modest Black neighborhood and used a career in technology to become an executive at a multi-billion dollar technology consulting company, I understand how even a small percentage of affluent whites could provide tremendous help to minorities through technology.

My First Letter to the *Daily Texan* about Affirmative Action

02/26/2012 03:49:18 AM

AUTHOR'S NOTE: The decision by the Supreme Court of the United States to review affirmative action in college admissions policies reminded me of a similar fight that occurred when I was a college student in the 1990's. Affirmative action is one of the few tools that can create a balanced playing field for all college applicants. However, it is often castigated by Blacks and non-Blacks due to, in my opinion, ignorance about the meaning of affirmative action. Furthermore, no one criticizes the institutionalized policies that help children of the dominant society get into college and succeed. It seems to only become a problem when policies exist that try to help black kids gain the value of a college education.

The next few posts cover the reprint of letters I wrote as a college student as well as my thoughts about affirmative action as an adult.

In light of the recent decision by the U.S. Supreme Court to review college affirmative action[70], I thought I would post two letters I wrote as a student at The University of Texas at Austin during the controversial Hopwood Decision which prohibited the university from using race as a factor in admissions. The Hopwood Decision was made in March 1996 when I was a junior electrical engineering undergraduate student at the university.

In response to articles and letters written to the *Daily Texan's*[71] Firing Line section (where letters from students were published), I wrote my own Firing Line letter which was published in the March 1, 1996 edition of the *Daily Texan*. It was titled "Column Was Flawed", and, although almost 16 years have passed since it was printed, my thoughts about the need for affirmative action at the university level remain unchanged.

---

[70] http://www.businessweek.com/news/2012-02-24/college-affirmative-action-threatened-by-u-s-high-court-case.html

[71] http://www.dailytexanonline.com/

As a black man, I have often experienced the negative consequences of people who speak and act out of ignorance.

K. Danial Williamson's column on affirmative action again demonstrated to me that many people have based their viewpoints on flawed logic.

I will not address his remarks that suggest Williamson has a limited knowledge and lack of respect for black America because I am sure other readers will do so.

My intent is to dispel many of the myths about affirmative action.

First, the hiring of anyone solely on the basis of race is illegal under Title VII of the U.S. Civil Rights Act of 1964 which states it is illegal for an employer to: "(1) fail or refuse to hire or to discharge any individual with respect to his compensation, terms, conditions or privileges of employment; or (2) to limit, segregate, or classify his employees or applicants for employment in any way which would deprive or tend to deprive any individual of employment opportunities or otherwise adversely affect his status as an employee because of such individual's race, color, religion, sex, or national origin."

Next, affirmative action was not meant to be a practice where Black Applicant X who has the same skills as White Applicant Y gets hired based on membership in a minority group. This is illegal. An affirmative action policy is one in which a business actively recruits candidates for employment from all spheres of society. After that it is up to the BUSINESS to decide who gets hired.

The only way for a business to be forced to hire more underrepresented employees is if that business has been found to have suspect hiring practices (this includes not hiring enough white employees).

Few businesses are forced to do this because of three reasons:

1. The business has to have more than 15 employees.

2. Overt discrimination has to be occurring in hiring practices.

3. A business under investigation has ample time to provide evidence that they actively encourage people of all backgrounds to apply for employment.

Affirmative action was designed to be a policy to combat racist and sexist hiring practices.

This brings me to the need for affirmative action.

Many of the high level jobs in corporate America are not held by people who go through the normal process of application, interview, job offer. It's done through what I call the Good Ole Boy Network. Perhaps an example will help me illustrate my meaning. Johnny's father is a friend of Bob who is president of God Bless America Enterprises, Inc. Bob likes Johnny because he's a nice kid who he's seen grow up. So Bob lets Johnny know that he can intern every summer and when he gets out of college he will have a place at GBAE.

Heck, he doesn't even have to do one interview. Just walk right in, take a seat in your office, and enjoy your salary!

This Good Ole Boy Network has been in operation for centuries and is made up of thousands of white men like Bob who love to hire swell white kids like Johnny. However, it doesn't work for everybody.

You see Tyrone also wants to work for GBAE. He sacked fries in high school, worked through college, and has to fill out two applications verifying he has no criminal record and go through three interviews.

Bob thinks Tyrone is a great black kid; in fact, he loves his three point shot. However, Johnny already has the job so Tyrone is out of luck like many other minority applicants who can't hook into the Good Ole Boy Network because their fathers aren't presidents, CEOs, or senators. It seems like some affirmative action could help them tremendously. Affirmative action is not about hiring unqualified minorities.

It's about giving everyone an equal chance to be considered for a job based on their abilities. Anything else is ignorance.

Anjuan R. Simmons Electrical engineering junior

My Second Letter to the *Daily Texan* about Affirmative Action

02/26/2012 04:19:31 AM

After seeing my first letter to the *Daily Texan* about affirmative action published, the debate about the use of race in college admissions continued to rage across the campus of The University of Texas at Austin. The conversation branched in multiple directions, and I decided to write another Firing Line letter in response to one written by another student. It was published on July 1, 1996 and was titled "Race the Marathon". I attempted to again present a logical view of affirmative action since so many student opinions seemed to be based on emotion instead of the racial reality of the United States:

Cecil Stickland's Firing Line letter (7/29/96) presented a valid viewpoint on racial separatism. I agree that the picture of the Mexican cameraman was taken too extremely by some people. I also understand the sensitivity some feel toward the depiction of minority groups.

But I want to comment on the last sentence of Strickland's letter: "Until we can see beyond the color of skin, until we can turn organizations like the NAACP into NAAAP (A for All) we continue to struggle." This sentence aspires for a noble ideal, but an ideal impossible in our present reality. Organizations like the NAACP, are essential for the survival of black people. Why? Because the social, economic, and mental effects of three centuries of slavery and oppression cannot be undone in three decades.

Many proclaim the need to forget race in order for us to advance as human beings instead of as racial groups. However, this mentality will only result in the continued dissolution of minority groups, especially blacks. Imagine a marathon run for the prize of human advancement. Some argue that the runners should all run together to win as a group. But there is disparity in the placement of the racial groups.

White runners are obviously winning. Twenty miles behind are the Asians, Indians, Jews, and others. Twenty miles behind these groups are Hispanics. And 50 miles behind the Hispanics are blacks.

Why are the blacks last? Sadly, they were used to build the route of the marathon and then held in chains while the other groups started the race. Eventually, they were freed, but a considerable gap had emerged between them and the other participants.

Strickland says I should stop fighting for my race, African-Americans, and fight for the human race. I wish I could. But my people are far behind in the marathon. Unless a concerted effort is made to advance black people, we will always be behind in claiming the prize. This effort is made more difficult by groups blocking our path by dismantling efforts such as Affirmative Action. And although we will have to run ten times as hard as everyone else, we'll continue to run and struggle for the prize.

Anjuan Simmons Electrical engineering senior

Why I Believe in Affirmative Action

02/27/2012 11:55:29 AM

AUTHOR'S NOTE: My experience fighting for affirmative action as a college student compelled me to write this post in early 2012.

Most of you probably associate me with technology. After all, I work as an information technology consultant, and a lot of the content that I post to Facebook, Twitter, Google Plus, my blog, and other online social networks covers technology. However, I also write and speak about minority advocacy issues, and, with Black History Month coming to an end this week, I thought I would discuss a topic about minorities that has gotten a lot of attention in the past week: affirmative action.

Before I continue, I want to warn you that I will discuss this already difficult topic in a very candid manner. I will also discuss how my views on affirmative action are tied to my personal experience with being called the "N-Word", but I will write out the full word because, well, it was always fully spoken or written out against me. If you don't like frank discussions about race or don't like reading the n-word spelled out, then I advise you to stop reading now. Actually, I assume that most of the people who would be offended have already stopped reading and have moved on to some other less challenging part of the internet.

An affirmative action case [72] is heading to the United States Supreme Court based on a lawsuit filed by a white female who was denied admission to the law school of The University of Texas at Austin. The white female, named Abigail Fisher, claims that less qualified minority applicants were admitted based on their race, and she was denied because she's white. For those of you who were, like me, students at UT in 1996, this lawsuit is nearly identical to what would become known as the Hopwood Decision. In that case, Cheryl Hopwood, also a white female, was denied admission to UT's law school, and she believed this was done due to preferential treatment

---

[72] http://www.star-telegram.com/2012/02/25/3762622/ut-reverse-discrimination-case.html

given to Black and Latino applicants. While the Supreme Court declined to hear Hopwood's case, the Fifth Circuit did rule in Hopwood's favor and race could no longer be used as a factor for admissions, recruitment, and retention programs in states under the jurisdiction of the court. This included UT, LSU, Texas A&M, and many other colleges and universities in Texas, Louisiana, and Mississippi.

I enrolled at UT in 1993 as a recipient of the Texas Academic Honors Award (TAHA), an academic scholarship that was part of UT's overall affirmative action program. This scholarship was designed to attract qualified Blacks and Latinos who could thrive despite the rigorous academic environment at UT. Many people think that affirmative action programs are designed to take things away from white people and give them to underserving minorities. They think of affirmative action programs as vehicles for denying white high school students on the honor roll admission to universities like UT while failing black students making C's and D's are admitted to the school.

However, the TAHA was designed to reward academically excellent minorities with high grades, high scores on standardized tests like the SAT, and demonstrated leadership ability both inside and outside their schools. I know this because I had to demonstrate these qualities when I applied for the scholarship. Fortunately, I was in the top 10 percent of my high school senior class. Actually, I was in the top 10 (I believe I was the 5th best student in my graduating class). I also had an excellent SAT score. It wasn't Dwayne Wayne's perfect score on the math portion of the SAT, but it was a great score (and higher than Abigail Fisher's SAT score of 1180). So, I, like other recipients of the TAHA, represented minorities who excelled in high school but may have lacked the financial resources that academically strong white students usually could access, primarily as beneficiaries of institutional racism. Despite having other academic scholarships, I definitely benefitted from the $5,000 per year the TAHA provided me during my four years as an electrical engineering student at UT.

The Hopwood Decision, which was rendered in March 1996, ended the TAHA scholarship and the other affirmative action programs at UT. I would retain my scholarship benefits until I graduated in 1997, but minorities who had planned to enroll at UT in the fall semester of 1996 would not have access to affirmative action assistance of any kind. Despite the fact that I would be one of the last students to receive the full benefits of the TAHA, I joined in the many protests against the Hopwood Decision that took place on the campus of UT. This included marches, and I also wrote two letters about the need for affirmative action to the Firing Line of the Daily Texan, the campus newspaper. I reprinted them on my blog, and you can find them here [73] and here[74].

Some of you may be thinking, "Anjuan, you and other minorities didn't really need affirmative action programs back in 1993, right? And, surely, they aren't needed now? We've come a long way. Times have changed, right?"

No, times have not changed. Allow me to share an example. A story that wasn't covered much last week concerned a baseball coach who was suspended last Monday for something he posted on his Facebook page. This coach, a white man named John Kelly[75], made a Facebook post that included this sentence:

I'm so sick of reading about this dumb stupid Nigger Whitney Houston.

When his post was reposted by the mother of a former player, it came to the attention of the board of the youth baseball league John Kelly worked for, and he was suspended from his position as president and banned from coaching for a year. However, I was fascinated by this statement from John Kelly regarding his use the word nigger in his Facebook post:

I didn't even realize I put it in until after I sent it.

---

[73] http://www.anjuansimmons.com/blog/2012/2/25/my-first-letter-to-the-daily-texan-about-affirmative-action.html

[74] http://www.anjuansimmons.com/blog/2012/2/25/my-second-letter-to-the-daily-texan-about-affirmative-action.html

[75] http://www.suntimes.com/news/metro/10838623-418/coach-benched-for-calling-whitney-houston-the-n-word-on-facebook.html

So, what does that mean? Does that mean that he subconsciously used an extremely hurtful and racist pejorative? John Kelly also stated this:

I do stand behind everything I said except the 'n'-word.

So, he stands behind calling a recently deceased person "dumb" and "stupid"? Like many white people caught using the word nigger, John Kelly also claimed that he is not a racist. He even said this:

I have some amazing friends who are black.

This to me is the key to why affirmative action is needed. Most racists don't know that they are racists. They think that because they don't have police dogs attack blacks or spray them with fire hoses like federal and state government law enforcement officials did in the 1950's and 1960's, they can't be racists. However, the truth is that racists have black friends; and refer to them as niggers when they don't think they will get caught.

Let me be clear. I don't think that all white people are racists. I don't even think that most white people are racists. In fact, I have a great deal of love for many of my white friends and have, in return, been shown a lot of love by them. However, I know that there are enough white people with racist mentalities who can, perhaps even subconsciously, hinder the progress of minorities who just want a chance to pursue their dreams. It was just at the end of last year that Countrywide[76], one of the largest providers of home loans, was found by the Department of Justice to have, in 200,000 cases, charged higher interest rates and fees to Blacks and Latinos than whites with similar credit ratings. Racism has transformed from Jim Crow to people like John Kelly. It's not overt racism that we have to fight. We have to fight against mental beliefs that many white people with power have about the inherent inferiority of minorities. These beliefs often only come to light from actions like an unwitting Facebook post or a federal investigation.

---

[76] http://www.nytimes.com/2011/12/22/business/us-settlement-reported-on-countrywide-lending.html?_r=1

Embracing My Blackness

I personally experienced this "mental racism" a year after the Hopwood Decision. It was May 1997, and I was a resident assistant in one of the campus dorms at UT. I was excited about my upcoming graduation and looked forward to starting my career at Andersen Consulting after I received my degree.

One day I returned to my dorm room to find a piece of paper pinned to my dorm room door. I turned the paper over to a UT police officer after reading it several times so I don't have a copy. However, I won't ever forget what was written on it. The top of the paper said this:

What's a nigger like you trying to get an electrical engineering degree? Shouldn't you be out robbing people?

Beneath these words were crude drawings of three figures. The figure on the left was a male looking to the right. Above the figure on the left were the words "You". The figure in the middle was a female bending over with her face down and her legs straight. Above this figure were written the words "Your Girlfriend". The female's head was pointed in the direction of the figure on the left and her butt was against the male figure on the right. Above the male figure on the right were written the words "Me".

While I was disturbed by the words and the included drawing, I wasn't surprised. The first time I was called a nigger was when I was in the fourth grade. One of my fellow students (let's call him Tim), objected to my use of a water fountain in the hallway and said something to the effect of "Nigger, you're taking too long at the water fountain!" So, I knew that some people would negatively assess me solely based on the color of my skin.

I never found out who left the racist picture on my dorm room door, but I did receive this anonymous email a few years later:

Message-ID: 10253934.957639809546.JavaMail.imail@spike.excite.com
Date: Sat, 6 May 2000 12:03:29 -0700 (PDT)
From: anonymous name eticxe_3@excite.com
To: asimmons@marconi.me.utexas.edu
Subject: Anjuan:apologies May 97 letter

Dear Anjuan (R. Simmons),

A while ago (about May 97) you may have received mail from me of an offensive nature. The letter was made anonymous. It was threatening too because of its meanness.

I wanted you to know that everything about that was just a prank. I didn't even know you and I had no ill will towards you. In fact, the way I planned it, I would just pick someone's name out at random. I came up with yours. Then, I thought of some theme to add to the letter to make it mean.

That's why it had the racist note to it. I'm not racist. For whomever I'd have picked, I would've added the appropriate theme. So please don't think that I have ill will towards you personally, or for your race or in any way whatsoever. I never did.

I feel very sorry right now about what I did whether I caused alot of trouble or none. At the time I didn't think anything about ir, I guess I thought it would just cause anger for a little while and that's it. But I thought about it and was thinking different now.

Again, I'm very sorry and I hope you can forgive me.

P.S. Whew! Glad I found your emails on the internet

As you can see, the person who left the racist letter on my dorm room door insisted that he/she was not a racist in the same way that coach John Kelly believes that he is not racist. However, this anonymous person questioned a "nigger" pursuing a degree in electrical engineering and included a violent drawing of him raping my girlfriend in front of me. Therefore, this was clearly a racist act. Like John Kelly, this anonymous person engaged in racism when he thought he/she couldn't be caught and then denied being a racist.

I've been asked by friends both in person and via online messages that I should stop talking and writing about racism and the need for programs like affirmative action that exist to help minorities both academically and professionally. They argue that such programs only result in division due to the perception that minorities receive unfair advantages. However, I strongly disagree. Affirmative action is not about giving unfair advantages. Affirmative action is about countering the unfair treatment of minorities that still exists in our society as well as correct the historical disadvantages that still slow our collective advancement. While I will be the first to celebrate a world where everyone is judged by the content of their character, I can't forget those 200,000 cases of Blacks and Latinos who have to pay more for their homes than whites simply because of the color of their skin. Nor can I forget the untold number of black kids who may have played for coach John Kelly while he inwardly thought of them as niggers. And I definitely can't forget Tim, who called me a nigger at a water fountain outside my fourth grade classroom or the anonymous person who used racism to intimidate me as I pursued my own academic goals. I cannot keep silent because racist mentalities have real consequences which can kill the dreams that many minorities have of owning a home, playing a sport, or of getting an education. To pretend that racism doesn't exist would betray those who need to hear about my own battles with racism. It's critical for them to understand that they, too, can overcome.

What the World Needs from Trayvon Martin

03/26/2012 07:07:29 AM

AUTHOR'S NOTE: The murder of Trayvon Martin and the subsequent acquittal of his killer didn't surprise me, but it still caused me to feel pain. I still hope that the killing of this young man can help this nation have honest conversation about race, but I am not very hopeful that will happen.

The murder of Trayvon Martin weighs on my heart in ways that only <u>two other events</u>[77] in my life have done. The first event occurred in middle school when a white student called me a nigger for using the water fountain for too long. The second event occurred in my senior year at the University of Texas at Austin when an anonymous person left a note on my dorm room door wondering why a nigger would study electrical engineering when I should be out committing crimes. The note also included a crude drawing of the anonymous person raping my girlfriend in front of me.

These are the types of events that change you. You're never the same. Life takes on a hint of bitterness and never quite returns to its previous sweetness. Other successive events in my life like getting married and the birth of my three children helped to slightly blunt the pain, but a part of me became forever hardened.

And then the news came about a young kid in Florida being shot and killed after buying iced tea and Skittles. Trayvon Martin was shot and killed by an overzealous neighborhood watchmen who was let go by the police without being searched, tested for drugs, arrested, or forced to surrender his gun license.

I'm sure that Trayvon was not a perfect kid. In fact, several people are digging into his online and offline history to find unsavory details about him. Sure, he had tattoos, a politically incorrect Twitter handle, and a less than healthy interest in "thug life". He had the penchant for making unwise

---

[77] http://www.anjuansimmons.com/blog/2012/2/27/why-i-believe-in-affirmative-action.html

decisions that define his age group. Trayvon Martin was an imperfect person.

Imperfect people can be victims, too.

These attempts to somehow justify Trayvon's murder or exonerate his killer remind me of the outdated view that only virgins can be raped. It's a consequence of the Madonna-Whore complex:

PERSON 1: "Did you hear that Becky was raped last week?"

PERSON 2: "Oh, no, that's horrible. Didn't she move in with her boyfriend last year?"

PERSON 1: "Yeah."

PERSON 2: "Well . . . it's not like she was a virgin, right?"

In Trayvon's case, it's the "Magical Negro"-Thug complex:

PERSON 1: "Did you hear that a black kid named Trayvon was killed a few weeks ago?"

PERSON 2: "Oh, no, that's horrible. Wasn't he suspended from school for something?"

PERSON 1: "Yeah."

PERSON 2: "Well . . . it's not like he was an Honor Roll student, right?"

It is illogical and irresponsible to minimize a person's tragedy due to that person's flaws. If flawlessness is the prerequisite for compassion, then we are all doomed to lives without pity.

I Am Trayvon

I never knew Trayvon, but we have a lot in common. Like Trayvon, I was an imperfect 17 year old. I was a straight-A student with perfect conduct grades, but I did plenty of things I had not business doing.

Like Trayvon, I was a black kid with a "funny name". I'm sure we both had the same experience of having to regularly explain to others how to pronounce our names. I was also a 17 year old kid with a girlfriend who cared about my safety just like Trayvon's girlfriend who talked with him mere moments before he was killed.

Trayvon's murder is personal for me because, in many ways, his story is my story. I was just fortunate enough to not run into the wrong racist.

My Sons Will Be Trayvon

Last week the President, despite surely knowing the political heat he would take, said, "If I had a son, he would look like Trayvon."

I have two sons, ages 7 and 5, and they will look like Trayvon in a few short years. I hoped that the things I had to do as a teen-ager to disarm the innate suspicion society has of black men wouldn't be necessary for them. Things like never taking a backpack into a store, always making sure I had a receipt for anything I purchased, and always being well dressed and well spoken.

Trayvon's death was a reminder that I'll have to comfort them when people fear them simply due to the color of their skin. Like when people cross the street to avoid them or when people say "I'll take the next one" when seeing them alone in an elevator. These are elements of the Black Male Experience that I hoped they would be spared. Because of Trayvon, I know I'll need to have the same uncomfortable conversations with them that my parents had with me.

What the World Needs from Trayvon Martin

Despite the media attention, many people wonder why black people are making a big deal about Trayvon. Well, in the same way that Trayvon's murder has focused and united many blacks, many racists have become focused and united as well. I spent five seconds doing a Google search and found this example (among MANY other examples) from thenewfascist.blogspot.com:

Trayvon Martin

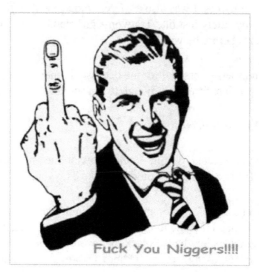

The nigger worship is in high gear now across our once-great country, but not all Americans are mourning nigger Trayvon Martin's death. I'm *celebrating* it! That dead nigger will never have the opportunity to impregnate a nigger sow and further pollute the earth with niggers. I hope Trayvon lived long enough to understand what happened when his victim, George Zimmerman, pulled the trigger and sent him to the big watermelon patch in the sky. *Fascism forward!*

What the world needs to learn from Trayvon is that carelessly taking the life of one person devalues all of our lives. Sure, he may be "just another dead black kid" to some people, but racism and prejudice have a tendency to grow and spread if left unchecked. You may not care about Trayvon's particular demographic, but what will you do when they come for you?

First they came for the Communists
And I did not speak out

Because I was not a Communist
Then they came for the Socialists
And I did not speak out
Because I was not a Socialist
Then they came for the trade unionists
And I did not speak out
Because I was not a trade unionist
Then they came for the Jews
And I did not speak out
Because I was not a Jew
Then they came for me
And there was no one left
To speak out for me

- Pastor Martin Niemoller

Comments

AUTHOR: Shareef
URL: http://shareefjackson.com
DATE: 03/26/2012 01:13:15 PM

This point is so powerful that I hope people read it twice: Trayvon's murder is personal for me because, in many ways, his story is my story. I was just fortunate enough to not run into the wrong racist."

THIS is the issue. It can happen to ANY of us if we happen to be at the wrong place at the wrong time. Doesn't matter what kind of degree you have, what your background is, or anything. It's the luck of the draw that we don't happen to be stalked by a dude like Zimmerman.

AUTHOR: Amani Channel
URL: http://www.webvideochefs.com
DATE: 03/26/2012 01:24:58 PM

All of us are Trayvons. We've all been in situations where someone (usually law enforcement) has been a little too aggressive. The sad thing is that these things continue to happen and only extreme cases bring attention to the problem. If Zimmerman had been a cop, there would be little if any discussion of the case, and even still it is questionable if he will be brought to justice. If Casey Anthony got off, I shudder to think that will happen here. I just hope folks keep it under control if the outcome isn't what folks are expecting.

AUTHOR: Anjuan Simmons
DATE: 03/26/2012 01:57:40 PM

@Shareef and @Amani: Thank you for your comment, gentlemen. Indeed, what happened to Trayvon could have happened to any of us. I hope we will honor Trayvon's memory by working toward better relations between the races no matter what happens to Zimmerman.

Brittany King
DATE: 03/26/2012 04:14:19 PM

Powerful read Anjuan!

AUTHOR: Anjuan Simmons
DATE: 03/26/2012 04:25:10 PM

Thank you, Brittany!

AUTHOR: andrea jackson
DATE: 03/26/2012 06:32:17 PM

Thanks! I never experienced overt racism til I moved to Brazoria County. I was floored.
I don't give a damn what Trayvon did in the past. Zimmerman didn't know it and at that moment, he wasn't doing anything. Zimmerman is a murderer. He disobeyed a direct order from the police...do not pursue. The fact of the matter is black boys are the most endangered species on the planet. I'm afraid I can't protect my son or yours.

AUTHOR: Nick Blaumann
DATE: 03/28/2012 11:02:26 PM

And what about whites who are called names and attacked by Blacks? Blacks are far more nasty and aggressive. Blacks do not fit into human society.

AUTHOR: GeorgeZimmermanFan
DATE: 03/28/2012 11:42:02 PM

Zimmerman had every right to follow and ask Trayvon questions beacuse Trayvon was on private property. Zim pays to live there, not Trayvon, and after a few burglaries in a supposed safe gated community, any unfamiliar face is a suspect.
That Trayvon thug got offended for questions and made the first move, no question about it. Zim did what anyone else would do, expect I would off shot that Trayvon in his head to make sure it was dead. You Blacks create your own stereotype. ZIMMERMAN=HERO

AUTHOR: BringSegregationBackToAmerica
DATE: 03/29/2012 03:07:24 AM

If you niggers don't like it here move the fuck to Africa!

AUTHOR: the truth
DATE: 03/29/2012 04:28:02 AM

your logic is distorted by your blackness, the reason blacks are viewed with suspicion is because they commit the majority of violent crime and it would be foolish not to keep your guard up around them. as a father myself i appreciate your point and it is a shame things have to be that way, but the problem lies with blacks themselves. stop the crime and violence (and on a less serious note stop the ignorance and lack of civility) and over time perceptions will change.
here is the absolute truth from a 40-something white man and i think it is profound. your people have been sold a bill of goods by your liberal handlers that exploit you. the idea that racism exists because you are a different color. now think how stupid is that? many races of color who are different and have different cultures are respected and flourish. how many orientals are viewed with suspicion? none! and we have fought wars against oriental nations not too far back. it is sad but blacks created the problem with their choices and behavior, the majority have not adjusted well to

civilized society. so we play a game modern society has inflicted. we say nothing but blacks are not trusted or accepted only tolerated, any neighborhood, shopping mall, restaurant etc...that reaches a level of around 20% blacks will empty of white people quickly, not because your skin is brown but because of the fear of crime, loud uncivilized behavior and general unpleasantness associated.

i feel i am a fair person, i believe a black man is entitled to anything he can earn and achieve and i would love to see blacks as a whole succeed and become more civilized. that is the American ideal, best man gets the job etc....but over 6 trillion dollars in wealth has been transferred to blacks (unearned) since the 1960's. AA has ensured college admissions and employment that was not earned. no stone has been left unturned by the government to aid and protect blacks and what has been done with it? the majority have squandered any opportunity to advance and earn respect and a place in our society, so they are merely tolrated because they have to be. speaking of Trayvon how many black kids are killed by other blacks? where's the race pimps when that happens? it is rare for a "white" to harm a black nowadays that's why it's big news and the media and race-baiters get all lathered up. but the truth is blacks kill other blacks all the time and no one seems to care and the majority of interracial crime is blacks killing, robbing, raping and beating the hell out of whites. the hypocrisy is astounding! if a black man was stopped and questioned at midnight in a wealthy white neighborhood we'd hear all about profiling etc...but what would happen to a wealthy white man in a black neighborhood at midnight? there is a reason things are the way they are and it starts with the personal responsibilty of all blacks. they will accept no blame for their conditions despite being helped more than any other race. i am beginning to think our ancestors had wisdom we have to relearn the the races cannot co-exist and must be seperated. after all you've had 150 years to step up to the plate and seem to be going backwards. you can think welfare & hip hop culture for that.

AUTHOR: Andybinga
DATE: 03/29/2012 05:36:21 AM

You forgot the part about witness seeing Trayvon on top of Zimmerman bashing his head into the sidewalk.

AUTHOR: J
DATE: 03/29/2012 05:54:45 AM

I am sorry for your sadness, but I was distracted by your comparison of the apathetic attitude towards Trayvon's death to the Madonna-Whore complex. It is a faulty analogy. In your example, Becky moving in with her boyfriend prior to her being raped is not a flaw in her character, or even a flaw for that matter. It is simply her decision to live with her boyfriend. However, in your example of the "Magical Negro" thug complex (which I have never heard before), the troubled student being suspended from school is the result of a negative flaw in an imperfect human. This attempt at demonstrating the correlation between these two complexes creates confusion when trying to understand the logistics on the topic.

But, to hone in on the emotions of your entry, I am sorry that you have been treated unfairly and witnessed discrimination. You shouldn't take it personally though. Many stupid people populate the planet. They speak or act on impulse, lacking any knowledge a priori/ a posteriori. If you try to understand their reasoning, you will drive yourself insane; moreover, you are searching for something that does not exist.

AUTHOR: Mooga Booga
DATE: 03/29/2012 03:29:41 PM

People dig information on the Holy Trayvon not because he is thus made guilty, but to counteract the fake image created by the media of Trayvon as some sort of an innocent child who couldn't possibly be guilty of anything. Now, you don't seem to be pissing and moaning about media lies in that direction, so why are you upset about people pulling the real trabone from below the holy but fake media image of him? He was killed not because he "made unwise decisions" in general, he was killed because he made yet another, specific unwise decision to attack a neighborhood watchman, who, to Trabone's misfortune, happened to be armed (with a legal weapon he was licensed to carry) and defended himself instead.

Btw, how many pissing and moaning articles did you write about a bazillion niggers killed by other niggers (with illegal guns they were NOT licensed to carry; over illegal crap like drug dealing etc.) just since the beginning of this year in places like Detroit, Philly, and so on? Why such selectivity of what weighs heavy on your heart?

69

Embracing My Blackness

The long and the short of it is, the Holy Traboon was a marauding thug and he was looking for trouble and he found it. And as far as your phony touchy-feely moralizing, the answer to you is, fuck off niggers.

AUTHOR: thetruth
DATE: 03/30/2012 04:57:21 PM

i noticed how you are now taking a break from decrying racial injustice. i think in the wake of the the Trayvon incident we should put a sharp focus on racial injustice. some points for discussion:
1) black males though 6% of the general population commit 52% of all violent crime. and interacial violence is overwhelmingly blacks assaulting whites.
2) despite 150 years and roughly 6 trillion dollars of wealth transferred, legalized discrimination in favor of blacks (AA) the majority of blacks still fail, cost our government a fortune in "assistance" cry racism and show no gratitude for the help they receive.
3) blacks are the leaders in crime, illegitimacy, illiteracy, being on welfare etc...they are rude, sullen, loud, uncouth and ill-mannered their prescence in any appreciable numbers at a location---instant ghetto.
4) they openly and legally discriminate all the time but would cry like babies
if the situation were reversed. BET, miss black america, united negro college fund, NAACP etc...if any of these same things were white only you would cry racism though you do the same thing.
these are just a few of the racial injustices i see, there are many more. but i would say any racism that exists in this country blacks are responsible for. they are more color conscience than any whites are, they have made no effort to help themselves, they use 200yr old events as excuses for failure in 2012. just the way the events regarding Trayvon have transpired says a lot. i don't know what happened and niether do you but i know it was more likely he was attacked and was merely defending himself than he shot someone for no reason. who needs a hassle like that?
as i have said i do not dislike black people; i wish them all the success and happiness they can attain, but i see these problems. blacks always want to see racism and cry about injustice. very rarely do i see blacks taking responsibility for their own actions and the small percentage who do will rarely address the problems blacks bring on themselves. Bill Cosby tried and he was shouted down. please remember it was white people who freed the black man, he did not free himself. civil rights came about because of

white elected officials. but many blacks are not free in their minds they do not try to improve themselves, they are content to act like animals and collect that "gubberment" check and the ones who do better never call them on it. if i were a black man i would be embarrased of my race and try to improve it. whites have done enough to help the black man it is time he helped himself.

AUTHOR: Mark
DATE: 04/01/2012 11:27:04 PM

Q: What's the difference between Mozart and Trayvon?

A: Mozart was good at composing, Trayvon is currently decomposing

AUTHOR: electrician the woodlands tx
URL:
https://plus.google.com/106262851303317459716/about?gl=US&hl=en
DATE: 07/10/2012 11:33:16 AM

This point is so powerful that I hope people read it twice: "Trayvon's murder is personal for me because, in many ways, his story is my story. I was just fortunate enough to not run into the wrong racist."

Statistically Speaking - Solving Problems of Color

01/11/2013 09:49:52 PM

AUTHOR'S NOTE: While I often call out the institutionalized racism in America, I do realize that African-Americans need to own our rehabilitation. This post lays out the problems that face African-American communities and my thoughts about how to solve them. Many of the tools I list are specific to Houston, but many of them have counterparts in other cities.

Our nation is one that thrives on statistics. It is difficult to open a newspaper or magazine and not find some statistical fact. Whether it is how many grams of fiber in your diet can supposedly reduce your chances of colon cancer, predicting who will win the Super Bowl, or learning the probability of dying in a plane crash, numbers give us a sense of control over the apparent randomness of life. Supposedly, if we can understand the chance that something might happen, then we can make decisions that favor our survival and prosperity.

However, statistics about African-Americans do not paint an attractive picture of Black society in areas such as crime, education, and health. According to the 2001 Federal Bureau of Investigation Uniform Crime Reports, African-Americans were arrested for 48.7% of murders, 53.8 % of robberies, 68.1% of gambling offenses, and 34.8% of rapes. Therefore, although African-Americans make up approximately 12% of the United States population, we are disproportionately represented in profiles of criminal activity. Furthermore, the 2002 results from the College Board showed that the combined average score for the math and verbal portions of the SAT was 857 for blacks. It was 1060 for whites. On the health front, according to combined information from the Centers for Disease Control, American Heart Association, and the National Institute for Health, we disproportionately suffer and die from cancer, diabetes, cardiovascular disease, high blood pressure, and HIV. In fact, AIDS is the leading cause of death among African-American women ages 25-34 and among African-American men ages 35-44. Another sad commentary on black sexuality is the fact that we are 27 times more likely to have gonorrhea and 16 times more likely to have syphilis than our white counterparts. Rounding out our survey of African-American statistics, we find that 49.7% of black women

72

and 28.1% of black men are obese. It seems that being an African-American can be hazardous to your health.

How should we as African-Americans view these "facts"? There are three general responses. First, we can choose to not believe these statistics and deem that they are completely false and gathered using biased methods by people who have an agenda against African-Americans. Second, we can admit that the statistics are somewhat true but are not due to intrinsic faults in African-American people nor problems with black society. Rather, the legacy of slavery and racism have contributed to African-Americans becoming the unhealthiest, most criminally inclined, and educationally challenged racial group in America. If slavery never happened and racism could magically disappear, then African-American success would mirror that of other ethnic groups. Third, we can believe the numbers are a valid commentary on African-Americans and prove our inferiority to other racial groups.

Clearly, the third response is unacceptable and the first response is too simplistic. The second one allows us to look at the numbers and accept what may be a painful truth. The preponderance of evidence supports the view that African-Americans are not succeeding at the same level as Caucasians and even other minority groups. One major reason for this is the legacy of American slavery (and its successors in Jim Crow laws, lynching, and segregation) which placed a huge roadblock in the path of African-American success. Furthermore, studies have shown that socioeconomic status has a large role in the differences between African-Americans and other races since it influences access to education, jobs, health insurance and other means of personal advancement and security. Groups with high education and income levels have fewer health problems and lower incidences of criminal behavior regardless of racial background. Therefore, poverty is another major factor in the inability of African-Americans to succeed as a group. However, simply working to improve our own individual socioeconomic status cannot be valid response.

Most of the people who read this article are African-Americans who do not have to deal with poverty. We, as well-resourced African-Americans, have found a way to attend schools of higher learning and obtain jobs that pay relatively high wages. We have beaten the odds and have achieved a relatively high level of success. So, how should we respond to these statistics about our African-American cohorts?

Embracing My Blackness

We need to take both an individual and a collective approach to the situation. As people born into the African-American race but fortunate to have risen above the odds, we can use our resources to help other black people. Many opportunities exist in the city of Houston to improve the lives of the less fortunate on a personal level. For example, the Star of Hope (http://www.sohmission.org) exists to help the homeless (who are overwhelmingly of African-American descent) by providing shelters for men, women, and children and services to overcome substance abuse, mental illness, and lack of education. Also, many predominately black centers of worship have youth, men, women, and prison ministries that seek to improve people's lives through support, programs, and religious worship. Although becoming involved on an individual level can have a huge impact, some problems can only be resolved by the collective efforts of a group. The NAACP (http://www.naacphouston.org/), 100 Black Men (http://www.100blackmen.org/), National Coalition of 100 Black Women (http://www.ncbw.org/), and other minority organizations have chapters that endeavor to improve the standard of living for African-Americans in Houston.

Although statistics about African-Americans commonly over-emphasize the problems of black people and can be misapplied without an understanding of the socioeconomic and political factors that disproportionately inhibit the advancement of African-Americans, they do point to problems in the black community. By becoming active on both an individual and a collective level, we can help paint a brighter picture of the African-American condition.

My Piece in Empower Me Magazine on Diversity and Agility

DATE: 04/22/2013 10:19:51 PM

AUTHOR'S NOTE: Trayvon Martin's death reminded me that African-Americans need to get organized when it comes to advocating for our rights. I didn't explicitly say it in this piece, but this post was one way that I want to use the tools I've mastered as a technology professional to help us get organized and start making progress.

I'm passionate about diversity and inclusion in the corporate world, especially when it comes to the technology sector. I believe that companies that embrace a variety of genders, races, religions, ages, and other protected statuses maximize their ability to create innovative products and services. I was happy when Entrepreneur Extraordinaire Adrienne Graham[78] asked me to write a post for her site Empower Me! Magazine[79] because it gave me a chance to combine a tech concept with diversity. I titled the post, "Diversity Through Agility" because I used elements of the Agile software development method to describe a way for organizations of any size to roll out diversity and inclusion initiatives. Here's the full piece:

I've had the privilege of working for large corporations that could afford to invest millions of dollars into diversity and inclusion initiatives. These companies roll out mandatory annual training about the importance of diversity and how to avoid creating hostile environments for protected statuses such as gender, race, religion, sexual orientation, etc. Although I left years ago, Accenture remains the company I spent the majority of my career as an employee. Accenture was so intent on creating a diverse workforce that it created a Chief Diversity Officer (now called Chief Leadership Officer) executive position.

---

[78] http://www.adriennegraham.com/

[79] http://www.empowermemagazine.com/

These corporations invest heavily in diversity and inclusion because they believe a strong return will be made in their investment. They realize that the world is becoming more diverse, and the inability to attract diverse job seekers will soon become a competitive disadvantage. Also, as a practical matter, some government contracts stipulate that bidding companies meet diversity requirements. Corporations that don't diversify their workforces disqualify themselves from billions of dollars in potential revenue.

If you are an entrepreneur, then you may not have the budget to create a Chief Diversity Officer or develop and deploy mandatory annual diversity training. However, that does not mean that you cannot improve the diversity of your organization. A methodology that has become popular in the software engineering industry can be tailored to small and mid-sized companies and used to quickly roll out diversity initiatives. It's called Agile.

What is Agile?

Agile is a methodology that focuses on delivering rapid results that improve over time. Instead of a long design and build process followed by testing the entire application (called the "waterfall methodology"), Agile focuses on small design-build-test cycles where chunks of the application are built and delivered.

Agile is an iterative development methodology where items are taken off a large backlog of product features, put into an iteration (often called a Sprint) lasting two to four weeks, and delivered as potentially shippable software. Since each iteration is a small time-box, the features put into it have to be well defined. During the iteration, progress is checked every day during a quick meeting called a Scrum or a Stand Up (i.e., everyone literally stands during the meeting). Software companies from Microsoft to Google have adopted Agile practices to quickly deploy software that can be nimbly altered based on changes in the competitive landscape, needs of customers, or technology innovations.

How can a software development methodology help entrepreneurs implement diversity initiatives? It can be done by taking the spirit of Agile and following these steps: Reflect, Roll-Out, and Review.

Reflect

Spend a few days thinking about what you can do to improve the diversity of your company, and create a Diversity Backlog listing your ideas. Try to be as specific as possible. For example, instead of writing "Have a company meeting about diversity", write "Have a company meeting where we discuss diversity goals in recruiting, hiring, and mentoring". You should be creative, but it's important to be as detailed as possible. As you add items to your Diversity Backlog, assign a priority (High, Medium, Low) to each item.

Roll Out

Once you have your Diversity Backlog, choose the items to roll out to the company. This choice should be based on what can be done in a two to four week iteration and the priority of each item in the Diversity Backlog. Have a daily Stand Up with your executive team to monitor progress. Each person provides the following information during the Stand Up: Accomplishments (work done since the last Stand Up), Goals (works planned to be done today), and Blockers (things that keep work from being done). The primary outcome of each iteration is to produce a set of Potentially Deployable Diversity Initiatives. End the iteration by rolling out the initiatives to your company.

Review

Review the results of your roll out with your executive team. Try to understand what went well, what could have been improved, and what new practices need to be started. Also, survey your employees to get their point of view. Take these findings and bake them into the next Reflect period.

Conclusion

Agile is a simple yet powerful approach that is designed to deliver specific results in a short amount of time. Entrepreneurs can take the power of Agile and methodically improve the approach their companies take to diversity, and this can be done regardless of the size of the organization.

Paula Deen, SCOTUS, VRA, Affirmative Action, and Trayvon

DATE: 07/13/2013 04:24:46 PM

A few people have asked me to comment on recent events related to racism and civil rights such as Paula Deen's racist comments, the recent SCOTUS decisions to weaken the Voting Rights Act and punt the fate of affirmative action to the states, and the George Zimmerman trial (including, among many things, the testimony of Rachel Jeantel).

I have much more to say than I can write, but my summarized response is this: power only respects power. Until groups that are disproportionately affected by workplace racism, unequal access to college, and racially motivated homicide learn to gain and use power, those groups will continue to fall behind in employment, education, and equal justice under law.

I find it odd that many who have spoken out against the SCOTUS's decision on the VRA have also disparaged the victory of the LGBT community in the DOMA and Prop 8 SCOTUS decisions. Whether you agree with the LGBT lifestyle or not, they have PUT IN WORK and used power to advance their causes. They have provided a model for getting things done.

While I respect everyone's right to demonstrate via actions like blacking out their social media profiles, wearing hoodies, or buying Skittles and Snapple, those actions do not result in socio-economic advancement. Trillions of dollars flow through the Black community every year, and we need to begin using our power to halt the erosion of our lives, our liberties, and our pursuits.

My Experience as a Black Man in America

DATE: 07/20/2013 07:52:02 PM

AUTHOR'S NOTE: I wrote this in July 2013 as I considered the acquittal of Trayvon Martin's killer and the remarks by President Barack Obama about the verdict. I wanted to show that most African-American men in the United States have a shared experience of suspicion by the dominant society.

I've already grown tired of the discussions about racial inequity in America because, frankly, the time for talk has long passed. It's time to discuss solutions.

However, I do want to comment on the reaction to the President's words yesterday about Trayvon Martin. The reaction has predictably broken along party lines, but I hope to explain why it is not surprising to me that even election to the White House does not allow a person to transcend being a Black man in America.

I, too, have experienced people locking their car doors when I, simply walking to my own car, pass their vehicles in the parking lot.

I, too, have seen women clutch their purses closer to them when I approach.

I have also seen women get off the elevator after I get on even though they are clearly going to a higher floor (because I notice a higher floor selected after they, the lone occupant of the elevator, exit).

I've even had police officers say they were looking for someone who "fit my description" even though I had just arrived at the location they were patrolling two minutes ago.

I've learned to not only expect such behavior but to accept it. I've learned how to navigate in a society that often views me with suspicion simply because I'm a black man in America. Because some people don't see my undergraduate degree in electrical engineering, or my MBA, or my nearly 20 year career in the technology profession, or the fact that I've travelled to six continents. To many, the only thought that goes through their mind when they see me is, "This nigger may try to hurt me."

This is the reality that I deal with every day. And, sadly, this is the reality I will have to teach my two sons to navigate in the hopes that they can survive and overcome it.

PART 2 – THE OBAMA EFFECT

Like many African-Americans, I was mesmerized by the ascension of Barack Obama to the White House. While I thought that it was possible I would live to see an African-American in the White House, I imagined it would occur in the final years of my life. I thought the country wasn't ready, the political games were too complex, and the selection of possible candidates left a lot to be desired.

When I saw the keynote that Obama gave at the 2004 Democratic National Convention, I thought he had the potential to make a successful run for the White House. However, I viewed the announcement in 2007 of his candidacy for President of the United States as a premature act. I thought he needed far more than one term as a member of the U.S. Senate to be a viable candidate. Furthermore, Hilary Clinton would be too strong for Obama to beat.

I was wrong. Candidate Obama proved to be an excellent campaigner, and I followed his progress with great interest. I began to fear that he would be killed if he continued to be successful. After he won his first term, I began to fear that the Affordable Care Act, Obama's signature domestic success, would be overturned. When it survived scrutiny by the Supreme Court, I feared that he wouldn't win a second term due to the nation's slow recovery from the recession that started before Obama took office.

This section contains the posts I wrote about Obama from his candidacy to his the end of his first term in office. From my concerns about the adequacy of his Secret Service protection to how Obama caused me to reevaluate the Presidency itself, I see that I codified my fears in my blog posts.

Maybe I should accept a simple truth: Obama knows more than I do and finds a way to win when everyone else (including me) thinks his defeat is certain. Perhaps then I can enjoy the rest of his final term in office.

Finally, I realize that Obama is far from a perfect President. However, I think he is the best person for these times and is one of the strongest examples that, no matter your origins, unimagined heights can be achieved through hard work and dedication.

Would President Obama Need More Secret Service Protection?

03/26/2008 04:24:48 PM

I posted this question to YouTube for the CNN Republican Debate in November where they took questions from YouTube.

While my question was not aired during the debate, I think it is an important question since the election of Barack Obama would truly be a historic event in America, and I think a lot of thought has to be put into protecting the first African-American President of the United States.

Many of the comments on my question (which can be found here[80]) were hostile to the idea of granting additional protection to Obama. The more civil comments made the reasonable argument that Barack should not be given any special treatment. I think these comments were made out of ignorance of what has been done in the past to protect an African-American candidate for President.

When Jesse Jackson ran in 1984, he received more death threats than any other candidate in the history of America combined[81]. Therefore, his Secret Service protection was larger than the others due to the tremendous amount of threats of open violence directed against him.

Obama was given "special treatment" when he began receiving Secret Service protection in March 2007 which was earlier than any other

---

[80]

http://www.youtube.com/comment_servlet?all_comments&v=cvdS1Gsqbuo&fromurl=/watch%3Fv%3DcvdS1Gsqbuo

[81]

http://www.indystar.com/apps/pbcs.dll/article?AID=/20080229/OPINION/80229 0310/1301/OPINION

presidential candidate[82] in the 2008 race. In fact, it was the earliest for any candidate [83]since the practice of Secret Service protection for presidential candidates was instituted after the 1968 assassination of Senator Robert F. Kennedy.

Mark Potok posted a message on the Hatewatch site stating that online expressions of hatred have steadily increased[84] as the success of Obama's campaign has increased. These posts sometimes include calls to assassinate Barack Obama to prevent him from becoming a "Nigger President". It is almost certain that the early granting of Secret Service protection to Obama is due to these threats.

So, if Barack Obama is receiving special protection as a candidate, then should special measures be in place if he successfully wins the general election?

I think the answer lies in understanding the history of violent threats against the holders of the highest political office in America. One can assume that the President of the United States is one of the most protected people in the world. However, one also has to realize that four Presidents have been killed while in office: Abraham Lincoln[85] in 1865, James Garfield[86] in 1881,William McKinley[87] in 1901, and John F. Kennedy[88] in 1963. Also,

---

[82] http://www.npr.org/templates/story/story.php?storyId=57314288

[83] http://www.bloomberg.com/apps/news?pid=20601103&sid=ajoVQoPnNSq0&refer=us

[84] http://www.splcenter.org/blog/2008/02/20/racist-attacks-on-obama-growing-more-heated/

[85] http://en.wikipedia.org/wiki/Abraham_Lincoln

[86] http://en.wikipedia.org/wiki/James_A._Garfield

[87] http://en.wikipedia.org/wiki/William_McKinley

[88] http://en.wikipedia.org/wiki/John_F._Kennedy

since the 1960's, Gerald Ford, Ronald Reagan, and George W. Bush were attacked while appearing in public. Ford was not injured, but Reagan was hit by gunfire. Bush was not injured when a grenade thrown at him failed to detonate[89]. So, despite the protection of the Secret Service, it is possible, even in the modern era, for attacks to get through and harm, if not kill, the President.

The tactics of the Secret Service are reasonably shrouded in secrecy, but I suggest, given the high level of threats against Obama, that a special investigation into their practices be instituted by Congress. Their security practices need to be reviewed and additional measures need to be instituted in order to minimize the risk of harm to Obama should he become President. I believe that even a numerical increase in the size of is detail would be a valid measure. For example, if, for a given event, the current President is assigned 10 Secret Service Agents, then Barack should have 15 assigned to cover him.

Just as Obama's election would signal a new era of possibility in America, his assassination would cast serious doubt on the ability of America to truly rise out of the racist hatred of its past. Therefore, I believe it is reasonable for him to receive additional protection if he succeeds in becoming the 44th President of the United States.

Comments

AUTHOR: Nelson
URL: http://wnelweb.blogspot.com
DATE: 03/31/2008 02:07:09 PM

You know what? I recant my earlier position on this topic. Previously, I had said that If Mr. Obama were elected, he should receive no more or less protection than any other president. At the time, this seemed like a tenable position, but after reading Mr. Hendricks's comment, I'm going with what he said. The amount of protection should be equal to the amount of threat, as would be true for any president. That kind of is what I meant the first time, but Mr. Hendricks put it much better than I did.

---

[89] http://www.cnn.com/2005/WORLD/europe/05/10/bush.georgia/

Pax,
Nelson

AUTHOR: Anjuan
URL: http://blog.transmyth.com
DATE: 03/26/2008 11:26:40 PM

Kevin,
Thanks for the comment as well as the post on your blog. Your point is well said: there is no "one size fits all" approach to protecting the President of the United States. However, some people (as seen in the comments on my YouTube post) obviously disagree.

AUTHOR: Kevin D. Hendricks
URL: http://www.kevindhendricks.com/2008/03/26/more-secret-service-protection-for-a-black-president/
DATE: 03/26/2008 11:04:36 PM

[...] Twitter friend Anjuan Simmons posted an interesting blog entry wondering if more Secret Service protection would be needed should Barack Obama become the first black president. The answer seems like a [...]

AUTHOR: Kevin D. Hendricks
URL: http://www.kevindhendricks.com
DATE: 03/26/2008 10:50:30 PM

Seems like a no-brainer to me. The level of security should match the level of the threat. It's not an issue of fairness--all presidents should get the same treatment, it's a matter of protection.

Kind of like in a war--you decide the size of your fighting force based on who you're fighting, not what you did in the last war.

What President Barack Obama Would Mean to Me

03/19/2008 11:11:35 AM

As I write this, Barack Obama[90] has a large delegate lead over Hilary Clinton[91] who is also running for the Democratic nomination. It is virtually impossible for Hilary to surpass Obama's delegate count before the Democratic National Convention[92] so it will probably be up to the super delegates to determine if Obama will become the Democratic Party nominee. Even if that happens, he will probably have a hard fight against John McCain[93] in the general election.

However, if Barack Obama does become the 44th President of the United States, it will clearly be a historic event. Selecting an African-American man to lead this country will communicate many things about the American people. Some may question if Obama is truly an African-American, but a honest inspection of his features shows any rational person that his genetic heritage has much in common with blood that flows in the veins of the descendants of African slaves. As a man whose bloodline also strongly links me to the survivors of the Middle Passage[94] and the rigors of slavery, his ascension to the White House would tell me a lot about America's past, present, and future.

An understanding of the significance of Barack Obama's Presidency must be rooted in an understanding of the history of African-Americans[95] in the United States. The bulk of this history involves slavery. Although present

---

[90] http://en.wikipedia.org/wiki/Barack_Obama

[91] http://en.wikipedia.org/wiki/Hilary_Clinton

[92] http://en.wikipedia.org/wiki/Democratic_National_Convention

[93] http://en.wikipedia.org/wiki/John_McCain

[94] http://en.wikipedia.org/wiki/Middle_Passage

[95] http://en.wikipedia.org/wiki/African_American

before the 18th century, it was in the 1700's that enslavement of black people became widespread and codified in the laws of the land. Due to the need for labor intensive work such as harvesting tobacco and cotton, slavery spread widely in the Southern states causing blacks to become a third of the population by the late 1800's. Slave codes[96] gave masters a legal right to brutalize their slaves and treat them as they were defined by law: property. The United States Constitution[97] counted slaves as 3/5th's[98] of the population for the purpose of allocating seats in the House of Representatives[99] to Southern States which gave those States a disproportionate amount of power in Congress. The harsh life of slaves caused many to oppose it, and this rift soon led to division including violent uprisings by Nat Turner[100], John Brown[101], and others. The Dred Scott[102] decision by the United States Supreme Court[103] in 1857 and the election of Abraham Lincoln[104] in 1860 along with other national events led to the start of the Civil War[105] in 1861.

The American Civil War led to the Emancipation Proclamation[106] in 1863

---

[96] http://en.wikipedia.org/wiki/Slave_codes

[97] http://en.wikipedia.org/wiki/United_states_constitution

[98] http://en.wikipedia.org/wiki/Three-fifths_compromise

[99] http://en.wikipedia.org/wiki/United_States_House_of_Representatives

[100] http://en.wikipedia.org/wiki/Nat_Turner

[101] http://en.wikipedia.org/wiki/John_Brown_%28abolitionist%29

[102] http://en.wikipedia.org/wiki/Dred_Scott

[103] http://en.wikipedia.org/wiki/United_States_Supreme_Court

[104] http://en.wikipedia.org/wiki/Abraham_lincoln

[105] http://en.wikipedia.org/wiki/American_Civil_War

[106] http://en.wikipedia.org/wiki/Emancipation_proclamation

and eventually to the ratification of the 13th Amendment[107] of the United State Constitution in 1865 which formally ended slavery in America and freed approximately 4 million black slaves. The ratification of the 14th Amendment[108] in 1868 and the 15th Amendment[109] in 1870 granted former slaves citizenship and the right to vote, respectively. This significant improvement in the legal standing of freed blacks was hindered by the realities of widespread illiteracy among the black population, segregationist Jim Crow laws[110], and often violent harassment by groups such as the Klu Klux Klan[111]. Decades of institutional racism[112] against African-Americans passed until the Civil Rights Act of 1964[113] and the National Voting Rights Act of 1965[114] helped to undo the legal framework that had historically denied African-Americans equal access under the law.

Against this historical tapestry comes Barack Obama, a man who, if born in the America of the 17th or 18th century would probably be able to work as a house slave based on his light skin tone. However, a house slave was still

---

107
http://en.wikipedia.org/wiki/Thirteenth_Amendment_to_the_United_States_Constitution

108
http://en.wikipedia.org/wiki/Fourteenth_Amendment_to_the_United_States_Constitution

109
http://en.wikipedia.org/wiki/Fifteenth_Amendment_to_the_United_States_Constitution

110 http://en.wikipedia.org/wiki/Jim_Crow_laws

111 http://en.wikipedia.org/wiki/Klu_Klux_Klan

112 http://en.wikipedia.org/wiki/Institutionalized_racism

113 http://en.wikipedia.org/wiki/Civil_rights_act_of_1964

114 http://en.wikipedia.org/wiki/Voting_Rights_Act_of_1965

a slave denied the essential freedoms upon which this country was founded. If he had been born in the late 19th or early 20th Century, he would be able to enjoy the free life that people of African descent were able to finally universally obtain. However, running for President of the United States would have been an exercise in foolishness and futility.

Obama's strong campaign shows that America is a country that may now be ready to close the doors of discrimination and open the doors of the White House[115] to an African-American man. Elevating a member of a group of people whose ancestors were once considered inhuman property to the highest office of the land would allow the United States to finally act in accordance with the principle that all people are created equal.

The election of President Barack Obama would demonstrate that this country can let go of the paradigms of the past and embrace a new future where everyone can fully participate in improving America regardless of any physical characteristic. Those who bring fresh ideas and are willing to work to bring them to life will have the opportunity to do so. As we continue to write the early history of the 21st Century, his Presidency will allow the creation of a bright future by a country that is truly united.

I am not naive enough to believe that the United States will transform into a Utopia[116] if Barack Obama wins the White House. He will face difficult times, and there are many challenges facing this country. However, I believe that Obama is the person who can uniquely motivate American citizens to work collectively to solve our national problems. After all, the very existence of a President Barack Obama would mean that anything is possible if one is willing to, against all hope, believe in hope and achieve a dream.

Comments

---

[115] http://en.wikipedia.org/wiki/White_house

[116] http://en.wikipedia.org/wiki/Utopia

AUTHOR: APGifts
URL: http://groups.yahoo.com/group/Generation-Mixed
DATE: 05/31/2009 09:27:13 AM

Hi Anjuan,

You are more than welcomed and please
do feel free to contact me directly at
REDACTED, if I can be of any
help in recommending resources which may
be of help or interest for your research.

Have a nice day.

-- AP

AUTHOR: Anjuan
DATE: 05/19/2009 04:14:30 AM

APGifts, thanks for your comments. You have inspired me to do more research into the specifics of how light skinned slaves were truly treated compared to darker skinned slaves. While my point did not address that specifically, I do have some fact checking to do. Thanks!

-Anjuan

AUTHOR: Nelson
URL: http://wnelweb.blogspot.com
DATE: 03/26/2008 08:10:35 PM

The fact that Mr. Obama is even running for president would have been unthinkable as little as fifty years ago. The fact that he could win is wonderful. If he does, I hope and pray he will be a good president on many levels. We as a nation have come a long way and have a long road ahead. Maybe he can help light the way.
Pax,
N.

AUTHOR: Anjuan
URL: http://blog.transmyth.com
DATE: 03/19/2008 10:15:40 PM

Thanks, Kevin! I hope that we can somehow move away from being such a divided country. I think this will come when we abandon the obsolete views that prop up the illusion of differences between people. I think that many Americans have very similar interests, hopes, and dreams. I also hope that Obama gets far more than 51% of the popular vote!

AUTHOR: Kevin D. Hendricks
URL: http://www.kevindhendricks.com
DATE: 03/19/2008 10:09:05 PM

Good words. I'm pretty excited about the possibility of a historic president, too.

As great as it would be if the U.S. elects a black man (or even a woman), I think the last 8 years have shown us that winning an election doesn't mean much for where the country is willing to go. All you need is 51% (or less) of the vote to win, and that leaves a lot of people who disagree.

But that's a minor quibble.

A Question About Obama and the Black Vote

11/21/2010 11:00:00 AM

I'm going through my Facebook backup and finding interesting things to post on my blog. This is something I was asked on my wall on April 12, 2010 at 7:43 am:

Q: With Obama taking 96% of the black vote during the last presidential election, it seems race spoke louder than politics for many voters. Did Obama's race influence your vote? Why or why not?

A: I've been open in sharing that I voted for Barack Obama to become the 44th President of the United States. I think of almost everything as a "weighted average" so, while Obama's race was a decision criterion, it was not given the most weight. There were several other factors that came into play.

Before I go into those factors, I want to be clear that I don't vote based on political affiliation. I am neither a registered Republican nor a Democrat. I am simply a registered voter. I voted for George W. Bush. Twice. I voted for Clinton in 1996. I was too young to vote in 1992, but I probably would have voted for George H.W. Bush.

I believe that the first duty of every American voter is to select the person who will best lead the country. Therefore, the person who demonstrates the best decision making skills during the campaign will draw my vote. I think that then Senator Obama made a series of decisions both before and during the campaign that impressed me. He took the unpopular position of opposing the war in Iraq early in his term as a US Senator. He strategically targeted the entire nation instead of the states with the biggest horde of electoral votes. Few can argue that he ran a brilliant campaign. McCain, on the other hand, made several strategic mistakes. Foremost of these was his selection of Sarah Palin as his running mate. While I admire many aspects of Palin as a person, I believe she was far from ready to serve as Vice President. McCain's decision to run with Palin immediately removed my ability to vote for him.

Second, for better or worse, we elect personalities as well as Presidents. I liked Obama's personal story as well as his skills as a leader. His devotion to his wife and daughters mirrored my desire to be a good husband and father. I have travelled the world, and I liked the fact that he had lived in different countries. So, the parallels between his life and mine were compelling.

Of course, I was also drawn to the possibility of electing an African-American. However, we should remember that Obama had to earn the black vote. We have seen black politicians run before (e.g., Jesse Jackson), but none of them had any real chance of winning. Barack had to show that he was an authentic person of color who could actually win the White House.

So, race was a factor in my decision to vote for Obama, but it was one of several factors.

I would also like to point out the fallacy of thinking of African-Americans as a monolithic voting block that will pull the lever for any black candidate. The African-American experience is a diverse one, and many black voters put a lot of thought into what they do during elections. We need only examine Arthur Davis who soundly lost the black vote[117] during his bid for Governor of Alabama. Just as African-Americans live different lives, we also vote in different ways.

---

[117] http://www.jackandjillpolitics.com/2010/06/good-riddance-to-artur-davis/?utm_source=feedburner&utm_medium=feed&utm_campaign=Feed:+JackAndjillPolitics+(Jack+and+Jill+Politic

My Thoughts about Government Healthcare

11/14/2010 06:03:07 PM

I'm going through my Facebook backup and finding interesting things to post on my blog. This is something I posted on my wall on March 22, 2010 at 9:04 am (via Formspring[118]):

Q: Do you support the current healthcare bill?

A: I don't think the federal government is capable of passing a bill that I completely support. But, yes, I support the current health care bill. Based on recent events, Congress agrees with my point of view on this topic (a rare occurrence).

Based on my observations, support or opposition to the health care bill is based on one's fundamental belief about whether the government should engage in social welfare programs at all. Many who oppose the healthcare bill are conservatives, and they will often cite Bible verses like 2 Thessalonians 3:10 which states,

"For even when we were with you, we gave you this rule: "If a man will not work, he shall not eat."

I usually respond by asking their opinion about Leviticus 23:22 which states,

"When you reap the harvest of your land, do not reap to the very edges of your field or gather the gleanings of your harvest. Leave them for the poor and the alien. I am the LORD your God"

or Deuteronomy 24:19,

"When you reap your harvest in your field and have forgotten a sheaf in the field, you shall not go back to get it; it shall be for the alien, for

---

the orphan, and for the widow, in order that the LORD your God may
bless you in all the work of your hands."

These verses indicate to me that social welfare was deeply ingrained in the
ancient people of God.

I have also observed that most people who are against the health care bill
have health care insurance. They have no idea what it's like to live every
day in fear of getting sick or even receiving a minor injury. They also don't
realize that they themselves are one pre-existing condition or major illness
away from medical bankruptcy.

So, yes, I support the health care bill. It is far from perfect, but it will help
millions of poor and unemployed Americans. The statement "America has
the best health care system in the world . . ." has always needed to have the
qualifier ". . . if you have money," added to the end for honesty. Perhaps we
can now remove the qualifier.

Does America Need a Pastor or a CEO?

12/18/2008 08:48:03 AM

AUTHOR'S NOTE: This post was not strictly about President Obama, but erroneous claims about his "secret Muslim faith" were a rampant during the early days of his campaign. Actually, they continued for his entire Presidency. In this article, I tried to think through the belief by most Americans that every President has to be a Christian.

The Presidential Election of 2008 brought a new found interest in politics. The historic campaigns of Barack Obama (offering the first African-American President) and John McCain (offering the first female Vice President) caused many people around the world to follow the political process in unprecedented detail.

What was not so historic was the emphasis on the religious views of both candidates. Despite his well-established Christian faith, Obama had to constantly deal with false rumors that he was a Muslim. While McCain never showed the overt displays of religious belief that George W. Bush displayed, his pick of Sarah Palin for his running mate was a clear bone thrown to Christian conservatives.

It is clear that it would be very difficult, if not impossible, for a person who professed to be an atheist to be elected President of the United States. This is due to the religious foundation of this country. Many of the early settlers of America were Puritans, and their views can be summed up in the famous speech by John Winthrop[119] in which he described the young country as a "City upon a Hill". This speech set forth the idea that the world would be watching America to see if it held true to its covenant with God. Furthermore, America's success or failure would be based on whether or not it maintained Christian principles and values. In many ways, the early Puritan settlers saw the new country as a congregation and not just a collection of colonies.

Naturally, the view of America as a church led to the belief that the

---

[119] http://en.wikipedia.org/wiki/John_Winthrop

President was, in many ways, a pastor who was responsible for nurturing the spiritual health and well-being of those under his leadership. George Washington underscored this belief in his Farewell Address[120] composed at the end of his second term as President (which set the precedent that Presidents would only serve two terms). In this address, Washington cautioned Americans against the idea that "that morality can be maintained without religion". By tightly connecting morality and religion, Washington enforced the idea that a moral President had to be a religious (i.e., Christian) person.

This idea of a "Christian President" continued in both explicit and implicit forms throughout the history of America. During times of national peril, Presidents drew from the Bible and Christian principles to guide and console the nation. Despite the fact that Article VI of the United States Constitution explicitly states that "no religious test shall ever be required as a qualification to any office or public trust under the United States" (commonly called the "no religious test clause[121]"), few Americans would be comfortable with an atheist as a President.

However, America has changed in many ways from its early days as a colony of those professing Puritan morals and values. The population of the United States is composed of many religious faiths including those who claim no religious faith at all. Should Americans still expect the President to be Pastor, shepherding the country through good times as well as bad times? Or, is America more like a corporation that needs a strong CEO who should only be expected to run the country well?

If Americans came to view the President as more of a CEO, then they would expect fiscal responsibility with the budget, a strategic vision for the country, a plan for defeating competitors, a marketing strategy to positively promote the country, and efforts to maintain high individual productivity and morale. Few Americans know whether or not the CEO of their company is a Christian so a President's personal faith would be irrelevant under this point of view.

---

[120] http://en.wikipedia.org/wiki/George_Washington%27s_Farewell_Address

[121] http://en.wikipedia.org/wiki/No_religious_test_clause

In the difficult economic climate of America, many Americans want a President who can solve their problems. Just as a person who is drowning does not check the Christianity of someone who dives in to save them before accepting their help, most citizens simply want a healthy job market, low taxes, and reasonable prices for goods and services. Imposing religious requirements on a President is a privilege that often only nations going through prosperous times can afford.

So, will the President of the United States be one day sworn in on the balance sheet and income statement of the country instead of a Bible? As America continues to diversify and go through tough economic times, such an outcome may not be far from reality.

How I Came to Terms with a One-Term Obama Presidency

08/23/2012 05:18:48 PM

AUTHOR'S NOTE: I mention this in the update I added to the post, but, of course, Barack Obama won re-election in 2012. However, I wrote this when before Election Day 2012, and I attempted to summarize what I thought was a strong first term.

Update: I wrote this before Barack Obama won a second term which, of course, I was overjoyed to see, but doesn't mesh with the premise of this post.

The 2012 Republican National Convention[122] kicks off this week in Tampa, Florida. I have been closely following the election contest between Barack Obama and Mitt Romney since the Republican primary season started. Most polls show the two candidates locked in a statistical tie, and I expect that this will be a close election. Baring some unforeseen scandal or catastrophe, we probably won't know who won until very late on Election Day.

Barack Obama could lose. While I am an Independent voter, I strongly support President Obama, and I hope he gets another four years in the White House. However, the economy continues to be a drag on his candidacy. Whether it's fair or not, Obama is being blamed for not turning a horrible economy into a fantastic economy. He simply turned a horrible economy into a mediocre economy. When incumbent presidents have Obama's economic numbers, they don't get re-elected. Despite the euphoria that many of us felt when we voted for him, many voters feel that they elected Superman and have been left with Clark Kent.

I have begun resigning myself to the possibility that Obama could be a one term president. Despite his high likability numbers, slowly improving economic indicators, and the Republican party's abandonment of women,

---

[122] http://www.gopconvention2012.com/

The Obama Effect

Blacks, Hispanics, and gays, Romney could ride the wave of economic dissatisfaction right into the White House. This would force Obama to join the ranks of other one term presidents like George H.W. Bush, Jimmy Carter, Gerald Ford, and Herbert Hoover. I have begun to accept that.

Barack Obama has been a historic president, and, despite a loss in November, his accomplishments have forever changed the social and political landscape of America.

On a personal level, I continue to feel an immense sense of satisfaction when I look at the faces of men who have held the office of president and see a black man's face at the end. While Obama is the 44th President of the United States, he is the 43rd man to hold the office since we have to count Grover Cleveland twice. The 42 men before Obama represented the privileged class that the framers of the Constitution originally envisioned as the leaders of society: white men. It is amazing to think that the first president may have owned slaves who were ancestors of the current president.

My wife recently told me something said by the daughter of one her girlfriends. The daughter said, "I guess I can't be a doctor because I don't see any black ones". Her statement spoke to the challenges that African-Americans face when raising black children in a predominantly white culture. While Blacks enjoy sending their kids to outstanding schools (which usually means white teachers), Blacks also realize that this limits the ability of their children to see black leaders and role models. As famed astronaut Sally Ride once said, "You can't be what you can't see". However, when African-American children see the face of Barack Obama, they are empowered to think, "I can be President of the United States. Because someone who looks like me did it."

The significance of Obama's time in office extends beyond the Black community. His election showed that America, while far from "post-racial", was willing to place the immense powers of the presidency into the hands of a black man. It may have taken one of the most unpopular administrations in recent history, an economy on the brink of economic collapse, and an extremely unpopular war to do it, but, nevertheless, an event happened that many of us thought would never occur in our lifetimes.

As a country, we made a giant leap closer to our declared belief that "all men are created equal".

Of course, Obama is satisfying to me not simply because of the color of his skin. He has proven to be a competent holder of the office who has avoided embarrassing scandals that have plagued other presidents (e.g., Lewinsky, Iran-Contra, Watergate, et al). Obama put together a complicated health care bill that passed (albeit, barely) strict constitutional scrutiny. His foreign policy accomplishments include the killing of Osama bin Ladin, contributing to the toppling of Gaddafi, and the dismantling of various terrorist organizations from senior members of al-Qaeda to hostage taking Somali pirates. While Obama has had an imperfect presidency, it has not been the presidency of a fool.

Obama has also strengthened civil rights in many ways. He has fought for equal pay for women, lifted "Don't Ask Don't Tell", and became the first president to advocate for marriage equality for same sex couples. These acts served to bring equality to distinct groups of people, but they also helped to dignify us all. Protecting the rights of the most vulnerable members of society strengthens those rights for all of us.

If Obama is a one-term president, I can find peace in knowing that he has already cemented his legacy as a staunch defender of America's national security, a tireless fighter for universal access to healthcare for all Americans, defender of civil rights, and symbol of the infinite possibility of the United States. I can live with that. Of course, I would prefer to live with four more years.

PART 3 – BUSINESS SCHOOL

I started business school at Texas A&M's Mays College of Business in August 2008. It was an amazing and rewarding experience. I decided to pursue my MBA because I have always thought of myself as someone who operates at the intersection of business and technology. My undergraduate degree in electrical engineering and my long history working in the technology sector provided me with many technology bona fides. However, I wanted to strengthen my business acumen.

My work experience allowed me to contribute to the classes in the MBA program in a way that went beyond the theory we covered in the textbooks. Whether it was accounting, finance, marketing, operations, or one of the other business functions we studied, I has some degree of real world exposure to them all.

Business school also allowed me to experience the effectiveness of diversity. The MBA program was composed of a great mix of men, women, Americans, and students from other countries. That diversity enriched our social and cultural interactions, but I believe it also increased the amount of innovation we could bring to our ideas and projects.

I didn't have time to write too many blog posts during my time in the graduate program, but here are a few that I thought were worth printing. They cover some of the key lessons I learned in business school, how I drilled down on my true personal and professional strengths, my search for the next chapter in my career after graduation, and, one of the greatest honors of my life, my selection to give the Student Speaker speech at our MBA commencement ceremony.

Three Key Lessons of the Mays MBA Program

11/14/2008 07:17:04 PM

AUTHOR'S NOTE: The MBA program had a communication class that spanned most of the program. I thought some of the writing assignments were interesting, and I posted some of the pieces I wrote for the class to my blog.

As the first term of the MBA program draws to a close, I find myself reflecting on the many lessons that I have learned over the past few months. Of these lessons, I can think of three that have made the biggest contribution to my success in the program.

Effective Teams are Essential to Success

Fortunately, I was assigned to work on a team with a great group of people. Although we have very different personalities, we have learned to appreciate healthy debate and focus on the overall success of our group. Also, my team developed a "divide and conquer" approach where one person took primary responsibility for a set of assignments, gathered input from the group, and managed the effort to successfully complete the work. Our approach led to high grades on our assignments that would have been difficult to achieve through individual effort. I look forward to maintaining relationships with all of them long after we complete the MBA program.

Don't Let the Opposition Cloud the Goal

Athletes must always know the location of the goal. Whether it is the basketball hoop, the uprights in the end zone, or the soccer net, a successful player always knows the location of the goal despite a cloud of opposing players. Similarly, a successful MBA student always keeps in mind the ultimate goal of the program: find a job commensurate with the skills gained in the curriculum. However, career management can easily take a back seat to the flurry and intensity of the academic requirements of the program. The BUAD 620 class has helped me to maintain focus on my career by forcing me to hone essential job search skills such as resume writing, interviewing, and developing professional presence.

Take Care of Home and Home Will Take Care of You

The time commitment of the MBA program makes it difficult to spend time with my wife and three children. I often leave my house before my family wakes up and return home once they have gone to bed. However, I always keep at least one day free during the week to fully engage with my family and remind them that they still have a husband and a dad. Although that day could be spent making progress on the myriad (and seemingly never-ending) MBA assignments, I find that I am a better student when I spend uninterrupted time with my family. A kiss from my wife, a hug from my kids, or simply sitting down to eat together makes it easier to return to Wehner and endure the demands of lectures, homework assignments, quizzes, and exams.

By continuing to implement the lessons of collaborate to success, focus on the end goal, and take care of home, I am confident that I will achieve true success in the MBA program that extends far beyond the classroom. These principles will also serve me very well in my post-MBA life.

AUTHOR: Anjuan
EMAIL: anjuan.simmons@gmail.com
URL: http://
DATE: 07/09/2009 12:01:03 PM

Hi Tina,
Thanks for checking out my blog! I'm glad that you found my posts to be informative. I admire your creativity and skills as a businesswoman, and I'm sure you're working at the top of your game!

Regards,

Anjuan

AUTHOR: Tina B
URL: http://www.tinabpoetry.com
DATE: 07/08/2009 01:12:02 PM

Hi Anjuan,

I'm just dropping a line to say that I think your blogs are well-worded and so true. I've read most of them already and look forward to reading more of your opinions and experiences in the future.

May God bless you as you continue in the Mays MBA program. I am sure success awaits you!

Take care,
Tina B

Strengths Synthesis

06/29/2009 02:42:20 PM

AUTHOR'S NOTE: One of the most compelling exercises I took part in during the program was an examination of my strengths. The idea of this exercise was that, all too often, people waste time doing things they aren't good at. It is far more effective to understand your strengths so you can use them and avoid wasting time on your weaknesses.

The three Strengths exercises (energize/drain journal and paper, StrengthsFinder online quiz, and the Strengthsfinder Workshop with Professor Busch) that I completed for BUAD 620 and the results of the Birkman test that I completed for MGMT 614 provided excellent insights into my personality. I discovered key linkages repeatedly revealing themselves in the results from these activities, and I found many overlapping elements that helped me understand my core strengths. This knowledge provided guidelines that I have added to my approach to meeting my professional and personal goals.

THE TEACH-INTELLECTION-DEVELOPER LINKAGE

Teaching was one of the energizing activities I derived from my energize/drain journal, and this links with the intellection and developer themes revealed in my top five strengths. As evidenced by my intellection strength, my appreciation for intellectual conversations explains my interest in the cerebral discussions that often occur when I teach others. Also, the developer theme explains my interest in seeing people grow as a result of my teaching efforts. Finally, my Birkman results identified a strong link to the literary area of interest which describes my fondness for abstract ideas and creative communication.

This linkage also explains why I feel drained when I lack knowledge about a subject. If I do not have a sufficient level of knowledge about something, then I am unable to teach others and help them grow. Therefore, ignorance prevents me from operating in my themes of intellection and developer. As a result of this insight, I was further convinced that I need to find a career path that allows me to educate others and invest in their growth and development.

THE TECHNOLOGY-INTELLECTION-CONNECTEDNESS LINKAGE

Using technology was another energizing activity I identified from the contents of my energize/drain journal. This also links with my intellection strength, but it also links with one of my other top five strengths: connectedness. One primary reason I am drawn to technology is the way it lowers the barriers between people. For example, with a cheap webcam and an affordable internet connection, two people can communicate and see each other despite being separated by vast geographic distances. Also, online social networks like Facebook allow individuals to reconnect with long lost childhood friends or become friends with those they would have otherwise never met. Technology is helping people understand that we are all connected, and our ability to participate in shared human experiences can be very enriching and powerful. This technology enabled connectivity is one reason I am so fascinated by the many ways technology changes the way people live and interact. Furthermore, my Birkman results showed a strong link to the scientific area of interest which reinforces my desire to work in the technology industry.

My tendency to become drained by new experiences may also be explained by this linkage. When I do something for the first time, I initially lack the ability to connect it with similar experiences that would provide me with insight into how to best perform the task. This disconnects me from a comfortable frame of reference, and I lose motivation and interest in the task. In the business world, when presented with a new idea or activity, I will have to seek connections between it and a similar experience. If I am unable to do so, then I will need to find colleagues who can help me see these connections.

THE FAMILY-BELIEF-CONTEXT LINKAGE

Spending time with my family was another energizing activity highlighted by my energize/drain journal, and this links with the belief and context themes shown in my top five strengths. Taking an active role in the success of my family is one of my core values. No matter how impressive the accolades I may gain in other areas of my life, they would all become meaningless if I fail as a son, husband, and father. Also, my deep interest in understanding my family tree and the lessons of my ancestors is explained by the context theme. I believe that I can better understand my present

107

circumstances by learning about my family history. It will be important for any company that desires my employment to respect my desire to balance my work responsibilities with the needs of my family.

My belief strength may also explain why I become drained by details. Having a strong set of core values helps me when I have to make obvious moral choices. However, my values do not always provide clear choices when I have to deal with the subtle nuances of morally ambiguous decisions. As a business professional, I will have to make sure I have multiple viewpoints to help me see a decision from multiple viewpoints. It will be important for me to work on diverse teams and respect and encourage the expression of perspectives even when they are contrary to my own.

CONCLUDING THOUGHTS

When I began the Texas A&M MBA program, I expected a rigorous education in the core business topics of accounting, finance, operations, strategy, and management. The program has provided such an education, but I was pleasantly surprised by the opportunities to take an introspective view of who I am as a person. The three Strengths exercises and the Birkman test provided the opportunity for me to become better acquainted with myself.

I have grown in many ways over the past nine months. Some of the growth was due to the confirmation of the skills that I knew were strong before I entered the program. These included information technology expertise, strong written and verbal communication ability, and effective leadership. It was comforting to know that these skills transferred from the professional world to the academic world in an intact state.

I also grew by being surprised by the areas in which I was weak. Despite my strong technical background and an overall strong mathematical aptitude, I have struggled in my accounting and finance courses. While I once thought I could adequately function as an accountant or financial analysis, I now realize that those would be very poor career choices!

I have also grown to love the culture and history of Texas A&M. Having gained my undergraduate degree from the University of Texas at Austin, I was apprehensive about my ability to fully integrate into life as an Aggie.

However, the awesome traditions of Texas A&M, the genuine friendliness behind the signature "Howdy" greeting, and the excellence of the faculty have converted me into a lifelong lover of this great campus.

My Blogworld Proposal

07/01/2010 05:29:40 AM

AUTHOR'S NOTE: I sent this proposal in the BlogWord not too long after I graduated from the MBA program. I'm including it here because, even though it wasn't selected, I still think it's a great proposal!

Description

Business school is a harrowing experience for any student. It is especially tough in the Texas A&M Full Time MBA program which lasts for 16 months instead of the usual 24 month long business school program. This curriculum requires class room instruction nearly every day of the week and includes grueling assignments including case studies, oral presentations, simulations, and group projects. Anjuan Simmons started the Texas A&M MBA program on August 8th 2008, and, in addition to the rigorous academic schedule, also had to maintain relationships with his wife and three young kids.

During this session, Anjuan Simmons shares how he used social media to survive the Texas A&M MBA program. He shares that one of the first things he did upon acceptance to the program was set up a blog to chronicle his experience in business school. While looking for other MBA blogs, he met a blogger who was in the class ahead of him in the MBA program. Anjuan shares that the friendship he formed with this student deepened when he meets her in person and provides Anjuan with a mentor throughout the MBA program as well as a business colleague after he graduated with his MBA degree.

Anjuan also shows how he used Twitter to chronicle his MBA experience and meet MBA students at other universities. He describes his use of Twitter to complete an assignment in his advanced marketing class that required him to keep a daily diary of interaction with brands. Anjuan also shares his Twitter evangelism and describes the converts he makes amongst his fellow business school students.

Another key social media tool that Anjuan describes is Linkedin. Anjuan shares how he used Linkedin to look for an internship during the summer of

2009. He also goes into detail about the ways that Linkedin helped him navigate job fairs and eventually get a permanent offer that he accepted right before he graduated from the MBA program.

Next, Anjuan covers how he used Facebook to expand his personal brand with his fellow students as well as with those outside the MBA program. He explains how this provided him with a support network that helped him through stressful periods like getting placed on academic probation after his second term. Anjuan goes on to describe that the thoughts, pictures, and posts he made on the walls of his fellow students deepened his relationships with them. His use of Facebook as a branding tool was instrumental in Anjuan's election by his fellow students to serve as Student Speaker during the MBA class's graduation ceremony on December 17th, 2009.

Anjuan concludes by sharing how his use of social media improved his life at home while he was in the MBA program. The long hours he spent away from his family were made easier to bear because his wife could follow his online profiles and better understand his graduate school experiences. This allows her to empathize with him and provide more moral support than may have been possible without social media.

In summary, Anjuan shares that blogging, Twitter, Linkedin, and Facebook helped him network, find employment, and expand his personal brand during his business school experience. This allows him to not only graduate from the Texas A&M MBA program but also to thrive during his time as a graduate student.

Session Takeaways

There are four things that the audience will learn from this session

First, blogs are a useful central hub for various social media identities. They will see how I used a WordPress plugin to bring my Twitter feed into my blog and link to my Linkedin profile. They will also understand my approach for cross posting content from my blog to Facebook.

Second, Twitter is one of the best networking tools available online. Session attendees will understand my approach for meeting someone, determining if they are on Twitter, and then interacting with them via @

replies, direct messages, retweets of their content, and introducing them to other Twitter users.

Third, the audience will learn that the usefulness of Linkedin as a business tool is not to be ignored. They will see how I set up my Linkedin profile and used recommendations to form a presentation of myself that is attractive to potential employers.

Fourth, session attendees will learn my personal view that social media loses its importance if it doesn't help us maintain the most important relationships in our lives. They will hear my description of how my wife went from hating social media because she didn't understand its usefulness to becoming a fan of the medium because it helped her empathize with my business school experiences.

7 Quick Lessons Learned from a day at a Career Fair

09/25/2009 06:58:46 AM

AUTHOR'S NOTE: When I wrote this, I was about three months from graduating from the MBA program and in the thick of looking for my next career position. I wrote this after one of the innumerable career fairs I attended during that time.

1. Hand sanitizer is key. You want a job not swine flu.
2. Comfortable shoes are also essential.
3. Drink plenty of water or risk losing your voice. It's hard to interview whispering like Batman.
4. Being told, "Go to our web site and apply there" is the new way of saying "we're really not interested in you".
5. Separating the booth area from the interview area by a 100 meter distance is cruel and unusual punishment.
6. Consulting companies and financial institutions give the hardest interviews. But, in the end, they pay the best.
7. I still believe that interviews are just conversations, and I had a lot of great conversations yesterday!

My Career Search

DATE: 09/10/2009 11:19:23 AM

AUTHOR'S NOTE: I, of course, didn't know it at the time, but I was offered (and accepted) a position at Deloitte Consulting right before I graduated from the MBA program. Nevertheless, this post captures some of the concerns I had about going back into the job market during a recession.

I will graduate from Texas A&M with my MBA in December. While I am very excited about this milestone, I am even more excited about the career search I am currently conducting.

I say "career search" instead of "job search" because I am not just looking for an employment opportunity. My goal is to find a company that will allow me to make the maximum contribution I can to their organization based on my skills and experience while also growing as a professional. After working as an information technology consultant with Accenture for more than a decade, I am ready to use the business acumen I have gained as an MBA student to maximize shareholder value for my next employer and continue my personal development.

The deep recession that has impacted the United States for over a year and the reality that we will probably have a jobless recovery[123] is depressing for many people who are looking for work. However, I am encouraged that many companies have spent the past few months streamlining their operations and focusing on their core business. Just like a major sickness is often an incentive for people to live healthier lives, I think that many companies have leveraged the recession to become better organizations. Therefore, I have hope that I will find many opportunities to serve these "leaner and meaner" organizations.

I offer companies a deep portfolio of technology skills, specifically in the areas of technical architecture and software integration. Also, not only do I excel at written and verbal communication, I have a passion for creating

---

[123] http://www.sfgate.com/cgi-bin/article.cgi?f=/c/a/2009/09/09/BUBV19KMG7.DTL&type=business

quality documentation and public speaking. Furthermore, I love leading teams, and I always make sure that everyone on my team furthers their personal goals while meeting the requirements of the project. Finally, any company for which I work will find me an enthusiastic supporter of the organization who will champion the corporate culture and community.

I am certain that my career search will be very challenging. With unemployment in the United States positioned to pass 10% and many companies unwilling to hire new employees, this is the gloomiest job outlook in many years. Nevertheless, I am confident the right organization is out there and ready for me to merge my career with its company.

Business School

What I Did This Summer

08/16/2009 04:13:57 PM

AUTHOR'S NOTE: The Texas A&M Mays Full Time MBA program is broken into two major parts with a summer between them. I wrote this in my communications class for an assignment about what I did during the summer.

My MBA Program asked the returning second year students to update their profile for a booklet that will be shared with first year students. I thought this was a good opportunity to think through what has been a surprisingly relaxing summer and wrote the following in my profile.

I turned down an internship this summer in order to spend more time with my wife and kids. The Texas A&M MBA program has been an excellent experience, and I have definitely grown as a business person. However, it is a very rigorous program, and I didn't get the chance to be the husband and father I wanted to be for most of the first three terms. Therefore, since this summer was the last time I had the opportunity for an extended break without significant work or school responsibilities, I invested a lot of time into my family. I also got the chance to pursue a few hobbies and interests of my own.

My wife is a college professor, and I got the chance to go with her to two academic conferences this summer. One was in Santa Fe, New Mexico, and the other was in Chicago, Illinois. These two parts of the country were almost direct opposites in terms of culture and geography, but I enjoyed both trips! Between her conference responsibilities, we took time to see a few tourist attractions and eat at a few nice restaurants. Outside of travel, we just took time to enjoy simple treats like going for walks around our neighborhood.

I have three children, and I really enjoyed hanging out with them. My oldest is four years old, and I got the chance to see him interact with his piano teacher as well as attend a basketball camp. We put all of our children in a two week swimming class at the YMCA, and they took to the water surprisingly well! Most satisfying of all, I got the chance to read them a bedtime story every night before they went to sleep.

116

Regarding my hobbies and interests, I enjoy public speaking, and I received opportunities to speak at Podcamp Houston (http://podcamphouston.org/wp/) and Caroline Collective (http://carolinecollective.cc/2009/08/03/c2-creative-presents-anjuan-simmons/) this summer. Furthermore, I am passionate about expanding Houston's position as a center for technology and innovation so I took part in various tweetups, social media breakfasts, and geek gatherings. Many of them took place at Coffee Groundz or the Houston Technology Center which are both in the Midtown part of Houston. This part of the city is quickly becoming a hub for the creative and tech crowds. I also made progress on launching a technology oriented video podcast called "Techlation" that will air on Houston Media Source (the public television station that serves Houston) and the internet.

I look forward to reconnecting with my fellow classmates in the MBA Class of 2010, and I eagerly anticipate meeting the MBA Class of 2011! I heavily network through social media so you can friend me on Facebook (http://www.facebook.com/anjuan) or follow me on Twitter (http://www.twitter.com/anjuan).

My MBA Graduation Speech - The Importance of Aggie Leadership

12/18/2009 04:22:44 PM

AUTHOR'S NOTE: Up until my MBA class, the President of the MBA Student Association gave the "Student Speaker" speech at the graduation ceremony of the class. Early in the second year of the program, it was announced that this would be changed, and the Student Speaker would be chosen via an election. I was very fortunate to be voted by my fellow MBA students to be the Student Speaker as our commencement ceremony. As the first paragraph explains, this post is the text of the speech I gave.

This is the text of the speech I gave at my MBA graduation ceremony from Texas A&M. I was honored to be the first student speaker elected by an MBA class to address the students, faculty, staff, family, and friends who attended our ceremony. The actual speech included a few ad libs, but this is the form of the speech that I prepared for the program. I'm posting this here because I believe that it is vitally important for CIO's to master communication. As I work to improve my public speaking skills, I will share examples like this of what I've written to prepare for speeches.

As prepared for delivery.

Howdy! Thank you, Dr. Blackwell for that generous introduction. Good morning faculty, staff, family, friends, debt collectors, future employers, and, most of all good morning to the Mays MBA Class of 2010! I want to acknowledge a few people before I begin. I would like to thank my family, many of whom are here today. I know you haven't seen a lot of me in the past 16 months so let me put to rest a few family rumors. No, I have not been kidnapped, and, no, I have not been in a witness protection program. I have simply been earning my MBA. Which, actually, in some ways, is not too different from the rumors! I want to send a special thank you to my kids who have been very patient with me and to my beautiful wife, Aneika, whose unwavering support and unlimited understanding have been instrumental in my success in the MBA program. In many ways, my ability to stand before you today is her victory. I would also like to recognize our military students. Many of the fundamental concepts of modern corporations are based on the military tradition, and you have provided living examples of that great tradition. Thank you for your service. I also want to thank our international students. Many of us have only dreamed of travelling around the world, but you brought the world to our program enriching it with your culture, your ideas, your values, and, of course, your good cooking. Finally, I thank all of my classmates for selecting me to be the student speaker. I am honored and humbled by your confidence and trust in me.

As I look at all of you seated in your robes looking so nice, all I can think is, "Wow". It has been a long journey, hasn't it? For those of you keeping score, exactly 500 days have passed since we first gathered in Cocanaugher to begin the MBA program. I have to be honest; I didn't know much about what it meant to be an MBA back then. In fact, I only seriously considered entering an MBA program after hearing a joke from a colleague at work. The joke went something like this:

One day an MBA student and a law student go camping. After a fun filled day of hiking, rowing, and enjoying nature, they set up their tent and go to sleep.

In the middle of the night, the law student wakes up her MBA friend and says, "Look up at the sky and tell me what you see".

The MBA replies, "I see a lot of stars."

The Law Student asks, "What does that tell you?"

The MBA thinks for a minute and then replies, "Astronomically speaking, it tells me there are millions of galaxies and potentially billions of planets. Time wise, it appears to be approximately a quarter past three. Theologically, it is evident that God is all-powerful and we are small and insignificant. Meteorologically, it looks like we will have a beautiful day tomorrow."

Quite pleased with herself, the MBA student asks the Law Student, "What does it tell you?"

The Law Student is silent for a moment and then replies, "Practically speaking . . . someone has stolen our tent."

So, I looked for MBA schools that not only provided a broad set of core business concepts but also provided the opportunity for practical application. I was fortunate to be accepted into the Mays MBA program. We have learned to analyze income statements, balance sheets, assembly lines, capital budgets, and stock portfolios. We have given seemingly endless oral presentations and written countless papers. However, we have also gotten our hands dirty through simulated marketing campaigns, Technology Transfer, and the consulting project. This program has combined education with implementation.

However, the most important aspect of the Mays MBA program is the production of leaders. This is vitally important in a time that has seen an unprecedented level of economic upheaval with sky high unemployment, a struggling international stock market, and many companies that are simply trying to survive. These are challenges that we haven't seen in this country since the Great Depression. There are uncertainties everywhere, but there is something that I know for sure: WE are the leaders that will guide this world out of our current troubles and into a brighter future.

Some say the solutions to the world's problems are higher taxes to reduce deficits. Others say that we need reform to improve our financial and healthcare systems. Many companies are trying to reorganize themselves to improve their operational efficiency or to leverage new technologies. Those are all noble activities. However, we cannot tax, reform, or reorganize our way out of our problems. We must LEAD our way out of our problems!

The good news is that leadership permeates this campus. In fact the Texas A&M University Purpose Statement is, and I quote, to "develop leaders of character dedicated to serving the greater good". Too many institutions stop at the first two words of that statement. They simply "develop leaders"□. But, Aggie Leaders do more than just lead. They lead with character and a desire to serve instead of being served by others. We can look across this country and see the many ways in which the Texas A&M Purpose Statement is being fulfilled. We can look at the Pentagon and see Robert Gates serving as Secretary of Defense and exhibiting the same outstanding leadership he demonstrated here as president of the University. Closer to home, we find another Aggie leader in Rick Perry who is the current governor of Texas. Not far from us in Houston we find Gary Kubiak who graduated from A&M in 1983 and will hopefully lead the Houston Texans into the NFL playoffs before 2083. It is now our turn to do our part to fulfill the Aggie Purpose Statement.

We are the next generation of Aggie Leaders, and I believe that there are three things that make us special.

First, we've learned to make hard decisions. George S. Patton said, "Be willing to make decisions. That's the most important quality in a good leader. Don't fall victim to what I call the "ready-aim-aim-aim syndrome.' You must be willing to fire." We all remember McAnally's accounting class that we had in the first term of our program. As I recall, at other schools a CPA is required to even enroll for a class as hard as hers. That was when many of us realized we were indeed in an accelerated MBA program! The rigor of the program forced us to make hard decisions. We didn't see much of our family or friends. Some of us ingested more caffeine than a healthy person should take. Furthermore, for many of us, simply deciding to pursue an MBA was the hardest decision of our lives. That decision meant leaving the stability of employment and giving up almost two years of compensation. Some of you have shared with me that even your closest friends criticized your decision to enter the MBA program. They felt that it was an unnecessary degree or that you couldn't afford it or that you were simply being vain and wanted three letters after your name. Yet, despite the difficulty of defying those who care about you, you decided to enroll anyway because you realized what every leader knows very well: every path to greatness is paved with difficult decisions and must often be walked despite the disapproval of others. When FDR decided to plunge America into World War II after Pearl Harbor, it was a difficult decision, but we are a far better country because of it and became the super power we are today. When John F. Kennedy challenged the nation to put a man on the moon and return him home safely, it was a difficult decision, but we enjoy the results of that decision in almost every aspect of our lives from advances in medicine to our global network of satellites. And, of course, Velcro. We will find that the difficult decision we all made to enter the Mays MBA program was worth it and has prepared us to do well in facing future hard choices as leaders.

Second, we have a leadership network both within our graduating class and in the global Aggie network. The best leaders spend a lot of time around other great leaders. To paraphrase something one of you told me, if you're the best leader in your group of friends, then you need a new group of friends. None of us are perfect leaders, and we will always have some imperfection in our leadership style. That is why having a leadership network is so vital. We will all encounter difficult problems out there that are bigger than our personal ability to solve them. Yet, we can take comfort in knowing that we have a portfolio of solutions in our class mates that are only a phone call, email, or text message away. We can all remember a time in the program where we had a tough assignment to complete. Maybe it was one of McAnally's financial statements, or Wesson's layoff exercise, or one of Krajicek's memos, but we all benefitted from getting feedback from a fellow student. It will be important for us to have a similar open environment of feedback in the future. After all, the MBA program provided a safe environment in which mistakes could be absorbed without widespread consequences. However, in the real world, mistakes could result in financial loss, lawsuits, or loss of employment. Our Aggie leadership network is the safety net we all have to protect us from ourselves. Not only that, but it's good to know you have friends in this tough economy. Even those of us who have jobs may find ourselves back in the job market sooner than we think. This can be a lonely experience, but when you have the Aggie network, you never have to lead alone.

Third, and finally, we have something that makes the Aggie MBA truly unique. And that is the importance of living by a code. Our degree plan does not include a course in ethics, but the importance of ethical behavior permeates the program. In fact, it covers this entire campus. I've already mentioned that the Texas A&M Statement of Purpose underscores the importance of leading with character. Also, our traditions like Silver Taps, Muster, Yell Practice, and Big Event are physical manifestations of our campus character and values. They all boil down to how critical it is to always act with integrity. If there is one truth that we must all take from our experience here it is that no achievement can truly be a success if it is obtained without integrity. This year alone has seen the downfall of successful people like Governor Mark Sanford, Senator John Edwards, and golfing legend Tiger Woods whose lives would have been much easier if they had maintained their integrity. They did not learn that it is only when you live a life of integrity that you can truly be free. You have the freedom to never have to remember what half-truth you told this person or that person. You have the freedom to never fear any investigations into your actions. You have the freedom to never be afraid that the people you care about will one day discover who you truly are; because the truth of who you are is on display every day. This freedom is rare, and, while it will repel some, it will also attract many others to you. In fact, you may be the first ethical leader that many people will ever meet. And, most importantly, you may be the only chance that some of them may ever have to become ethical leaders themselves because of your example. This is an awesome responsibility, and it is one that few have. Treasure it, and you will find that you can improve the world simply by your presence in it.

Our ability to make hard decisions, the Aggie leadership network, and our personal integrity are what set us apart as Aggie leaders. After today, many of our paths will diverge, but these three traits will always allow us to have a unified journey toward leadership excellence.

Gandhi said, "We must become the change we want to see." I challenge all of you to become the leaders you want to follow.

Thank you, good luck, and Gig 'em!

Comments

AUTHOR: vani
DATE: 02/18/2010 03:02:00 PM

Anjuan,rnrnI have actually moved to a higher position in the collections business, I am not a debt collector any more and am working as a collections strategist and work with the leadership in making key decisions for the portfolio.rnrnMy long term career goal is to get to a key leadership position where I can contribute, learn and lead. rnrnI know that this seems very vague. All I know about me is that I have always been dedicated to the idea of continuous learning and feel that I strengthen my professional abilities every time I take on new challenge and learn a new set of skills.rnrnI did finish my graduation in Arts through correspondence (never really got any Au2019s or Bu2019s) and now am dreaming to move up to a management position.rnrnI am obviously not that great on any of the subjects covered under GMAT and need someone to guide me from scratch. rn

AUTHOR: Anjuan Simmons
URL: http://www.AnjuanSimmons.com
DATE: 02/18/2010 02:19:00 PM

Business School

Hi Vani,nnIt depends on your goals. What do you want to do with your career right now? Do you want to continue as a debt collector and advance to higher positions in that field? Or, do you want to change careers and do something totally different?

AUTHOR: Vani
DATE: 02/18/2010 02:12:00 PM

really a great speech, I am really motivated to work towards earning an MBA now.

I am 32 years old and have struggled my way up in my career. I started my career post high school and worked and grew up from a door to door salesmen to a debt collector to lead strategist now. It took me almost 13 years to reach here.

Do you think MBA ia a good choice for me

PART 4 – TECHNOLOGY TRANSLATOR

I've always enjoyed helping people use technology. I truly believe that technology will become one of the great enablers of human potential. Helping people understand the ways that technology improves their lives gives me the opportunity to show them better ways to reach their goals. This includes personal goals like finding friends who share similar interests or professional goals like finding a career that mirrors their passions. Or, it could simply be the goal of finding a good place to eat lunch. We're living in the Social Information Age where the power of computers, the global platform of the internet, and the personal connectivity of social networks combine to bring endless possibilities.

However, my love for technology does that blind me to the reality that many technologies are too hard to use. While some companies like Apple understand the need to create products at the intersection of art and engineering, too many technology providers release products when they should be releasing experiences. I call this the "experience gap" where the potential of a strong technology product is marred by the unpleasantness of using it.

I try to fill this gap by being a friendly person who helps people understand how to get around the unpleasantness of certain technologies and seeing their usefulness. If I frame the technology correctly, I can help others see the beauty of the experience through my personality and desire to help.

My initial blog posts covered my thoughts about innovative ways to use technology or explanations of various technological concepts. I also wrote a few "how to" posts. However, I prefer to help people think strategically about technology rather than provide step-by-step instructions about how to use a particular piece of technology. For example, instead of writing a post about "How to Use Instagram Video", I would rather write about "Using Instagram Video as a Marketing Channel". Or, to use an analogy, I'd rather be "Car and Driver" magazine than the automobile manual in the glove box.

I added the "Technology Translator" tagline to my blog years ago because that captures how I see helping people with technology. It's my passion for facilitating technology conversation for the benefit of the end user.

Tech School: Time Travel via The Internet

09/25/2007 04:18:33 AM

AUTHOR'S NOTE: I naturally enjoy helping people with their technology problems, and I published a few "Tech School" posts soon after I started blogging. These posts contained my thoughts about certain aspects of technology as well as how to solve some of the common technology problems that plague most consumers.

For those of us in our 20's and 30's we can be called perhaps the first generation that can review our lives online. Never before has a generation had so many ways to learn about the past.

Want to know how you looked as a child? There are many photo-sharing sites like Flickr and Picasa that many parents and grand-parents have used to upload decades of pictures. Do you wonder what your relatives were like back in the days before you knew how to walk or talk? You combine search sites like Wink.com with Ancestry.com to research aunts, uncles, cousins, etc.

Have you lost touch with childhood friends from elementary, junior high, or high school? It is very likely that they have joined social networking sites like MySpace or Facebook. Finding female classmates is slightly more difficult if they have gotten married and changed their last names, but most social networking sites have a group feature that allow alumni to identify and find each other. You can even find old friends who have gotten into instant messaging and save airfare and cell phone minutes by walking down memory lane via test message.

Do you long for those Saturday morning cartoons for which you woke up at 6 AM to watch, but you can't remember their titles? Simply check out YouTube where you can find clips and even full episodes of those animated commercials designed to suck money out of your parents' bank accounts and fill your bedroom with soon-to-be-discarded toys. You can even go on Wikipedia to find episode summaries and links to websites where adult people like yourself dress up like the characters from Voltron . . .

Whether such examinations of the past are good or bad for our already narcissistic culture, I cannot say. However, it is amazing to know that there

126

is almost no aspect of our past that cannot be researched and investigated via the Internet.

Tech School: How to Avoid Owing $200,000 to the RIAA

10/09/2007 01:17:13 AM

AUTHOR'S NOTE: While the RIAA has backed off from pursuing legal action against people who illegally download music, I think this article provides tips for those who want to maintain some level of anonymity online. I don't condone illegal downloads of any kind, but I think that we should all know how to protect our privacy as much as possible.

In a case that strikes a dangerous precedent, <u>Jammie Thomas</u>[124] was ordered to pay $222,000 to the RIAA for willful copyright infringement. Thomas was found guilty of making copy written recordings available over the Kazaa file-sharing network.

Except for those related to Donald Trump, the outcome of this case raised the hairs on the back of the necks of millions of people who have used file-sharing software like Kazaa, eMule, eDonkey, and BitTorrent. Could a lifetime of garnished wages be in your future if you use these peer-to-peer networks?

Since there are many applications of file-sharing networks that fall under the realm of fair-use (such as the spread of Linux distributions and other open source software), I'm writing this post to share ways to increase your anonymity while still using peer-to-peer networks.

NOTE: To be clear, I do not condone the use of file-sharing software to distribute copy written material. These tips are to be used to distribute material that the owner would not mind being shared for free. Since many peer-to-peer software packages install with default values that could make you a false-positive to the RIAA, I am writing this to protect those who want to engage in fair use while reducing the chance of being a defendant in a court of law.

---

[124]http://arstechnica.com/news.ars/post/20071008-thomas-to-appeal-riaas-222000-file-sharing-verdict.html

1. **Username:** Pick a username that is completely different from any other online ID. Your file-sharing software username should not match the ID you use for Hotmail, GMail, Amazon, eBay, or any other internet site. One damaging piece of evidence used against Jammie Thomas was the fact that the ID she used for Kazaa matched an ID she used at other sites.

2. **No Uploads:** It is bad karma to not allow other file-sharing users to upload files that you have downloaded, but federal law states that "making available" copy written material is illegal whether the material has been downloaded or not. If you disallow uploads (yes, and thereby becoming a leech), you cannot be accused of distributing the intellectual property owned by someone else. Remember that a lot of peer-to-peer software allow upload by default so you will have to check the preferences to find the right parameter to select to disable uploads.

3. **Share Wisely:** If you ignore my advice about not allowing uploads, make sure you carefully select the folders on your hard drive that you share. Download to one folder and allow uploads to another folder that clearly does not contain copy written material.

4. **Encrypt:** Few file-sharing applications provide encryption so you will have to use tools like TOR. Be aware that TOR rarely works by simply installing the software. Be prepared to undergo a fair amount of education and geeking around its innards before your traffic is encrypted. However, I do suspect that this ruling will result in the creation of peer-to-peer clients that have encryption built in as well as other privacy features.

5. **Secure Your Network:** Use a router between your computer and your cable/DSL modem. This will make it difficult (although far from impossible) for agents of the RIAA to probe your system. It is a good idea in general to use a router since the network address translation inherit within all routers protects you from random attacks over the internet.

Following these tips will not guarantee a lawsuit free life, but they will improve the chance that you can enjoy the legal use of file-sharing networks without fear of sending $1500 dollar checks to the RIAA for the next 30 years.

Tech School: Backup Essentials

11/17/2007 06:49:51 AM

We live in a culture of denial that results in an unwillingness to accept the truth. For example, many people refuse to be tested for HIV and other STD's despite having multiple sexual partners. Also, many people don't want to see their credit report even though they have several maxed out credit cards. Furthermore, despite overwhelming evidence that a partner is cheating, many people hesitate to find out the truth and simply turn a blind eye. The idea seems to be that bad news can't hurt me if I don't know about it. The problem is that the truth will eventually catch up with you, and this particularly applies to the world of computers. Here is the truth about your hard drive that you don't want to hear: one day it will die taking your documents, pictures, music, videos and other (usually irreplaceable) data with it. The corollary to this truth is this: you have no way of knowing when that day will come; it could be tomorrow. Yes, a hard drive failure is in your future if you own a computer. The only way to protect yourself is to back up your data.

Backing up the data on your computer is like flossing your teeth. Many people know that they should do it, but they often skip the activity. We all lead busy lives, right? Right, until your dentist tells you that you have gum disease and will spend your golden years drinking your steaks. Yes, backup is a boring tedious task that few will applaud you for doing. And how exactly should you do the backup anyway? Well, it is as easy as answering those classic Four W's and an H we learned in middle school: Why, What, Where, How, and When (listed in that order for a reason). By the way, I have already gone over the "Why" so, let's dive into the second W.

What

Computers have a lot of data on them, and their storage capacity increases every year as technology advances. Furthermore, the cost of storage continues to drop dramatically. This results in even more data being stored on our humble hard drives. However, you don't have to backup all of it. The programs installed on your computer usually have registry entries that will require re-installation if the hard drive fails. Therefore, you don't have to worry about backing up program folders (just make sure you keep the original installation discs and any applicable product keys). I suggest that you have all of your data in one place. Windows makes this easy with the "My Documents" folder which is the default location for storing personal data. This is a good place to put everything that you want to back up including documents, spreadsheets, music, pictures, and videos. The benefit of having one place for all of your important files lies in the fact that you only have to backup from one location on your hard drive. If you want to be more sophisticated, you can create a separate partition for storing your data. This is what I do because I format and re-install Windows once a year (to get rid of "bit rot"), and I can format the main partition and install Windows on it without worrying about destroying my data since it is stored on another partition. An even more sophisticated approach is to have a separate physical internal or external hard drive. This allows you to back up your data and also have two spindles available to the computer: one for the operating system and one for your data which should provide a performance increase to your computer. Whether you use the "My Documents" folder, a separate partition, or a separate drive, the key is to have one place to store your important data.

Where

A backup is essentially a copy of your data. Once you put all of your data in one place on your computer, you have to decide where to put the copy of that data. You have a number of options. Most computers have a CD burner so you could burn the copy to a CD. However, unless you use rewritable media, you have to swap in a blank CD before doing the backup, and you are limited to 700 MB. Most people have larger storage needs so you can burn your copy to a DVD if your computer has a DVD burner. This allows you to store up to 4.7 GB of data. However, again, unless you use rewritable DVD's, you have to put in a fresh DVD before doing the backup. A more flexible solution is the use of a USB key which can provide storage capacity equaling or surpassing what is available on DVD. There is also the convenience of making multiple copies to the flash drive without having to swap it out. If you have a large amount of music, pictures, or video on your computer, then you may need to make use of an internal or external hard drive. These have the benefit of providing a very large amount of storage (up to 1 Terabyte). However, no matter where you choose to store your backup copy, it won't help you if your house burns down. Therefore, for the maximum protection, I recommend keeping another backup location somewhere else (like work) and make sure you keep your backup of your backup up to date. An easier, though possibly more expensive, solution is to use an online backup service like Carbonite[125].

How

Now that you have your data in one place and a place to put your copy, you need to determine how to move your files from your central storage location to your backup location. Windows has a built in backup utility, but I don't care for it. It makes one big "glob" that you have to mount in order to see what is inside of it. I prefer to backup the actual physical files because I can then see them in the backup location. Therefore, I recommend free tools like SyncBack[126] or SyncToy[127] which let you backup from a source to a target location. They can even synchronize between the two locations taking into account changes made in both places. However, I usually do a one way backup because my policy is to only make changes in my central storage location and have those changes overwrite the backup version.

When

How often should you run your backup? I suggest at least once a week. Both SyncBack and SyncToy can be scheduled to run at weekly intervals. Once you do your initial backup, subsequent backups usually operate on a smaller set of files (the ones you have changed). Therefore, when your hard drive crashes, you can restore from the backup and lose no more than a week's worth of information on the small number of files that you modified since the last backup. However, if you frequently change a large number of critical files, then you may want to back up more often even possibly adopting a daily backup schedule.

Now, you are prepared for the day your hard drive spins its last breath

---

125 http://www.carbonite.com/

126 http://www.2brightsparks.com/downloads.html#freeware

127
http://www.microsoft.com/windowsxp/using/digitalphotography/prophoto/synctoy.mspx

never again to see the data stored on it. Instead of that day be one of weeping and gnashing of teeth, you can calmly go to your computer store of choice, buy and new hard drive, and copy your backup to it without breaking a sweat.

Comments

AUTHOR: HeavyGod
URL: http://heavy-blog.com/
DATE: 11/27/2007 08:40:52 AM

Really good and really interesting post. I expect (and other readers maybe :)) new useful posts from you!
Good luck and successes in blogging!

AUTHOR: Dave Friend
URL: http://www.carbonite.com
DATE: 11/26/2007 10:40:47 PM

Hi Anjuan, I'm Carbonite's CEO, and thanks for the mention in your blog. The thing about burning DVDs or copying your data off to an external hard drive and then taking to a friend's house is that almost nobody has the discipline to really do this on a regular basis. As you know from using Carbonite, if you're using an online backup service, you can install it and then forget about it. It just works away in the background all the time. Unless you're an IT professional or totally obsessive, it's the only way that you're really going to protect your data.

Regards,

Dave Friend

CEO, http://www.carbonite.com/"

AUTHOR: Nelson Webber
URL: http://wnelweb.blogspot.com/
DATE: 11/20/2007 11:36:25 AM

Well, I do love open source technology. It's the one area where the old maxim, 'you get what you pay for' usually does NOT apply!
Pax,
N

AUTHOR: Anjuan
DATE: 11/20/2007 07:37:55 AM

Yeah, it takes time for Wordpress to catch up. I think it checks frequently for updates, but if you happen to do something right after a check the lag is noticeable. Open Source Content Management Systems - gotta love 'em!

AUTHOR: Nelson Webber
URL: http://wnelweb.blogspot.com/
DATE: 11/20/2007 01:54:28 AM

Well, **NOW** they are. Never mind.
N.

AUTHOR: Nelson Webber
URL: http://wnelweb.blogspot.com/
DATE: 11/20/2007 01:52:44 AM

FYI, the comments for this blog are not showing up.
Pax,
N

AUTHOR: Nelson Webber
URL: http://wnelweb.blogspot.com/
DATE: 11/20/2007 01:51:04 AM

Yeah but **YOU** know how to make 'em work! I do enjoy assembling them though, it's a bit of a hobby. Both of my PC's are home builds. I would have built my laptop, too but it wasn't worth the effort really... And I don't know where to find out how to build one!
If you ever have any assembly questions esp. AMD (only chip I ever use) rigs, I'm your man.

I'll let you know how it goes. Turns out the MoBo is on back order at TigerDirect. New chip (AMD Athlon 64 X2 3800+ Socket 939 (Manchester)) is on its way, however.

Pax,
Nelson

AUTHOR: Anjuan
URL: http://blog.transmyth.com
DATE: 11/19/2007 10:31:03 PM

Nelson,
I'm glad to hear that someone else uses Syncback. I like it for its power and simplicity.

I hope you get your other PC up and running. You surpass my tech cred; I have replaced RAM and drives on several occassions, but never an entire Motherboard!

----- COMMENT: AUTHOR: Nelson Webber EMAIL: wnelweb@gmail.com IP: 24.127.0.51 URL: http://wnelweb.blogspot.com/ DATE: 11/19/2007 06:57:21 PM

Thanks for the tips. I use "synchback" and have it programmed to automatically do its good work. Unfortunately, I haven't been able to do it recently, because I accidentally killed the other PC to which I'd been backing up. I know, I know, get a good USB flash drive also. I have one and I use it, too.

If you're interested, I killed my other PC by attempting to upgrade the processor. I think I may have cracked the MoBo while re-stalling the heatsink. Now neither the new chip nor the old one work. Machine spins up the DVD drive and I think I hear on of the hard drives staring to spin, but that is as far as it goes. SO I sent off for a new upgraded MoBo and more powerful chip. I wish I knew how to fix the old one, but I don't.

Pax,
Nelson

Tech News: Self Google-lation

12/17/2007 04:15:38 PM

SUMMARY

Several news sources reported yesterday that many people are using Google to search themselves. Citing a report released Sunday by the Pew Internet and American Life Project, 47 percent of American adult internet users have searched for information about themselves using a search engine like Google. The people most likely to self-Google were under 50 years old and usually well-educated and compensated.

MY TAKE

I don't think this is news since "vanity searches" have been a known entity for a while now. However, many companies are late to the game when it comes to following technology trends (hence, "w00t" as word of the year by Merriam-Webster despite the fact that it is now old school slang) so I should not be surprised. I do think more people are searching for themselves online to make sure they control their identity. As a blogger, I like to see searches for "anjuan" come up with my blog postings or other things that I have published online. So, I think a more interesting story would cover ways to make sure that search results for your name produce the hits that YOU want other people to see. That is an essential part of creating a strong online personal brand identity.

Comments

AUTHOR: Nelson
EMAIL: wnelweb@gmail.com
URL: http://wnelweb.blogspot.com
DATE: 12/19/2007 02:57:58 AM

I've done it and I'm not ashamed to admit it!

Bye the way, I like the latest format; pretty sharp lookin'.

Technology Translator

Pax,
Nelson

4 Rules for Driving with Technology

01/04/2008 02:34:12 PM

The end of 2007 brought the tragic story of Craig P. Bigos who struck and killed a 13-year-old boy with his car. Bigos did not even know that he hit the child until the next day because he was typing a text message while driving.

As mobile devices become more powerful and vehicles gain more media and gaming capability (which was one of my predictions for 2008), the driving experience will potentially be more dangerous than ever before. We are already seeing the impact of technology distractions by the results of a study showing that drivers on cell phones slow traffic. In order to reduce the number of vehicular tragedies in 2008, I propose these rules for driving with technology.

#1. Always Keep At Least One Hand on the Steering Wheel

While we all learned in Driver's Ed that both hands should be in on the wheel at the 10 o'clock and 2 o'clock positions, I know it is impractical to enforce. So, this rule mandates that you always have at least have one hand on the steering wheel at all times. Despite your vaunted ability to drive with your knees, keep in mind that you are directing a vehicle weighing hundreds if not thousands of pounds moving at high rate of speed. You wouldn't operate a jackhammer with your knees, would you? Therefore, save two-handed text messaging and "pinching" photos on iPhones for extra-vehicular time.

#2. Always Hold Mobile Phones with Your Right Hand

I thought about making this a corollary to Rule #1, but it is important enough to stand on its own. If you have to hold a mobile phone to your ear in order to use it, then hold it in your right hand. The reason for this rule is the importance of peripheral vision. If you are using your left hand to hold the mobile phone to your left ear, then you are cutting off the field of vision on the left side of the car. This increases the blind spot on the left side of the car and also further complicates the already difficult maneuver of making a left turn (since you usually have to cross the oncoming lane of traffic). A better way to implement this rule is to purchase a wired or

Technology Translator

Bluetooth headset which does not restrict your field of vision while using a mobile phone. It may even make sense to invest in a mobile phone hands-free car kit that lets you operate your phone via voice commands similar to Microsoft's Sync technology.

NOTE: For countries where vehicles drive on the left side of the road, **reverse this rule**.

#3. Always Keep Both Eyes on the Road

Although this sounds obvious, I have seen too many drivers operating their vehicles while reading, turning around to discipline children, and other activities that distract from watching the road. Vehicles cover an incredible amount of ground in just a few seconds, and removing the faculty through which we receive the most information from the driving experience is foolish. Doing so at highway speeds is idiotic. Before you know it, that vehicle that was 100 meters away when you last saw it is now crashing into your front fender because you didn't see its break lights flash. So, no more reading email, watching DVD's, and checking the navigation system while you drive at 80 miles per hour.

#4. Never Wear Headphones

While it may seem odd to wear headphones inside of a car because, well, you usually have a car stereo, I have seen a surprising number of people wearing those little white ear buds while driving. This removes the sense of hearing which is almost as bad as losing your sense of sight when it comes to driving. Drivers receive many sound-based warnings including sirens from police and emergency vehicles and the honking of the horns of other drivers letting you know that you are about to merge into a tractor trailer. Instead of wearing those Bose noise canceling headphones while you're behind the wheel, use a device that will send music on your MP3 player to your car stereo system.

I hope that these four simple rules will allow us to safely enjoy our automobile technology. Let's all make a resolution to not be the next Craig Bigos.

Comments

AUTHOR: Anna
URL: http://annakristine.wordpress.com
DATE: 01/17/2008 03:20:15 AM

These are very interesting ideas. I would like to see them implemented and tested to see how effective they are. I think that driving with headphones has been shown to be dangerous, and when I see someone (usually a teenager) driving along with iPod ear buds in, I usually cringe inwardly!

Twitter

01/08/2008 11:32:25 AM

AUTHOR'S NOTE: Twitter is now a well-known service, but it wasn't in January 2008 when I wrote this.

This is a quick post to mention a tool called Twitter[128]. For those who do not know, Twitter is a micro-blog tool that is used to send quick 144 character answers to the question "What are you doing?" It sounds simple, but it is actually a powerful tool.

I have started using it quite a bit because it seems to be what all the cool kids use . . . Seriously, it is a very useful information gathering and networking application. I have seen some people use it to give updates on what they are doing and others market their endeavors (blog posts, podcast updates, etc.). The people I follow on Twitter are scattered around the country, and I enjoy receiving updates over such a wide geographic area. It is another way in which the Internet removes borders and makes the world smaller.

I am looking for a Wordpress plugin to add my twitter updates to this blog, but I do not want it to clutter the interface. If you want to follow me on Twitter, my username is simply "Anjuan" (without the quotes, of course).

---

[128] http://twitter.com/

Protecting Yourself from Googling Employers

01/22/2008 11:17:28 PM

Whether we know it or not, we all have a "personal brand". Your personal brand is the set of all the thoughts and feelings people have when your name is mentioned. While this varies from person to person, we all have general characteristics that are projected on a regular basis.

You want your personal brand to be one of the first things a person thinks about when trying to solve a problem. Just like many people think about Tylenol when they have headache, or they think about Kleenex when they want to blow their nose, your personal brand should be thought of when a problem that lies within your area of expertise is needed. This could be starting a company, fixing a technical problem, or replacing the tile in a bathroom. A large part of networking is communicating and enhancing the image of your personal brand.

That Internet has made it easier to maintain a strong personal brand, but it is also harder in many ways. The main challenge is taking control of your online personal brand. Employers are increasingly using search engines like Google to gather personal information about potential employees. It will be increasingly important to exert as much control over what turns up in search results as you possibly can. Your future occupation may depend on it.

Here are eight tips for controlling your online personal brand and protecting yourself from those who may use search engines to check up on you.

1. **Choose an Identity and Stick with It.** While the Internet provides the potential to maintain multiple identities, it is important to choose one. You can still have your lushychocolate@aol.com, but you also should create an identity that can be used by the general public. The best identify for this is simply your name (first.last@aol.com). This is easy if you have a unique first name, but the combination of your first and last name should allow must people a suitable level of uniqueness.

2. **Create a Personal Website.** Hosting sites such as GoDaddy offer cheap domain registration services. Ideally the URL of your website should be the same as your name. I wish someone would have given me this advice

143

before anjuan.com was purchased by a restaurant in Japan. I don't recommend using the same company to register your domain and also host your site so you'll also need a web host. You can find help doing that at Web Hosting Talk.

3. Twitter. Twitter is a popular Internet service that allows you to send short status messages to your friends. It sounds simple, but Google seems to highly rank Twitter posts. So, set up a profile using your name as the label. My Twitter profile is the first hit when I search Yahoo for my name. However, I am always aware that anything I type in Twitter could be seen by a potential employer. So, make sure you keep that in mind as well.

4. Join Facebook and Myspace. Again, your profile on these sites should be your name. Most search engines give high rankings to social networking profiles that are often updates. Also, make sure that you form relationships within each social network because, well, that is what they are for. However, make sure you appropriately use the privacy control of these social networking sites. Both Facebook and Myspace are generally closed to non-members (or can be hidden from viewing by people you do not know), but you should be careful to protect any potentially embarrassing information.

5. Start a Blog. The name of the blog doesn't have to be the same as your name, but your updates to the blog should be marked with your name. That allows for regular updates to your page to be spidered by search engines and that will improve your overall ranking. Also, comment on other people's blogs. This will allow you to network with other bloggers, and gather additional readers further enhancing your personal brand.

6. Start a Podcast. This can be hosted on your blog, your website, or some other site. However, it's important that your name is tied to the podcast. Also, your podcast should cover topics for which you have a great deal of passion. This will help people know how to associate your name to something you are good at doing. I have yet to do a serious podcast, but I am currently designing one.

7. Join New Web Sites. I know that it seems that every day brings a new web site, especially those of the social networking variety. However, protecting your personal brand means expanding it as new services come online. This is akin to the California Gold Rush, but, instead of finding gold you are staking your claim to your brand. Many of these sites offer a customized URL (e.g., yourname@newsite.com) that you should use to promote your name. Also, you may also be surprised to learn that you enjoy the new way that these sites offer to expose your personal brand. Speaking of that, I need to join tumblr.

8. Track Progress. After a few weeks of updating your web site, sending out tweets, adding Facebook friends, creating blog entries, and producing podcast episodes you'll be ready to check your progress Search for your name using the major search engines (Google, Yahoo, and MSN). You should start to see entries with your name at the top of the search results. For Google, you can set up a Google Alert that sends an email to you whenever your name is mentioned online.

Following these tips will give you greater control over what people find out about you on line. Personally, I have been happy with what I see when I type my name in search engines. The results include links to this blog, my Twitter page, a product review I did a few years ago, and only one false positive near the bottom of the first page. Fortunately, a few less than professional things I posted back in college don't come up on at least the first few pages of search results. I hope that the contents of these hits provide searchers with the crux of my personal brand: technology enthusiast working in the information technology industry.

Comments

AUTHOR: Nelson
URL: http://wnelweb.blogspot.com
DATE: 01/24/2008 02:32:02 AM

You know I never thought to do this until just now. I googled my online name and got 957 results. Amazing.
You've outlined some really great things to do to create one's self on the web. Thanks!
Pax,
Nelson

7 Geekentine Tips

02/12/2008 11:33:52 PM

*AUTHOR'S NOTE: Yes, I wrote tips to help Geeks on Valentine's Day. *shrug**

Valentine's Day is a little over 24 hours away so there is little time to come up with an innovative gift for your partner. You can do the usual and make a last minute stop at Wal-Mart on the way home to rifle through the slim pickings at the flower shop, grab a not-quite-appropriate greeting card, and pick up the last of the heart shaped candy boxes, but, as a geek, you can do better.

Here are seven creative ways for you to use your geekiness to show how much you appreciate your significant other. They are listed in order of difficulty (in terms of planning and cost) from lowest to highest. By the way, I initially posted these in my Twitter stream, but I thought they would make a good blog post for people who don't follow me on Twitter.

#1. Remotely access your home computer and write a love note that your significant other will read when he/she logs in.

#2. Install a startup program that, when your significant other starts his/her laptop, plays a video of you praising him/her.

#3. Use PhotoStory to create a video tribute and post to Youtube. You can find one that I did for my wife a couple of years ago here.

#4. Hide small gifts around your partner's home/car/job/etc and send text message hints about where to find the next gift.

#5. Use Orb to create a streaming Internet audio playlist of your partner's favorite songs. This beats burning a CD.

#6. Video your partner's friends & family, edit it into a "This is Your Life" video, and rent out a movie theater to show it.

#7. Use ustream to live stream a video that your partner thinks is previously recorded and then suddenly appear and fly to Paris together.

I must admit that I have only used about half of these ideas, but I can attest that they worked wonders for my relationships! Using these tips will allow your significant other to truly appreciate the benefits of having a relationship with a geek!

Comments

AUTHOR: Anjuan
URL: http://blog.transmyth.com
DATE: 02/24/2008 02:28:44 PM

Thanks, Anna and Nelson!

AUTHOR: Nelson
URL: http://wnelweb.blogspot.com
DATE: 02/24/2008 02:47:17 AM

Wonderful ideas! Thanks.

AUTHOR: Anna
URL: http://annakristine.wordpress.com
DATE: 02/23/2008 02:23:27 PM

Haha. Those are great. My favorite is #6; that would be awesome!

Three Ways to Learn from Twitter

04/15/2008 05:59:14 PM

AUTHOR'S NOTE: Unfortunately, Twitter's fairly recent decision to restrict it's API has crippled or destroyed most of the resources I mentioned in this post.

While Twitter is doing well more than a year after its "coming out" at South by Southwest 2007, it is not a mainstream tool. Most of the praises given to it consists of "preaching to the choir" since most of the people who write about it are in the same demographic as most Twitter users: tech enthusiasts. If you ask an average person in the streets of any major city around the world what they think about Twitter, I am sure the overwhelming response would be, "huh?".

This is a shame, because Twitter is a great learning tool. Due to the nature of Twitter and the manner in which third parties have used its API, there are three ways to learn a great deal about any subject by using Twitter.

1. The Wisdom of the Crowds

The learning potential of Twitter is directly proportional to the number of people you follow. This goes against what many Twitter users (Jason Calacanis comes to mind) seek to do: gain as many followers as possible. Instead of trying to horde followers, I suggest following as many people as you can (to be honest, Jason does follow a huge number of people). As you follow more people, you will inevitably see who they interact with via the use of the "@" symbol in their tweets. For example, the following Tweet came across my Twitter stream a few minutes ago:

Mickipedia: @boboroshi I went to HS in VA beach. going home to deal with some family stuff.

Obviously, I follow Mickipedia since the update appeared in my stream, but I don't follow boboroshi. I use Google Talk to receive updates from my Twitter feed (all I had to do was add twitter@twitter.com as a Google Talk contact). This allows me to send commands to Twitter via Google Talk. You can also issue commands by using SMS to interact with Twitter. Since Mickipedia usually offers interesting updates, I assume that boboroshi

148

probably does the same. In order to learn more about boboroshi, I send the following command to Twitter via Google Talk:

whois boboroshi

The whois command simply asks Twitter to send profile information about a user. By doing so, I get this response from Twitter:

John Athayde, since Mar 2007.
bio: www.boboroshi.com/about
location: Washington, DC
web: http://www.boboroshi.com

So, I know that boboroshi's real name is John Athayde. Clicking the links in his profile shows me that he and I share the same interests so I type the following command into Google Talk:

follow boboroshi

Follow is another command that is used to tell Twitter that I want to receive updates from a user. Twitter responded with the following:

You'll receive a message every time boboroshi updates. To silence, send 'off boboroshi'. For more commands, send 'help'.

So, I have expanded my Twitter network simply by adding a person who follows someone I follow. Since I tend to use the whois command to find people who have interests similar to mine, my Twitter feed tends to contain a lot of technology related updates. As the people I follow post thoughts and URL links, I receive information that I often would not encounter.

2. The Track Command

Getting updates by following a lot of people does have a drawback. I often get a lot of random information that does not center around one topic. However, what if I want to know if someone tweets (i.e., posts a message on Twitter) about a certain topic? Instead of waiting for someone I follow to tweet about a topic, Twitter offers the track command.

Technology Translator

Let's say that I want to learn what people on Twitter are saying about the Democratic presidential candidates. Using Google Talk, I can enter this command into Google Talk:

track barack Obama

Twitter responds with:

You'll now receive updates matching 'barack obama'. To stop, send 'untrack barack obama'.

Since I have a track on Barack Obama, I received this update from ryanbrenizer (who I do not follow).

(ryanbrenizer): loves Barack Obama giving Gob's "COME ON!" as a political line.

As you can see, Twitter lets me know that this is a tweet resulting from the track command by putting the name of the user in parentheses. By using the whois command, I can determine if I want to add ryanbrenizer to the list of people I follow (in line with point #1).

Of course, I can also put a track on "hilary clinton" to keep up with what is being said about her.

If I ever forget what I'm tracking, I can enter this command into Google Talk:

tracks

And Twitter will send the following:

You are tracking: "veronica belmont", "tom merritt", "molly wood", "neha tiwari", "kevin rose", "anjuan", "amber macarthur", "vonage", "barack obama", "hilary clinton".

Yes, you can see that I keep up with my favorite Internet personalities as well as a vanity search and a few other terms.

If I get tired of receiving updates on a particular term, I can stop tracking it. So, if I no longer want to keep up with what the Twitterverse is saying about Kevin Rose, I can type the following:

untrack kevin rose

And Twitter will send this response:

You'll no longer receive updates that match 'kevin rose'.

By using the track command, I can receive targeted updates about the subjects in which I am most interested.

3. Third Party Websites

Twitter's publication of their API means that websites and applications can use Twitter to expand its capabilities. There are several web sites that do this in innovative ways, but I want to focus on two: Quotably and Tweetscan

Quotably provides a way to view the conversations of a particular Twitter user. For example, if I wanted to see what Dave Winer has been discussing on Twitter, I can go to quotably.com and enter his Twitter username:

After clicking the "Follow" button, I get a list of not only the conversations that Dave started but also those in which he participated via replies.

Tweetscan is similar to the Twitter track command. However, instead of having to wait for someone to tweet about a subject, I can use Tweetscan to immediately receive a list of tweets about a topic. So, let's say I wanted to use my earlier example of seeing what Twitter is saying about Barack Obama. I can enter this search term into Tweetscan.

Clicking the Search buttons results in the following:

So, in many ways, Tweetscan is like Google for Twitter.

Conclusion

By following large numbers of people based on their interests, making use of the built in track command, and using third party tools like Quotably.com and Tweetscan.com, Twitter becomes a powerful tool for learning about any topic. I think that this functionality is what will help it become a mainstream success.

The Puppy Linux Solution

12/17/2008 07:23:09 PM

AUTHOR'S NOTE: I've always been a fan of lightweight operating systems because they allow old hardware to be repurposed for specialized uses. This post captures my description of a lightweight OS called Puppy Linux. Fortunately, there are even easier options these days like the credit card sized Raspberry Pi computers.

I have a laptop in the kitchen that I use to look up recipes, catch up on feeds in my RSS reader (Google Reader[129]), check the weather and do general web surfing. It's not a powerful computer at all being an ancient Dell Inspiron 4100[130] with in Intel Pentium III clocking at 1.2 GHz and 256 MB of RAM. While these were impressive specs when the laptop came out in 2001, they are quite wimpy by today's standards.

I initially tried to run Windows XP[131] on the laptop, but waiting 15 minutes for the machine to boot up became hard to bear. Additionally, every task took forever to complete so I realized that, despite my very limited requirements, the laptop needed a more forgiving operating system. So, I then tried Windows 2000[132] which improved the performance of the laptop, but it still often took up to a minute just to launch a web browser.

It then occurred to me that a lightweight operating system would be ideal for my laptop. However, such an option was not available from Microsoft and nothing from Apple would run on a Dell laptop even if they had a solution. So, I decided to look to the Linux world and eventually found Puppy Linux[133].

---

[129] http://www.google.com/reader

[130] http://www.hardwarecentral.com/hardwarecentral/reviews/article.php/927071

[131] http://www.microsoft.com/windows/windows-xp/

[132] http://en.wikipedia.org/wiki/Windows_2000

[133] http://www.puppylinux.com/

Puppy Linux is a lightweight Linux distribution that has a very small footprint. The distribution is only 85 MB and can be run as a live-CD meaning that it can run from a CD-ROM drive instead of from the actual computer hard drive. This offers the convenience of trying Puppy Linux without modifying the resident operating system on the computer.

I downloaded the Puppy Linux distribution (version 4.1.2), burned the resulting .ISO file to a CD, and then inserted the CD into my kitchen laptop. I initially ran it from the CD and used the option to load the entire Puppy Linux operating system into RAM. Doing this required 128 MB of RAM, and my laptop had 256 MB which was plenty of room. The installation went very smoothly being composed of a number of wizards that stepped me through each step. Soon, I was greeted with the Puppy Linux desktop.

The interface was clean and similar in layout to Windows XP with a Menu button in the place of the Start button, and applications ran in a task bar. Clearly labeled icons on the desktop indicated which applications I should use to browse the file system, write a document, or browse the web.

Since the main use of my kitchen laptop is to surf the internet, I clicked the icon for the "browse" which launched SeaMonkey[134], the native web browser in Puppy Linux. It was clearly based on the same Mozilla source code that underlies Firefox, but it looked a couple of years out of date. At first, I was unable to get online, but I clicked the "setup" icon on the desktop, found the entry to marked "connect to the internet or intranet..." and configured my Ethernet adaptor to use DHCP. This fixed the problem, and I was soon browsing the web using SeaMonkey.

SeaMonkey did a good job of faithfully rendering web pages. I was also pleasantly surprised to find that it also played flash content on sites like YouTube[135] and Hulu[136]. However, the main benefit was that

---

[134] http://www.seamonkey-project.org/

[135] http://www.youtube.com/

[136] http://www.hulu.com/

SeaMonkey (along with the overall operating system) ran extremely fast. Since a CPU can quickly access RAM, the operating system was very smooth and responsive. I launched some of the other native Puppy Linux like Abiword[137], the word processor, and it also ran well. I found that I could open multiple tabs in SeaMonkey and still achieve great performance.

Although SeaMonkey was a decent web browser, I yearned for the familiarity of Firefox. I used Puppy Linux's package manager, PETGet and found Firefox 2.0.0.7. This was not the very latest version of Firefox out in the wild, but it provided the classic Firefox look and feel. I found that Firefox ran as responsively as SeaMonkey, and I realized that I had found a great operating system for my old kitchen laptop.

Although my kitchen laptop is rarely turned off, I didn't want to have to configure DHCP and install Firefox in case I had to reboot the machine (which would wipe out RAM and force me to run the Live CD again). So, I formatted the NTFS hard drive of the laptop into a Linux friendly ext3 format and installed Puppy Linux to the hard drive. This allowed me to enjoy the speed of Puppy Linux while maintaining the settings I liked despite the occasional shutdown of the laptop.

If anyone has an old PC that is used for light tasks like web browsing or word processing, then I think that Puppy Linux is a great solution. It is fast, easy to learn, and has a wide variety of applications despite its small size.

Comments

AUTHOR: Anjuan
DATE: 01/05/2009 04:38:45 AM

I mentioned this on Twitter, but thanks again for commenting on my blog! One thing I enjoy about social networking is the ability to get to know people of similar interests and figure out cool solutions!

---

[137] http://www.abisource.com/

AUTHOR: tony
URL: http://mtony75-2.blogspot.com
DATE: 01/02/2009 03:47:31 PM

Great article. I'm guessing the window manager was either KDE or gnome.
Will have to find a old laptop and create a recipe kiosk.

AUTHOR: Anjuan
DATE: 12/21/2008 02:56:58 AM

Artie,
Thanks for sharing your tips. I will update Firefox per your suggestion.

AUTHOR: Artie
DATE: 12/20/2008 01:45:28 PM

Nice post. Just use the update function in Firefox to get the latest version.
Maybe you can use some of my tips at http://www.murga-
linux.com/puppy/viewtopic.php?t=36014

Artie

AUTHOR: Anjuan
DATE: 12/18/2008 04:50:13 AM

AG,
Thanks for the clarification.

AUTHOR: AG
URL: http://bkaeg.org/blog
DATE: 12/18/2008 03:45:57 AM

SeaMonkey _is_ Mozilla. Since Firefox is a registered trademark of
Mozilla Corporation, it really isn't Free as in Free Speech. So,the Debian
Project and other Linux
Distros http://en.wikipedia.org/wiki/Iceweasel" rel="nofollow">re-branded
it. This prevents anyone from running afoul of the Mozilla trademark.

iPhone 3 or 3GS?

07/09/2009 08:40:00 AM

AUTHOR'S NOTE: This is obviously a dated post, but some of the principles it contains still apply today.

I was asked this question by a friend:

I am buying an iPhone. Is the 3GS worth the extra $100 over the 3G? Should I get the Apple Care warranty or roll with the standard? Will you tell me the must-have apps so I don't limit myself to Maps and Urbanspoon?

My response:

I assume you don't already have an iPhone and you're already using AT&T as your carrier. If those are both true, then I would recommend getting the iPhone 3GS. This is primarily due two key features that were introduced with the 3GS: the ability to capture and playback video and the better hardware (processor, memory, and graphics chip) that was introduced in the 3GS. There are a few other cool features of the 3GS (like the anti-oil screen, compass, and voice control), but for me the key improvements are video capability and hardware.

Regarding the warranty question, you get one year of hardware repair coverage and 90 days of technical support (both calculated from the date of purchase) when you buy an iPhone. Apple Care just extends those to two years. I'm not a big fan of buying additional coverage simply because I rarely use them. If you think you'll call Apple's support a lot or if you just want peace of mind, then I say go with Apple Care.

I have to admit I'm not very familiar with iPhone applications beyond the big ones. It also depends on what services you use and if they have an iPhone interface. For example, I have a Slingbox at home so the iPhone Slingplayer would be key. However, that wouldn't be the case for someone without a Slingbox.

Some of the top apps I've read about are Beejive (multi-protocol instant messaging), Fandango (local movie listings), Pandora/Last.FM (streaming

157

music), and Yelp (similar to Urbanspoon, but it can't hurt to try it out to compare). Some good games a podcast I listen to just recommended are Mass Effect Galaxy and Hero of Sparta. Keep in mind that games that take advantage of the improved hardware specs of the 3GS haven't appeared yet, but you should see them soon.

I hope that helps!

Quick Lessons From a Day at South by Southwest

03/13/2010 05:33:30 PM

AUTHOR'S NOTE: I wrote this after experiencing South by Southwest Interactive for the first time in 2010.

So, I am almost at the end of my first full day at South by Southwest Interactive. It has been an amazing experience. Here are a few things I have observed:

1. The WiFi network has been strong and stable. Considering that thousands of geeks are constantly pegging it to Tweet, Facebook, blog, Flickr, etc., it has held up like a champ. In fact, I have turned off 3G on my iPhone (making it use Edge) and now use the SXSW WiFi to get online.

2. The Austin Convention Center is a bit difficult to navigate. There are easy to understand signs everywhere, but it takes time to adjust to such a cavernous structure.

3. Free food is everywhere, but it is well hidden. I would run into people offering free food or drinks, but it was almost always unexpected. This is probably by design to avoid a deluge of foodies seeking grub non gratis.

4. Panels are great but Core Conversations provide more knowledge. I'm probably biased, but I got more out of the Core Conversations. Panels provide one to four people a platform to broadcast their ideas, but the Conversations allow more people to share their expertise. It's the difference between using text messages and using Facebook. You get more diversity of opinion.

5. "Geeks looking good" is possible. I think we see technology enthusiasts and other creatives shedding the image of socially challenged unwashed fanatics. We are becoming much more suave and sophisticated. Well, most of us.

Nestle: A Social Media Destruction Case Study in 6 Lessons

04/05/2010 04:33:00 PM

A few weeks ago, I had the honor of conducting a panel at South by Southwest Interactive 2010[138] called "How Social Media Can Destroy Your Business Model[139]". It was the culmination of months of effort that began when I submitted the idea to South by Southwest using their online PanelPicker[140]. To say that the experience was absolutely stunning would be an understatement. My panel would not have been as successful without the help of the person I picked to co-present, Kami Watson Huyse[141]. You can find the presentation that she and I put together for our panel here[142].

---

[138] http://2007.sxsw.com/interactive

[139] http://panelpicker.sxsw.com/ideas/view/3635?return=/ideas/index/interactive/q:anj uan

[140] http://panelpicker.sxsw.com/

[141] http://myprpro.com/about/about-communication-overtones/

[142] http://www.slideshare.net/kamichat/how-social-media-can-destroy-your-business-model

I was happy to have more than 200 people attend my first SXSW panel.

This is me, audience member <u>Shashi Bellamkonda</u>[143], and Kami listening to a question from the crowd.

The execution of the panel had its imperfections (you can find a transcript of the Twitter channel for those who posted to our #sxswdestroy hashtag <u>here</u>[144]). There were early complaints about the lack of microphones (an issue I reported in my panelist feedback survey to SXSW). However, once Kami and I started putting forth the great content that we had planned for our session, the audience calmed down and began enjoying the experience. By the time we wrapped up, many people came up after the panel and confirmed that it was a great success.

---

[143] http://twitter.com/shashib

[144] http://wthashtag.com/transcript.php?page_id=10288&start_date=2010-03-13&end_date=2010-03-14&export_type=HTML

As the days passed after the end of SXSW, I wondered what would be the next company to experience social media destruction? Kami and I had many relevant and recent examples of companies that had lost customers, eroded their brand value[145], or had to deal with embarrassment based[146] on not having an effective social media strategy. However, I thought that many long weeks would pass before I had a case study to analyze in light of the content of my panel and the great discussion we had during the session.

It turns out that I didn't have to wait long. Just a few days after my panel concluded, Nestle was committing many of the errors (many of them unforced) that I discussed during my panel. This article[147] ("Nestle Takes a Beating on Social-Media Sites") in the Wall Street Journal serves as an excellent write up of what happened to the company. I'll use it to analyze what Nestle did to make the company an easy social media target by taking block quotes from the article and deriving lessons from them.

Protesters have posted a negative video on YouTube, deluged Nestlé's Facebook page and peppered Twitter with claims that Nestle is contributing to destruction of Indonesia's rain forest, potentially exacerbating global warming and endangering orangutans. The allegations stem from Nestlé's purchases of palm-oil from an Indonesian company that Greenpeace International says has cleared rain forest to establish palm plantations.

At first glance, this seems to be a simple problem of having an international supply chain that sources palm oil from a partner that allegedly causes environmental harm in a third world country. I've seen this before when large oil companies like Shell pollute the environments of third world countries like Nigeria where they operate to drill for oil. Surely, something like palm oil would be far less of a public relations nightmare,

---

[145] http://consumerist.com/2009/04/dominos-rogue-employees-do-disgusting-things-to-the-food-put-it-on-youtube.html

[146] http://mashable.com/2010/02/14/southwest-kevin-smith/

[147] http://on.wsj.com/cyNdcv

right? Wrong.

Lesson #1: Small groups of well-organized protesters can use social media to make even small business problems into large public embarrassments.

The power of social media lies in its ability to give anyone with very small resources a global platform for their message. Even fifteen years ago, to take on a huge international company like Nestle required a radio or television tower at best or a printing press at worst. Now, it is a simple matter of uploading content to YouTube, Facebook, or Twitter.

Nestle says it had already decided to stop dealing with the firm, which supplied just 1.25% of the palm oil Nestle used last year. It says it bought only a tiny fraction of the firm's output, so any impact was negligible, and that it is working toward buying only environmentally sustainable palm oil.

Lesson #2: You cannot defend yourself against a negative social media campaign with facts.

Companies love to respond to negative publicity with facts. You see it in their press releases and in the words of their spokespeople. Facts do not protect your company. That's like a bank teller explaining to a bank robber that the bank had only been robbed once in the past five years. That fact does not help in the present situation.

Lesson #3: Who is Nina Backes?

"We, like Greenpeace and many others, abhor destruction of the rain forests, and will not source from companies where there is verifiable evidence of environmental damage," says Nestle spokeswoman Nina Backes.

The Ninas on Facebook

I did a search for Nina Backes on Facebook and Twitter. The only hits were teen-age girls posting self-portraits taken with camera phones and other nondescript pictures. So, I assume that Nina Backes, Nestle spokeswoman, did not use Facebook and Twitter. If the person you're using to speak for your company in the midst of a social media public relations crisis has no presence on the top two social media sites, then you've asked a blind, deaf, and mute person to host your press conference. And that person is not Helen Keller[148].

---

[148] http://en.wikipedia.org/wiki/Helen_Keller

Lesson #4: You cannot pull content from online social media sites.

In the protest's first days, Nestle asked Google's YouTube video site to remove the mock commercial, citing copyright infringement, Ms. Backes says. YouTube pulled the video, but it continued to spread on the Web.

When it comes to companies, social media cannot be created or destroyed. It can only be engaged. Pulling content only signals that you have something to hide. It is far better to join in the discussion and face the protests head on with credible company representatives.

Lesson #5: Threatening users of online social networks is the same thing as threatening your customers.

Nestle also told Facebook users it would delete their comments from its Facebook page if they included the altered logo.

No company would argue that threatening customers is a valid way to manage customer relationships. Companies must be willing to respectfully communicate with customers; even when they are angry. That is the only way to work through issues and eventually come to terms with which everyone can agree.

Lesson #6: One day a company will suffer real economic loss due to making a mistake when it comes to social media. Pray it isn't yours.

[Nina Backes] says it is too soon to judge whether sales of KitKats or other Nestle products have been affected by the protests.

The trend is clear. The growth of social media web sites like Facebook and Twitter is real and will continue to dramatically grow. This will only make it a more potent weapon to be used against companies. Only by mastering the medium can companies not only defend themselves against social media attacks but use it to achieve positive business results.

Comments

AUTHOR: Anjuan Simmons
URL: http://www.AnjuanSimmons.com
DATE: 04/07/2010 08:11:18 PM

Thanks for the comment, Kiratiana! I think that PR people can be private if they choose to do so. However, they should not represent the company when responding to social media incidents. That's like a person who wants to be a sports reporter, but they never take part in or watch sports!

AUTHOR: Kiratiana
URL: http://Kiratianatravels.com/
DATE: 04/07/2010 04:28:26 PM

Wow! That was really interesting! I think the part about the spokesperson not having a social media presence really struck me the most. I have known PR people who wanted to be private and PR people who are all over twitter. Your argument is definitely in favor or people being on social networks. Those pictures were also pretty sad!

Great post!

Protecting Your Child Online

04/18/2010 05:15:35 PM

It's 2 A.M., do you know who's looking at your child's Facebook profile? Children and teen-agers are putting an unprecedented amount of information about themselves on online social networking sites like Facebook[149], Twitter[150], and YouTube[151]. These sites are popular because they provide a global platform for communicating to the world. That is why marketers, public relations professionals, entrepreneurs, and other people who seek to reach a global audience have embraced online social networking sites. However, this global platform also attracts a demographic that often lacks the decision making skills to properly protect themselves from online danger: children.

Children of all ages are exposed to near ubiquitous access to the internet. Children lack the maturity to deal with the exposure provided by online social networking sites. This leaves them vulnerable to those who would exploit this vulnerability in order to bring harm to a child. This includes child predators, stalkers, or even other children who may use sites like Facebook as a platform for bullying[152]. It is important that parents and guardians understand how to protect their children from the potential risks of maintaining an online presence. There are three simple steps that can be done to protect children who participate in online social networks.

1. Relationship Matters

Spending quality time offline will provide a foundation for moderating online relationships. The first step in protecting your child online is making sure you have a healthy relationship offline. Children need to feel that open

---

[149] http://www.facebook.com/

[150] http://twitter.com/

[151] http://www.youtube.com/

[152] http://www.mercurynews.com/peninsula/ci_14901574

lines of communication[153] exist before they feel comfortable discussing their online activities. If you only check in on your child to get sound bites of their life, then you probably don't know your child very well. They may resist further probes into the detailed facts of their lives, but children inwardly yearn for such attention because it is a sign that you really care.

By having a strong relationship with your child, you earn the right to have open discussions about what they do and are exposed to online. This allows you the freedom to ask about the people they interact with online, and it gives your child the freedom to come to you when they have questions about any online situations they encounter.

The importance of strong relational ties also extends to your child's friends. It is very likely that the same kids who are close friends with your child in real life are also friends with them on online social networking sites. By understanding the backgrounds and interests of your child's friends, you can get a better grasp of the type of people they will attract. Since online social networking sites are usually designed to reduce the degrees of separation between people, online predators who are drawn to the friends of your child will often come into closer virtual proximity to your child.

2. Privacy Acts

Parents and guardians hold the key to the online safety of children. One of the first principles a parent or guardian needs to explain to a child is the importance of privacy. We live in a celebrity obsessed culture, and many people involved in social media measure their own internet fame[154] by how many people are friends with them on Facebook, follow them on Twitter, watch their YouTube videos, comment on their blogs, etc. Children are particularly prone to this desire to have large numbers of online followers because this is often tied to popularity in the real world.

I recommend that parents and guardians set a rule for very young children that they only maintain online connections with people they actually know.

---

153 http://parentingteens.about.com/od/parentingclasses/a/communicate2.htm

154 http://www.wired.com/culture/lifestyle/magazine/16-08/howto_allison

That means that it is fine to have online connections to other students in their school system or their peers with whom they engage in extracurricular activities (e.g., sports, religious activities, volunteer groups, etc.). However, if they want to connect to anyone they don't know in real life, then they need to explain to you why such a connection is necessary.

How can this rule be monitored? I believe that children under the age of 13 should be required to have at least one parent or guardian be connected to them on any online social network in which they participate. That means you should be friends with them on Facebook, follow them on Twitter, subscribe to their YouTube channel, etc. That gives you visibility to the child's circle of online of friends and the ability to question any connections they make.

Parents and guardians also need to understand how to help their children understand the privacy settings of the online social networking sites they use. I recommend that children under the age of 13 should protect their tweets on Twitter[155] meaning that people need to request to follow them on Twitter. Facebook is a more closed platform than Twitter, but some of the privacy settings are set to be open to everyone by default. In general, these need to be changed to Only Friends.

Parents also need to make sure their kids understand that their password should not be shared with anyone. I also think that it is fine if children don't reveal their passwords to their parents. Strong relationships require an atmosphere of trust, and it is important that children believe that some aspects of their privacy are protected. However, if there are any signs that a child is engaged in inappropriate online activities, then the parent has the right to forbid access to online social networks for a set period of time.

3. Block First but Tackle if Necessary

Parents and guardians can do a lot to protect the online activities of young people. However, even if you tightly restrict the number and type of people you child interacts with when using online social networks, it is likely that they may encounter some objectionable content or behavior. This can take

---

[155] http://askowen.info/2008/04/how-do-i-protect-my-tweets/

the form of pictures or videos that show their peers engaging in activities that go against the values you want your child to follow. Or, someone may seek to embarrass your child by making negative comments about them online or posting unflattering pictures. It is also possible that YOUR child may be the one that is trying to hurt someone using an online social network!

It's important to first talk with your child and come to an agreement that the behavior is inappropriate. If you've done a good job building a strong relationship with your child, then they will come to you when they see something online that disturbs them. This will help them buy into the assessment that the behavior is wrong and needs to be addressed. Many people who do things like try to bully others online are looking for a reaction. By not reacting, that person is robbed of the outcome they sought to obtain though their behavior. So, encouraging your child to not respond to the online activity is often a good first step.

If the person doing the inappropriate behavior is not a close friend of your child, you probably should advise your child to block their account. However, "defriending[156]" someone is often seen as an offensive act, so it is probably a good idea to have your child directly address the person about their behavior whether it is a good friend or not. You can coach your child on how to do this, and such experiences are often valuable teachable moments for helping your child deal with future interpersonal contacts. Yet, you should be prepared to speak with the parent or guardian of the offending child if your child is uncomfortable doing this.

If the offensive behavior persists despite repeated attempts to block the person from interacting with your child, then tackle the problem head on by reporting it to the administrators of the online social network. Facebook makes this easy by including a "Report This" on almost every page whether it is your child's wall or inbox. Other sites have similar mechanisms for reporting bad behavior.

You should be prepared to call the police if the behavior is particularly egregious or if you believe that your child's life is in danger. Law

---

[156] http://www.urbandictionary.com/define.php?term=defriend

enforcement is becoming more aware of the growing threat of online harassment, and officers are getting better at dealing with these issues. However, be prepared to present of evidence of the behavior by taking screenshots and printing out examples of what is happening to your child.

Finally, if your child is the one who is doing the bullying, then you should immediately address the issue. Explain that they should only say things online that they would tell someone in person. If that is not deterrent enough, then consider removing their access to the internet (including mobile devices with online access) until they demonstrate the maturity necessary to have the privilege restored.

By building strong relationships, protecting their privacy, and blocking (and reporting when necessary) inappropriate behaviors, parents and guardians can set safe boundaries for the online identities and activities of their children.

The Business Case for Location Based Services

05/05/2010 07:22:19 AM

AUTHOR'S NOTE: Gowalla is no longer a location based service, but, at the time of this writing, Foursquare is still a dominant player. While the information in this post is a little dated, I still think that businesses haven't leveraged the full potential of location based services.

While still operating in a niche, location based services are quickly becoming the next big thing in social media. Services like Foursquare[157] and Gowalla[158] are racking up thousands of users that are willing to broadcast their exact location to their online friends.

How Location Based Services Work

After creating an account, these services use the GPS chip in most PDAs[159] and smart phones[160] (and even many feature phones[161]) to determine the user's location. The user can then check in at a location which alerts everyone connected to that user that they are there. Other users can then go to that location and also check in to alert other friends.

Foursquare and Gowalla both add a gaming aspect to checking in by making users compete for rewards. Foursquare allows users to earn "badges"☐ which track the achievement of certain tasks like checking in from a boat or checking in at several museums. If a user checks in at a certain location more than anyone else, they become the "mayor"☐ of that

---

[157] http://foursquare.com/

[158] http://gowalla.com/

[159] http://en.wikipedia.org/wiki/Personal_digital_assistant

[160] http://www.phonescoop.com/glossary/term.php?gid=131

[161] http://www.phonescoop.com/glossary/term.php?gid=310

location. Gowalla also tracks achievements and allows users to become "founders" of a location, but more than one user can be a founder of a given location. In general, I prefer the competitive aspect of Foursquare more than that of Gowalla.

The Value to Businesses

While I don't see location based services taking off for very large companies, I think that small businesses and retail shops can benefit from them. For example a restaurant recently drew over 150 customers[162] who were seeking Foursquare's elusive "Swarm Badge"☐ which is achieved by 50 or more Foursquare users checking in at the same place at once. While it is unlikely that every one of the people who showed up bought something from the restaurant, many of them did. Similar location based campaigns would work for other retailers ranging from shoe shops to hair salons.

The Social Web

I first experienced the power of Foursquare and Gowalla at South by Southwest Interactive 2010. It was amazing to see where my online friends were checking in which helped me decide what sessions and parties to attend. Like Twitter[163], location based services are hard to understand unless a lot of the people you know in real life use it. I can see these services becoming very popular on college campuses where a large number of young people lead very social lives.

In fact, a recent study[164] showed that college students experienced withdrawal symptoms when forced to go without media devices[165] like cell

---

[162] http://blog.steffanantonas.com/case-study-how-to-use-foursquare-to-draw-a-crowd-into-your-restaurant.htm

[163] http://twitter.com/

[164] http://withoutmedia.wordpress.com/about/111109-words/

[165] http://arstechnica.com/media/news/2010/04/college-students-struggle-to-go-without-media-for-24-hours.ars

phones, text messages, televisions, eBook readers, email, and Facebook for 24 hours. These students reported feeling "uncomfortable" □, "alone" □, and "secluded" □ [166]. In many ways, the negative feelings described by these students were due to the loss of personal connections [167] that were made possible by text messages, email, Facebook, and Twitter. Location based services add a geographic layer to these connections which I think will deepen the social ties that young people currently make via social media. Companies that construct an effective location based services strategy will be able to offer innovative products, services, and marketing messages to this new generation of consumers.

Comments

AUTHOR: Anjuan Simmons
URL: http://www.AnjuanSimmons.com
DATE: 05/05/2010 11:21:00 PM

Thanks for the comment. I agree that the analytics that location based services offer can be a huge source of both customer incentives and target ted suggestions. Right now, the value proposition has not been fully realized, but I think that many online social networks are starting to get it. That is why Facebook and Twitter will probably expand their services to become more location aware.

AUTHOR: geekycyberdad
DATE: 05/05/2010 06:54:17 PM

Last night I tried a new restaurant because of a mobile coupon that I got through an app called Yowza. I think the real business case of location based apps is in finding ways to capitalize on the "when" and "where" of potential customers. Foursquare has begun to embrace this with many

---

[166] http://www.healthnews.com/family-health/social-media-addiction-possibility-for-your-teen-4207.html

[167] http://www.nydailynews.com/lifestyle/2010/04/27/2010-04-27_college_students_are_addicted_to_social_media_and_even_experience_withdrawal_sym.html

businesses offering special offers to frequent users. Just imagine the possibilities if they moved down this road even further and offered up suggestions on where to go based on your past check-ins and those of your friends.

Used correctly, location based services can be of huge benefit to consumers and businesses of almost any size alike.

Summer Computer Maintenance

07/12/2010 04:46:20 PM

It's the summer which hopefully means that well deserved vacations are being enjoyed. This is also a great time to perform basic computer maintenance on your system that is often ignored during busier times of the year.

Back It Up

Backing up computer data is a lot like flossing. It's something most people know they need to do, but they often forget to do it. However, it takes one computer meltdown to communicate the need to keep a copy of the essential files on your system. External hard drives are relatively inexpensive, and you can even find 1 TB models for under one hundred dollars. Once you connect the external drive to your computer, simply copy the files you want to safeguard to it. For additional peace of mind, you can take the external drive to work or keep it in a safe deposit box just in case a catastrophic event like a house fire occurs. That will keep often irreplaceable files like pictures, audio files, and financial documents safe. You can also invest on online backup services like Carbonite[168] or Mozy[169].

Let It Breathe

Since they are machines, we sometimes forget that air is an important factor in system performance. Proper airflow is needed to make sure that the heat generated by computer components is removed from the cases that house them. If you have desktop, now is a good time to rearrange the desktop items around it and make sure that the ventilation holes are not blocked.

You can also buy a can of compressed air from a local computer or hardware store. This is a handy tool for blowing air over the keyboard of

---

[168] http://www.carbonite.com/

[169] http://mozy.com/

your laptop to remove any debris that has fallen beneath the keys. For desktops, unplug the cord, remove the case, and blow out the dust that probably covers the motherboard, fan, and other internal components.

Boost Your Performance

One of the cheapest yet most effective ways to boost the performance of a computer is add additional RAM (Random Access Memory) to it. The RAM chips inside your system provide what is essentially a "scratch pad" to temporarily store calculated values in memory. However, RAM chips come in different varieties so you need to know what kind of RAM your system supports before buying more. Fortunately, websites like Crucial.com[170] will help you do this once you tell it the manufacturer, product line, and model of your system. Adding RAM to a desktop can be done by most individuals, but you probably need to enlist the services of a professional to add RAM to a laptop.

Another effective way to boost the performance of your system is to format the hard drive and reinstall the operating system. Before doing this, you'll need to make sure you have completely backed up your data and locate the installation discs for the operating system and all of your applications. Most operating system installation programs include a utility for formatting the hard drive and are wizard driven which makes them easy to understand. Once you complete the installation of a fresh version of your operating system, you'll find your computer running like the day you first turned it on!

By backing up your data, ensuring proper ventilation of your system, and boosting system performance, you'll find that your computer will emerge from the summer ready to handle anything you throw at it!

---

[170] http://www.crucial.com/index.aspx

A Question about a Hard to Remove Virus

AUTHOR'S NOTE: The next few posts show my answers to technology questions I received from people in my social network. You'll see how I formalized this process later in this book by holding "Tech Tuesdays" where I gave out free technology advice to anyone who asked a question.

11/04/2010 01:16:15 PM

I'm going through my Facebook backup and finding interesting things to post on my blog. This is something I was asked on my wall on July 15, 2009 at 2:44 pm:

Hey Anjuan. A friend of mine got a virus on here yesterday and has been having a hard time getting rid of it. She's run a couple of antivirus' but her system is still crashing. Any suggestions? (I know it's not Tech Tuesday but it's an emergency - she works from home!) Thanks!

Sure, I hope I can help! Is she sure she has a virus? Is an antivirus program giving her a warning that she is infected? I'll assume that's the case, but people sometimes think they have virus when it could be another issue.

I'll assume she's running Windows Vista. She should try booting into Safe Mode. She can do this by rebooting the computer and holding the F8 key while it's starting up. She'll get a window called "Windows Advanced Options Menu" where she can select Safe Mode. This is a very minimalistic mode where Windows will run just basic operations. If she can successfully use Safe Mode, I recommend she immediately copy the data off of the computer onto an external hard drive.

Once her data is safe, have her try running the anti-virus while in Safe Mode. Hopefully, that will clear up the infection.

Her response:

REDACTED Thanks! It was a link that she saw as a friend's status telling her to watch a home video. When she clicked it it set it as her status and then kicked her off facebook and started showing porn, then shut her

system down. She ran Norton, and then another one she found online on a forum about that virus, but it's still giving her a hard time.
I'll forward this to her.

A Question About Saving Video to Your Hard Drive

11/08/2010 11:00:53 PM

I'm going through my Facebook backup and finding interesting things to post on my blog. This is something I was asked on my wall on November 9, 2009 at 12:02 am:

Hey Anjuan. A friend of mine asked this question... "Does anyone know how to save a video to their hard drive. I want to save my television debut from Fox 26 but don't know how. Please help." Can you help?

There are a number of ways to do this, but I think the easiest approach is to use a computer TV Tuner. This is basically a device that you connect to your computer which allows you to record television shows or to plug video equipment to your computer (usually via component cables).

I have used such a product from ATI (which is now owned by AMD). You can find a list of such products here:
http://www.amd.com/us/products/pctv/tv-wonder-tuners/Pages/tv-wonder-tv-tuners-for-the-pc.aspx

However, the product that is the easiest to use is a USB device that you simply plug into the USB port (after installing the included hard ware). Here is a direct link to such a device:
http://www.amd.com/us/products/pctv/tv-wonder-tuners/Pages/tv-wonder-hd-600-hi-speed-usb.aspx

The benefit of this device is that your friend can actually use it to directly record the television program on the computer. It acts as a personal video recorder and can download channel guides and schedule future recordings.

There are two drawbacks to this approach. One is that money will have to be spent (although the USB devices should cost around $80). The other is

Technology Translator

that you need a fairly high end computer (I would recommend a dual core processor and at least 2 GB of RAM).
I hope this helps!

182

A Question about Cloud Computing

11/10/2010 05:13:51 PM

I'm going through my Facebook backup and finding interesting things to post on my blog. This is something I was asked on my wall on November 16, 2009 at 2:14 pm:

Anjuan - this is a bit early for ur weekly I.T. Tuesday session .....
Can you please give me a tiny summary of "SaaS Cloud ERP" -
actually im wondering if Im mixing up the term... does "SaaS Cloud
ERP" exist or isit "Cloud Computing" and "SaaS ERP" .... Thanks!!

I think you're combining a few terms. I'll take them separately in order from the general to the specific.

Cloud computing: In general, this refers to the ability to provide computing over the internet. If your recall from our computer networking Visio diagrams, the internet is usually depicted as a cloud, and that is why it's called "cloud computing". Capabilities provided by cloud computing include services like platform as a service, software as a service, web services, utility computing, and others. So, think of it as a rather broad category.

SaaS: This stands for Software as a Service which is a type of cloud computing. SaaS provides software applications that are hosted by a third party provider and usually accessed via a web browser. Google Docs are an easy to understand example of this.

ERP: This stands for Enterprise Resource Planning. In general, it is a class of software applications that manage business data and business functions. A traditional (and popular) example of ERP is SAP.

So, SaaS Cloud ERP would mean an ERP application that is provided as a service over the internet. I'm sure there are certainly vendors that provide such a service. However, I am not convinced that cloud computing is anywhere near the level of robustness needed for most major enterprises. However, that is another discussion.

A Tech Question About Spokeo

11/15/2010 10:46:44 AM

I'm going through my Facebook backup and finding interesting things to post on my blog. This is something I was asked on my wall on March 30, 2010 at 5:50 am:

Q: www.spokeo.com. What is the good, the bad, and the ugly? I'm a bit surprised by the easy access of non-volunteered personal information to this particular site and would like to get your take on it.

A: Spokeo and other "people-finder" web sites generally provide publicly available information (like phone numbers, addresses, etc.) for free and charge for more detailed private information (like social network profiles, cell phone numbers, and email addresses). They are good when used like the white pages in a phone book and allow people to reconnect with people they already know (or knew in the past).

One of the drawbacks of these sites is that they often publish old data. So, they are often very unreliable.

The information published by these sites is easy to access because public records are often stored in easy to access databases. But, a person can make certain information private by, for example, requesting an unlisted phone number. However, some information will always be public due to freedom of information laws. This makes information that is very personal (like how much someone's house is worth) freely available to the public.

Overall, I think these sites are useful as long as you are aware that the data may be outdated or completely wrong.

Why Wi-Fi is Necessary on Mobile Phones

01/13/2011 10:05:26 AM

A Facebook friend asked me this question earlier this morning:

Anjuan, let me ask you a question. I got the Samsung Epic from Sprint. It has wifi. I already have internet on my phone so why is the wifi necessary?? No one seems to know why exactly...

Since this may be something other people may wonder about, I decided to post my response here:

@Michael: There are two major benefits to Wi-Fi. The first benefit is speed. When you access the internet on Sprint's network, you are using it along with millions of other Sprint customers. So, your online experience will change based on how many of your fellow Sprint customers are hitting the network. Conversely, a Wi-Fi connection usually has to only support you and, sometimes, a handful of other people. So, you'll get better download and upload speed.

The second benefit is control. This is similar to the speed benefit. While Sprint may offer unlimited data plans, they are not legally obligated to give you the best bandwidth for your online needs. For example, you may find a GPS navigation app that you like due to its features and accuracy. Sprint could detect that you're using that app and degrade its performance on the network so that you're more inclined to use Sprint's preinstalled GPS app. The recently passed FCC rules are supposed to limit this behavior by carriers, but that only applies if their behavior is challenged in court. When you use Wi-Fi, you are completely off the Sprint network and can fully control the user experience of apps that connect to the internet.

I hope that helps!

UPDATE

He made this follow up comment:

Technology Translator

Wow Anjuan, that really cleared up alot for me. I suppose when Im on wifi it doesnt matter about the 4g. On my phone I cant use both at the same time. Im sure the wifi is way better than the 4g by far. Thank you so much.

And here was my response:

I'm glad that my comments were helpful. Also, while Sprint currently offers an unlimited data plan, it is possible that they may introduce tiered pricing in the future. That means that you will have a cap on your data usage and be subject to additional charges if you go over that cap. Wi-Fi usage would not count against your data usage so using Wi-Fi would be the way to go if Sprint implements a tiered pricing arrangement.

The Very Best iPad Apps

05/26/2011 02:12:20 PM

AUTHOR'S NOTE: This is another post that contains dated information, but some of the recommendation still hold up.

A friend on Facebook recently asked me this question:

Hi Anjuan! I know you are an expert in this area - what do you recommend as the very best iPad apps? :-)

Here is the response I shared with her:

I'm happy to help, of course!

So, I assume that you have the iPad 2 which has better hardware than the first iPad as well as front and rear facing cameras. My recommendations apply to the first iPad as well, but some of them are meant to show off the faster speed of the iPad 2.

With tens of thousands of apps, it's hard to only pick a few, but here are my favorite iPad apps. I've grouped them by functional area so let me know if there are other types of apps you prefer, and I'll look for more options.

PRODUCTIVITY
* Dropbox (free): Lets you synchronize files between your desktop/laptop and your iPad.
* PenUltimate ($2): This is a great app that turns your iPad into a literal notepad where you can take notes with your finger or, if you have one, a stylus.
* Evernote (free): This lets you organize various types of media into folders. It synchronizes with the desktop version.
* Wunderlist HD (free): A task manager.
* MarketDash (free): Tracks your stock portfolio.

READING
* Instapaper ($5): Let's you save web pages for later reading. This is nice if you browse a lot of web sites but don't always have time to read all of the content.

* Flipboard (free): This takes content from URL's shared on Facebook, Twitter, and RSS feeds and lays them out in a very nice magazine format. It's great for news junkies like me. I recommend at least giving this one a try since its free.
* Pulse (free): This is another nicely done new reader.
* CNN for iPad (free): Yep, like I said, I'm a news junkie.
* Financial Times (free to download): I've noticed your preference for the Financial Times, and this app gives you access to its great content. However, you'll have to have an FT.com subscription.
* Kindle (free): Great if you have books in Kindle format.

SOCIAL MEDIA

* Friendly (free): Facebook has yet to create an iPad app like the one they have for the iPhone so the developers behind Friendly created an alternative that mimics the Facebook user interface.
* TweetDeck (free): I don't think you use Twitter, but, if you decide to use it one day, this is a nice iPad 2 client.

LIFESTYLE

* Epicurious (free): This is a well done cookbook app.
* BigOven (free): Another cookbook app.

AUDIO/VIDEO

* TuneInRadio ($1): Lets you listen to online radio stations like NPR or your favorite local stations.
* Soundhound (free): If you've ever heard a song and couldn't identify it, Soundhound is a great app that listens to the song and identifies the title, artist, and usually a copy of the lyrics.
* Pandora (free): Pandora lets you create stations based on your favorite artists
* Netflix (free): This really only makes sense if you use Netflix, but, if you do, the iPad app is amazing.

GAMES

* Angry Birds Rio HD
* Fruit Ninja HD
* Paper Toss World Tour HD
* Jenga HD

That's all I have time to list for now. I hope this helps!

How do I Protect My Computer on Urban WiFi?

09/17/2011 11:14:45 PM

I received this question from one of my Facebook friends:

Hi Anjuan,

I was thinking about using the free wifi offered by our city to a businesses but Im worried about someone hacking in my computer and getting account #'s ect. Is there anyway to insure that doesn't happen or is it just best not to use it. It would save me 50 bucks a month.

Thanks

Here's my response:

Thanks for the question! What version of Windows are you using? If you're using Windows Vista or Windows 7, then both have a great built in Firewall that you want to be sure that you turn on before logging into the city wifi. Also, Microsoft offers a free antivirus application called Windows Defender. You can download it here:

http://www.microsoft.com/windows/products/winfamily/defender/default.mspx

I recommend running Defender at least once a day to catch anything that may make it through your computer's firewall.

I hope that helps!

Anjuan

Why Every Tech Entrepreneur Needs to "Hello World" .. . and More

11/30/2011 05:41:35 AM

This post was inspired by Dorian and Adria. I thank both of them!

One of the most rewarding aspects of online social media is the opportunity to be inspired by people you would never know if sites like Twitter and Facebook didn't exist. Social networking has brought people into my life who encourage me as we share our experiences navigating the complexities of life.

I was recently reminded of the power of these shared experiences by posts by two Twitter friends, Dorian Dargan[171] and Adria Richards[172]. Although they, to my knowledge, don't know each other, their posts hammered home a lesson that every tech entrepreneur needs to learn. The lesson is simple: tech entrepreneurs need to know how to program.

Dorian sent me a Twitter DM earlier today with a link to his post Why I Am Learning to Program[173]. Follow the link and read it. I'll wait. Done? That was good stuff, right? This is the line from Dorian's post that really resonated with me:

Unfortunately, however, inspiration in and of itself simply isn't enough to make one's world-changing idea a living, breathing thing.

Dorian is exactly right. Inspiration, no matter how lofty and grandiose, cannot, by itself, lead to creation. Inspiration is amazing, but products have to be created based on the harshness of reality. That reality can only be

---

[171] https://twitter.com/#!/dtothathird

[172] https://twitter.com/#!/adriarichards

[173] http://doriandargan.wordpress.com/2011/11/24/why-i-am-learning-to-program/

understood if inspiration is applied to the actual process of making, and that is especially true when it comes to technology entrepreneurs.

Architects are better able to design buildings when they have personally built things and have experiential knowledge of brick and mortar, hammer and nail, and saw and wood. Conductors are better able to guide the orchestra when they intimately know every piano key, violin string, drum membrane, and woodwind hole. Similarly, tech entrepreneurs are better equipped to add doses of realism to their ideas and can more competently guide the work of their programming teams when they know how to program themselves.

I am not suggesting that tech entrepreneurs need to be the best programmers on the team. In fact, if that's the case, then they probably need a new programming team. However, tech entrepreneurs need to know how to code, and their knowledge should go beyond a simple "Hello world" program. Tech entrepreneurs should understand the difference between good code and bad code and should be actively involved in code reviews. This is the only way to make sure that the spirit of the entrepreneur's vision survives the transition from idea to syntax.

Adria wrote two blog posts about her efforts to learn how to program. The first one was written last year and is called 11 Reasons Why I'm Learning Ruby on Rails[174] and a follow-up post was written in June of this year titled I'm Back Learning Ruby on Rails[175]. You should also read both of these posts. I'll wait again. Now, you see why I enjoy reading Adria's stuff, right? Her posts are right in line with Dorian's thoughts about the importance of "idea generators" also being "code generators".

Although Dorian and Adria are on the Ruby on Rails tip, my programming experience is with PL/SQL and Visual Basic (well, VB through the Siebel Tools IDE). As someone with "tech entrepreneur bones in my body", I have been inspired by these posts from my two friends to also dust off my

---

[174] http://butyoureagirl.com/6313/why-im-learning-ruby-on-rails/

[175] http://butyoureagirl.com/10090/im-back-learning-ruby-on-rails/

programming skills and get back to building things in code. After all, I can't expect my future customers to trust my products if I don't intimately know how they work, right?

Comments

AUTHOR: Natasha Tygart
URL: http://weheartit.com/natashatygart
DATE: 12/02/2011 06:15:45 AM

Programming is one of the things I hate to do. Unfortunately (for me), there are really times when you have to learn them and use them in the future.

Question About Buying a New Computer

04/24/2012 09:45:16 PM

One of my Facebook friends recently asked me this question:

Hey Anjuan. How are you and fam?

Im looking at getting another computer. What do you think about this?

This Averatec All-In-One desktop features a 18.4-inch WXGA TFT LCD (1680 x 945) screen, AMD Athlon 3250 1.5GHz processor, and 2GB SDRAM memory. This desktop computer is a great way to conserve space while keeping the Convenience of a desktop computer.

My response:

Sorry for the late reply. My family and I are doing well. How are you and yours?

Whenever I get a question about buying a desktop/laptop, I always have to ask, "What do you plan to do with it?" If you want to mostly surf the web, do light Microsoft office type work, and consume media (movies, music, etc.), then almost any product on the market (including the one you mentioned will do). However, if you want to do more intensive tasks like editing video, playing video games, etc., then you probably want to get better specs like an Intel processor and 4 GB of RAM. In that case, you probably also want to get a major brand name like HP, Toshiba, Dell, or Samsung.

Also, keep in mind that a few developments in the computer industry make this a bad time to buy a computer. The next version of Windows (Windows 8), Mac OS (Mountain Lion), and Intel's latest processors are all coming out in the next few months. It may be better to wait (if you can) until after the summer to see what new machines debut with these updates.

I hope that helps. Let me know if I can provide more information.

Technology Translator

Regards,

Anjuan

Advice to a Facebook Friend about a Career in Technology

05/31/2012 03:57:27 PM

A Facebook friend recently asked me about getting into the technology industry:

Hey Anjuan. I don't mean to bother you but I'm reaching out to you in hopes that you can provide me with some advice in getting into the IT field.

I'm 29 years old and have always been interested in electronics, computers, pretty much technology in itself. I don't have much job experience in the field except for work that I've done for friends and family which consists of desktop support help. I have an associates degree (AA) I received from my community college and am now working towards my bachelors degree.

Here's my reply:

Thanks for the message. I think that picking up a certification like A+, Cisco, or MSCE would be a good first step. Those certifications do carry weight, and you can narrow your job search to opportunities that ask for them.

I think that technology security will be a big area for a long time so continue to focus on that. Other big areas include Cloud Computing and Mobile.

Once you get in the door and get some experience, you probably should start looking at how technology projects are created and executed. As we become a more global world, hands-on technical work can be outsourced. However, good management and leadership is much harder to send overseas.

I hope that helps.

Technology Translator

Comments

It is a good blog for the all people they are give the best and information about he career guidance in technology.I learn so much from this blog.Thanks to give this.

Master Your Inbox with the D.R.A.F.T. Method

03/03/2013 11:00:20 PM

I have a lot of email accounts. I have a work account as well as several personal accounts on Gmail, Hotmail, Yahoo, and even an old AOL email address. At one point, I was receiving hundreds of emails per day, and my multiple inboxes were seas of unread mail with islands here and there of the few messages I was actually able to read. A friend of mine named Scott Hanselman[176] made me aware of the term "psychic weight" [177]. That is the burden that impossibly full inboxes (and other electronic notifications) have on the mind: so much email, so little time.

I know I'm not alone in struggling under the psychic weight of what feels like a million messages. There's even a term for what people do to deal with the problem: email bankruptcy[178].

There have been a number of solutions proposed to solve the email overload problem, and the most famous is probably Merlin Mann's "Inbox Zero[179]" concept. This is the idea that inboxes should be regularly zeroed out to free yourself from the mental burden of so many unread messages. Merlin proposed a five step system: delete, delegate, respond, defer, do. I like Inbox Zero, but I don't think it really covers the way to not only truly get control over an overflowing inbox but to also pro-actively reduce the rate of incoming messages. It also doesn't provide a nifty acronym; unless D.D.R.D.D is a word.

I've come up with my own system for email management, and it does have a nifty acronym: D.R.A.F.T. It stands for **Delete, Reply, Archive, Filter,**

---

[176] http://www.hanselman.com/blog/

[177] http://www.hanselman.com/blog/PsychicWeightLifeIsPending.aspx

[178] http://gawker.com/254608/

[179] http://inboxzero.com/

and **Transform**. You apply the method by starting with the first message in your inbox and deciding whether to delete it, reply to it, archive it, filter out similar messages, or transform it (yes, like Optimus Prime). Some messages require more than one action to be used, but the overall goal is to unshackle your productivity from your inbox and direct it toward more efficient tools like your calendar, To Do List, knowledge base, etc. More importantly, you'll be less tempted to tend to the care and feeding of an overflowing inbox after work when you should be doing important things like spending time with the people you love (or your therapist).

The Pre-D.R.A.F.T. Principle

Before we get into the D.R.A.F.T. email management method, I have to make sure you understand one key principle: **Fire and Forget**. That means that you only deal with an individual email once. You may apply more than one action from the D.R.A.F.T. method to an email, but once you've dealt with it, don't go back to it.

Delete

Your first goal for every email should be to delete it. This is especially true for those emails that flood into your inbox because you signed up for the free newsletter of a person or business you can't even remember. One of the best ways to organize your inbox in a way that facilitates deletion is to sort your inbox by sender or by subject. If you use Outlook or some other desktop email client this is usually easy to do. It's a bit harder if you're using a web based email system through a web browser, but there is usually some workaround. For example, to see all messages by a particular sender in Gmail, hover over the sender's name in your inbox and then click "Emails" in the window that pops up. You'll be taken to a screen where all messages from that sender are displayed, and you can delete away.

Reply

If you can't immediately delete an email (if, for example, it's an email from your boss, significant other, probation officer, etc.), then your next goal should be to immediately reply to it. If writing your reply takes more than one minute, add it to your To Do List. Your inbox should not be a replacement for a To Do List!

So, you may ask, "What if I immediately reply, and that results in another reply from the original sender?" I'm glad you asked because that is why **The Two Reply Rule** exists. If your reply triggers another reply, then reply again. If that triggers yet another reply, then pick another communication channel because **email is clearly not working.** I've seen emails with more than twenty replies going back and forth. After the second reply, a phone, telegraph machine, or sign language should have been used. Email is not the medium for deep discussions!

To clarify **The Two Reply Rule**, here's how it works:

1. Person A emails Person B
2. Person B sends a reply to Person A
3. Person A, apparently not satisfied with Person B's reply, sends a reply to Person B's reply.
4. Person B sends another reply to Person A
5. Person A, again apparently not satisfied with Person B's reply, sends a reply to Person B's reply.
6. Person B stops this madness and reaches out to Person A via some other channel (phone call, instant message, physical visit, smoke signals, etc.).

It's perfectly fine to send a summary email of the discussion, but don't try to have the discussion using email.

Archive

Perhaps you may not be able to delete an email due to its importance, or you can't immediately reply because a reply may not be warranted. Maybe the email is an interesting article that you actually want to read later. I personally don't get interesting emails like that, but, hey, I respect the concept. What I don't respect is leaving those emails in your inbox. Archive those suckers out of your inbox and continue to convince yourself that you'll read them later.

Filter

Deleting, replying, and archiving messages in your inbox will go a long way toward getting you to an empty inbox. However, those actions can only occur after the damage has been done (i.e., the email lands in your inbox). It is far better to pre-emptively keep emails from getting into your inbox altogether. One of the best ways to do this is to set up a filter that automatically performs an action on a message based on criteria you establish. Does the office cafeteria send a weekly menu? Create a filter that automatically files those emails into your "Gross But Convenient Lunch Options" folder. Does that runner girl at the office (who you don't even work with) keep emailing you with requests to fund her next 10k or half marathon? Email her your bank account and routing number with the subject "Use Wisely" and automatically filter those messages into your "Pay It Forward" folder.

Another way to pre-emptively keep email out of your inbox is to unsubscribe from email newsletters. If someone wants to get information to you, then they should publish an RSS feed and let you subscribe to it via Google Reader[180] or some other RSS reader (but, c'mon, Google Reader is the best). Don't let those email newsletters clutter your inbox. Filter them out

Transform

A lot of people think they have an email overload problem, but they really have a time, task, and file storage problem. As I said earlier in this article, your inbox is not your To Do list because tasks simply get buried and searching for them makes them even harder to complete. Furthermore, your inbox is not a calendar reminder to set up a meeting. Your inbox is also not your file storage system. I know we all get great attachments full of amazing content in our inboxes, but it is a disservice to the greatness of those attachments to keep them trapped in your inbox.

So, transform those messages! Instead of waiting to schedule a meeting, immediately add it to your calendar and use the body of the email to create the agenda for your meeting. Then Delete or Archive the email. If the email

---

[180]

https://accounts.google.com/ServiceLogin?service=reader&passive=1209600&continue=http://www.google.com/reader&followup=http://www.google.com/reader

is a task that takes more than a minute to do, add it to your To Do list and then get the email out of your inbox (if it takes less than a minute, do it immediately). If the email has a great attachment, detach it from the email and put it in a file storage area or inside your corporate knowledge base. I prefer Dropbox for the former and a wiki for the latter.

Delete, Reply, Archive, Filter, and **Transform** make up the D.R.A.F.T. Method. Like any other method, it is only useful if it is used, and you have to use it over and over again to make it a habit. It will take some time, but you'll have a much more manageable inbox if you D.R.A.F.T. your emails.

Don't you love that empty inbox feeling?

How My iPad Replaced My Laptop

04/24/2013 01:50:50 AM

If you and I walked into a conference room within the past year, you, like most people, would probably assume that the black device I had with me was a laptop. However, once I opened the device, you would see a keyboard (not too unusual) with a screen that looked like the device ran iOS. You may even ask me, "How did you get the iPad operating system running on your laptop?" And I would answer, "Oh, this isn't a laptop. It's my iPad in a keyboard case."

Here's my iPad in its Clamcase.

I decided to use my iPad as my laptop replacement about a year ago because, at the time, I was traveling a lot and needed a lightweight computer to use on airplanes. I usually didn't have to pull it out of my backpack before my belongings went through the x-ray machine, it turned instantly on, and the iPad had enough battery life to make it through any flight.

However, I was able to fully realize the potential of my iPad when I purchased a keyboard case for it. The iPad is great for consuming content, but I needed a device that also excelled at content creation and data entry. The iPad's virtual keyboard is responsive, but I wouldn't even consider writing long form content on it. At the time, the ZAGGfolio[181] was a very popular keyboard case for the iPad, but a few Google searches led me to the Clamcase[182]. The ZAGGfolio had a nice keyboard, but it seemed way too flimsy to use in places ranging from cramped airplane seats to hotel sofas to conference room tables. I needed a sturdy solution and the Clamcase was the best one I could find.

After I solved the data entry problem with the Clamcase, I then had to find a way to use the iPad for the business function I do the most: taking copious notes at long meetings. I could type using the Clamcase, but I wanted to also write as if the iPad was an infinite notepad. That required two solutions: a stylus and a note taking app.

Having used Wacom tablets in the past, I knew I could trust the quality of their iPad styli. I chose the Wacom Bamboo Stylus Duo[183] which provided a writing implement that felt good in my hand and responded well to the capacitive touch screen of the iPad. This stylus also provided a ballpoint pen on the opposite side from the digital tip in case I ever needed to write on actual paper.

---

[181] http://www.zagg.com/keyboard-cases/index.php

[182] http://clamcase.com/

[183] http://www.wacom.com/en/products/stylus/bamboo-stylus/duo

This is my Wacom Bamboo Duo stylus.

The note taking app was harder to find. I tried popular apps like <u>Penultimate</u>[184] and <u>Bamboo Paper</u>[185]. However, one app outshined them all: <u>Notability</u>[186]. Notability provided an experience that was almost like using a pen to write on paper, and it had a clean interface. I also liked that fact that it integrated with cloud services like Dropbox. I use Notability several times every day, and I don't even consider other note taking apps.

---

[184] https://itunes.apple.com/us/app/penultimate/id354098826?mt=8

[185] https://itunes.apple.com/us/app/bamboo-paper-notebook/id443131313?mt=8

[186] https://itunes.apple.com/us/app/notability-take-notes-annotate/id360593530?mt=8

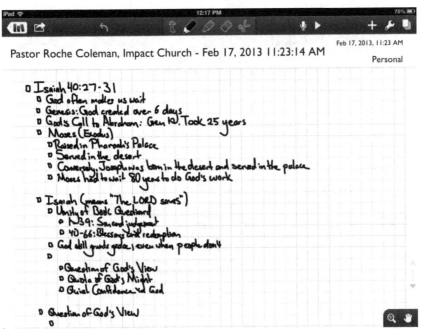

*Due to client confidentiality, I can't show my business notes, but here's a
sample of sermon notes I've written using my iPad, Notability, and my
Wacom Bamboo Duo stylus.*

FOREWORD
BY JEFF SUTHERLAND

Scrum Firsts
- Company: Objective Technology
- ScrumMaster: John Scumniotales
- Product Owner: Don Roedner
- Creators: Jeff Sutherland

Product Owner Responsibilities
- ☐ Product Vision
- ☐ Business Plan
- ☐ Revenue
- ☐ Road Map
- ☐ Release Plan
- ☐ Product Backlog

The product owner is a new role for most companies and needs this book's compelling and easily understandable presentation. When the first product owner was selected, I was a vice president at Object Technology, responsible for delivering the first product created by Scrum. The new product would make or break the company, and I had six months to deliver a development tool that would alter the market. In addition to creating the product with a small, carefully selected team, I had to organize the whole company around new product delivery. With only a few months until product shipment, it was clear that the right minimal feature set would determine success or failure. I found that I did not have enough time to spend talking with customers and watching competitors closely so that I could precisely determine the right prioritized feature set up front and break those features down into small product backlog items for the team.

I had already delegated my engineering responsibilities to the first ScrumMaster, John Scumniotales, but now I needed a product owner. I had access to any resource in the company, so I selected the best person from the product management team for the role I had in mind: Don Roedner. As the first product owner, Don had to own the vision for the product, the business plan and the revenue,

xv

Notability also lets me write on and highlight any PDF file. Here's an example from a book I read about Agile Project Management.

I enjoyed taking handwritten notes on my iPad with Notability, but I also needed a way to do create documents, spreadsheets, and presentations. I purchased the parts of Apple's iWorks suite that performed these functions: Pages[187] (word processor), Numbers[188] (spreadsheets), and Keynote[189] (presentations). These apps performed exactly as I expected

---

[187] https://itunes.apple.com/us/app/pages/id361309726?mt=8

[188] https://itunes.apple.com/us/app/numbers/id361304891?mt=8

[189] https://itunes.apple.com/us/app/keynote/id361285480?mt=8

and usually converted files created by their Microsoft Office counterparts without a hitch.

While I don't do it often, I sometimes like to create forms that colleagues or customers can fill out on my iPad. The forms didn't have to be complex, but I wanted the ability to create text boxes, check boxes, radio buttons, combo boxes and other basic form fields. I found the FormsConnect[190] app which met my basic form needs and even offered a few advanced features. I also liked FormsConnect's ability to sync with DropBox.

The iPad is powerful, but there are times when I need a full desktop. For example, there are some sites (especially ones that use Flash) that don't work well on the iPad whether you're using Safari, Chrome, or any other browser. Also, there may be a desktop application I need to use that doesn't have an iPad app version. In these situations I'm glad to have the ability to remotely access a full desktop using Mocha RDP Lite[191] (for accessing Windows machines) and Mocha VNC Lite[192] (for accessing Macs).

As I used the iPad more for work, I began to realize how it could meet non-work needs. I'm the father of three kids ages 8, 6, and 5, and I film a lot of their activities. I wanted a way to easily and quickly edit video clips into a movie with fairly high production values. I purchased another Apple app, iMovie[193], which far exceeded expectations. I can edit clips with finger swipes, pinches, and double taps. I even started a video series about people in my social network called 2°[194] which I edit completely on my iPad (the video is filmed using a webcam attached to my Mac Mini and a program

---

[190] https://itunes.apple.com/us/app/formconnect/id432653695?mt=8

[191] https://itunes.apple.com/us/app/remote-desktop-lite-rdp/id288362576?mt=8

[192] https://itunes.apple.com/us/app/mocha-vnc-lite/id284984448?mt=8

[193] https://itunes.apple.com/us/app/imovie/id377298193?mt=8

[194] http://www.anjuansimmons.com/2-show/

called Call Recorder for Skype[195] which I use to record the Skype interviews).

Of course, I have a lot of fun on my iPad as well. After working for the first few hours of a flight or late at night in a hotel, it was nice to blow off some steam. I use VLC (which Apple pulled from the App store in 2011) to watch movies recorded in almost any format, Downcast [196]for audio and video podcasts, and the built in iTunes app for music.

The most popular social media sites have apps exist on the iPhone, Android phones, and other types of tablets, but I think that the iPad versions of Facebook[197], Twitter[198], and Linkedin [199]have the best designs and features.

When I travel with my kids, I like a few "pass and play games". These are games where you pass the iPad around when it's someone else's turn. Uno[200], Scrabble[201], and Peggle [202]are a few of my favorites.

Whether I need to take handwritten notes, collect form data, remotely access a PC or a Mac, edit videos, watch movies, listen to music, update my social graph, or play games with my kids, my iPad has become a more than

---

[195] http://www.ecamm.com/mac/callrecorder/

[196] https://itunes.apple.com/us/app/downcast/id393858566?mt=8

[197] https://itunes.apple.com/us/app/facebook/id284882215?mt=8

[198] https://itunes.apple.com/us/app/twitter/id333903271?mt=8

[199] https://itunes.apple.com/us/app/linkedin/id288429040?mt=8

[200] https://itunes.apple.com/us/app/uno-hd/id364368518?mt=8

[201] https://itunes.apple.com/us/app/scrabble-hd-for-ipad/id363306776?mt=8

[202] https://itunes.apple.com/us/app/peggle/id314303518?mt=8

competent replacement for my laptop. In fact, in some ways, it's better than any laptop I've ever used.

PART 5 – TECHNOLOGY DIVERSIFICATION

If you're a minority in the technology industry, it doesn't take long to understand the obvious: the industry lacks diversity and has an almost laughable level of homogeneity. The lack of diversity gets worse as you progress up the career ladder. I have walked into many boardrooms and found myself to be the only minority in the room. I've consulted at some companies when I was the only person of color in the building (except for the janitor).

Some argue that there is no need to push for greater diversity in the technology industry. They claim that the industry is a meritocracy, and people of high ability will do well. However, I've seen the many ways in which this is not true. Most job opportunities in technology are obtained through personal relationships. Since America is still very much divided along color lines, those opportunities are divided as well. Often, it's not the most qualified person who gets the job. The person who gets the job is often the one with the best personal network, and the strongest personal networks are made up of people with white skin.

Furthermore, it's a natural human tendency to hire and advance people who look like you. Since white men are the predominant demographic in the technology industry, they tend to hire and promote white men. Unless a concerted effort is made to break this natural human tendency and truly seek out the best talent, companies will not be filled with the best and the brightest. They will simply be composed of carbon copies.

Through social media, I've met amazing people of color and women who are technologists, and I have become passionate about doing what I can to make the technology field more diverse. These efforts are sometimes met with hostility, particularly from members of the dominant society who have gained positions of power and influence in the technology industry. However, if we truly want to maximize technological innovation, then we must maximize the representation of minorities and women in the technology sector.

Black, Male, and in IT

01/17/2008 07:54:05 PM

AUTHOR'S NOTE: Keep in mind that I wrote this in early 2008, and many of the technology shows listed in this article no longer exist. This was one of my earliest efforts to chronicle my experiences as a black technologist.

I have spent the past few hours thinking about what it means to be an African-American man working in the information technology industry. This was caused by hearing an offhand remark said by someone who was a guest on one of my favorite podcasts, Buzz Out Loud[203]. I posted my thoughts to the Buzz Out Loud Forum[204], and I have to admit to not being surprised that many of the people who replied had no idea what I was talking about. Now, I absolutely do not think that the person who made the comment is a racist. In fact, I have a tremendous amount of respect for her. However, I also realize that she has no idea how what she said could be seen as racially insensitive. This leads me to the conclusion that it is very difficult for Non-Blacks to understand what it is like to be a Black person.

I followed the path that many people who work in Information Technology took. I had an early interest in computers, and I purchased my family's first computer (a Commodore 64[205]) from a flea market using my allowance when I was in the fifth grade. I was a straight A student and joined Math and Science Clubs. I grew up reading Tolkien[206], collecting comic books, and watching Star Trek: The Next Generation[207]. I majored in Electrical Engineering in college. The number of computers and gadgets in my house is limited only by my budget and the tolerance of my wife.

---

[203] http://reviews.cnet.com/8300-11455_7-10.html

[204] http://forums.cnet.com/5204-10152_102-0.html?forumID=97&tag=more

[205] http://en.wikipedia.org/wiki/Commodore_64

[206] http://www.tolkiensociety.org/

[207] http://en.wikipedia.org/wiki/Star_Trek:_The_Next_Generation

However, I work in an industry with very few African-American men. Out of the thirty or so supervisors I have had in a decade of working as an information technology consultant, only one was an African-American man. Every now and then I still encounter a client who can't believe that I am there to represent my company. I have to go out of my way to prove my credentials and competency in those situations.

This even affects the frequent travel that that I do as a traveling consultant. For example, when I enter the expedited boarding lane for frequent fliers (and I have flown hundreds of times), I am sometimes told, "Sorry, Sir, this is for Elite members only". Also, it seems that restaurant hosts sometimes sit me at the back of their establishment near the bath rooms or the kitchen. I have also seen Non-Black patrons, although they entered the restaurant after I did, get seated near the front and also served before I do.

There are few men who have reached the top of technology companies that I can look up to as role models for members of my race who have made it. Even the technology podcasts I listen to rarely have black hosts or even black guests. I have never seen or heard a black person on Cranky Geeks[208], Attack of the Show[209], TWiT[210], Tekzilla[211], or Mahalo Daily[212]. If I was an alien observing the world through these podcasts, I would think that Black people did not exist!

I think that part of the reason that Non-Blacks have trouble understanding the Black experience is lack of exposure. This is especially true for White people. How many White people have invited a Black person over to their house for dinner let alone have one spend the night? However, this "lack of

---

[208] http://www.crankygeeks.com/

[209] http://www.g4tv.com/attackoftheshow/index.html

[210] http://twit.tv/

[211] http://revision3.com/tekzilla

[212] http://daily.mahalo.com/

understanding" is only in one direction because I invite White people into my house every time I turn on the television, rent a movie, or read a newspaper. There they are being the perfect father, saving the world, or being elected to a position of power and leadership. Conversely, the image of Black people in the media is often the thug, pimp, or lazy low level employee.

Is this the fault of some evil conspiracy to keep African-American men down? No. However, I believe that racism still negatively affects African-Americans today. Yet, we need to take responsibility for ourselves and work to improve our condition. I will increase my efforts to mentor young African-American men and encourage them to consider pursuing a career in information technology. I will also redouble my efforts to be the best representative I can be of African-American men in my career field. After all, I may be the first and only impression of African-American men that many Non-Blacks will see. Maybe making a positive impression will not only help people understand African-American male technologists, but also help them be more sensitive to issues of race.

Comments

AUTHOR: Liz
URL: http://lizburr.cm
DATE: 01/20/2008 02:19:36 PM

I am so glad you wrote this entry. I worry about these issues a lot, being a Back female in the web/tech industry, and knowing of other Black web/tech professionals and the issues they face. Some people like to pretend the nuances of racism are not existent in these situations, but they are. I don't let them hold me back, or bother me too much, but you can't turn a blind eye to them either.

AUTHOR: Anjuan
URL: http://blog.transmyth.com
DATE: 01/18/2008 12:11:34 PM

Thanks, Nelson. I look forward to that day as well!

Technology Diversification

AUTHOR: Nelson
URL: http://wnelweb.blogspot.com
DATE: 01/18/2008 12:08:02 PM

I look forward to the day when race need not even be an issue or concern. I don't mean that race should be ignored: cultural history is very important. It's good to know where you came from. However, if a person shall be judged, let it be so by his or her actions and accomplishments and personality and relationship to other persons rather than by physical characteristics.

Pax,
Nelson

3 Reasons Why the Technology Industry Needs More Diversity

06/09/2010 10:00:21 AM

Yesterday, I had the pleasure of having lunch with 50 high school students and serving on an industry panel where they asked questions of me and eight other graduates of the School of Engineering of the University of Texas at Austin. This was part of the My Introduction To Engineering (MITE) Summer Camp[213] that is a part of the University's Equal Opportunity in Engineering program. These juniors and seniors were selected based on high academic performance and an interest in a career in engineering. They also represented underrepresented racial groups such as women, Latinos, Asian Americans, and African-Americans.

I had an amazing time speaking with these students! They were bright, articulate, ambitious, and we laughed and discussed what it's like to be an engineering student at UT's Ernst Cockrell School of Engineering[214]. Interacting with them reminded me of why it's important to have more diversity in the engineering field as well as the overall technology industry.

Diverse Backgrounds Lead to Diverse Solutions

When people come from different backgrounds, they bring with them fresh ideas that a group made up of homogenous individuals often fail to grasp. As Greg Papadopoulos[215], former Chief Technology Officer at Sun Microsystems wrote in this article[216]:

---

[213] http://www.engr.utexas.edu/eoe/precollege/mite

[214] http://www.engr.utexas.edu/

[215] http://en.wikipedia.org/wiki/Greg_Papadopoulos

[216] http://news.cnet.com/2010-1022_3-6122825.html

Technology Diversification

Here's the crux of the issue for me: We as engineers do indeed passionately argue for approach A versus B, and we are limited by the perspectives of those participating in the process. In what I call the "Nerd-Y Syndrome," when those participants are mostly nerdy guys, you get designs that are most appealing to, well, nerds with Y's (as in Y chromosomes).

I'll change the last few words in the quote to "white nerds with Y's". The only way to produce products with designs that benefit from the best thinking and appeal to the most people is to have a diverse group create them.

Think of the Manhattan Project[217] which was designed to create the first atomic bombs. This project was greatly helped by Jewish physicists and mathematicians who fled Germany as the Nazi regime took control of academia. This decimated the scientific ability of Germany and encouraged prominent physicists like Niels Bohr[218] to contribute to American efforts to produce the first nuclear weapons. The Nazi destruction of diversity made it all but impossible for them to achieve the scientific achievement of nuclear fission while allowing more inclusive countries like the United States, Canada, and the United Kingdom to succeed. In general, talent moves from areas of low inclusion to those that are highly inclusive, and diversity is the best way to attract the best talent.

Diversity Leads to Socio-Economic Empowerment

Although the world is still emerging from the latest economic recession, it is clear that technology will be an area of growth for the foreseeable future. Every industry uses technology to some degree, and technology will be needed to improve operational efficiency and lower costs. Those who gain skills as technologists will find a strong market for employment.

If efforts are made to create a diverse workforce, especially for underrepresented groups, then that will allow financial resources to flow to

---

[217] http://en.wikipedia.org/wiki/Manhattan_Project

[218] http://en.wikipedia.org/wiki/Niels_Bohr

new parts of the economy. This will provide those communities with the ability to better educate their members which will hopefully result in more technologists entering the market. Therefore, a self-perpetrating cycle will begin that will allow the creation of an even more diverse workplace environment.

Diversity is the Key to International Business

As our world becomes increasingly global, countries will continue to interact with each other in trade relationships. This is especially true for the technology industry where suppliers are often spread across vast geographic distances. Technology companies that have diverse employees will find it easier to interact across international boundaries.

When people think of international trade, they usually focus on geographic challenges in moving products or services across the globe. However, there are other factors that equal or exceed the difficulty of distance. The CAGE Distance Framework defines Cultural, Administrative, Geographic, and Economic Distance as the four primary factors that cause challenges in doing business across borders (source: Business Standard[219]).

While not explicitly described as an industry affected by cultural distance, technology companies often provide products and services that are used by people across various languages, ethnicities, religions, and social norms. The explosive growth of the iPhone and iPad in countries outside of the United States[220] demonstrates that corporations need to have a strategy for competing around the world instead of only in their home country.

Companies with diverse employees in their technology function at all levels will find it easier to create such an international strategy. Having people that represent various international cultures allows an organization to more

---

[219] http://www.business-standard.com/general/pdf/113004_01.pdf

[220]
http://online.wsj.com/article/SB10001424052748704269204575271280092834098.html

easily bridge cultural distance. Only by having a diverse workforce can a company approach a culturally diverse world.

Innovative solutions, socio-economic empowerment of underrepresented groups, and international business opportunities are three powerful reasons for greater diversity in the technology workforce. I plan to continue my personal contribution to making sure that people of all genders, ethnicities, and cultural backgrounds see engineering and technology as viable and exciting career paths. I hope that everyone who reads this does the same.

Comments

AUTHOR: Briana
URL: http://www.urbanbellemag.com
DATE: 07/31/2010 09:27:28 AM

Anjuan, this is so true. It's funny; I've heard a few people saying not enough black people (and other races too) are not "into" technology. Not true! I'm very deep in social media, as I'm sure you are too. I think since the companies haven't been hiring us, we're beginning to do our own thing. I was reading a post on Urban Belle Magazine, an online magazine for women of color, that young black students are excelling in school AND entrepreneurship: http://www.urbanbellemag.com/2010/05/young-black-and-successfulblack.html. We're taking matters into our own hands. Just look at Angela Benton at Black Web Media. She took matters into her own hands and is building herself an empire. So if the big dogs don't come to us, we'll do it ourselves. Great post!

AUTHOR: Anjuan Simmons
URL: http://www.AnjuanSimmons.com
DATE: 06/11/2010 12:05:10 AM

This has now been fixed. Thank you!

AUTHOR: Michael
DATE: 06/10/2010 12:13:07 AM

Just wanted to let you know that the links on your "about" page to your fb and twitter pages are broken

Bridging the Digital Divide in Africa

11/02/2010 01:22:10 PM

AUTHOR'S NOTE: As a technologist of African descent, I have always been interested in Africa becoming a tech hub. This is a piece I wrote to outline steps that can be taken to take advantage of the amazing technological promise of Africa.

Africa has 333 million mobile subscribers, and it is one of the fastest growing markets for wireless phones. However, less than ten percent of the continent's population has access to the internet. Compare that to the 77.3 percent of the users in the United States who have access to the internet. Africa's low broadband penetration limits the ability of its nations to harness the economic growth that often accompanies the spread of internet access. Also, the cost of internet and phone service in Africa is the highest in the world. Despite these challenges, efforts are underway to bridge the digital divide in Africa by expanding broadband penetration and building services that leverage the increased connectivity of the African population.

Laying the Foundation

The future of Africa's internet access can be found under the sea. That is where 14 fiber-optic cables will soon link the continent to European and Asian data centers. These connections will triple that amount of bandwidth that is available today.

However, high speed connections have to go beyond the coastlines. Countries like Rwanda are spending millions of dollars[221] to set up a fiber optic infrastructure. This will allow communities within African countries to more easily communicate with each other as well as with the world outside of Africa. By improving internet access, Africans will gain access to the most important commodity in the modern world: information.

---

[221] http://kristof.blogs.nytimes.com/2010/10/27/rwandas-road-of-progress/

Technology Diversification

The Mobile Solution

As fiber optic connections lower the price of internet access, companies are creating services to benefit African mobile subscribers. For example, M-PESA (the M stands for 'mobile' and pesa is Swahili for money) was created by Sagentia[222] to provide a solution to the banking problem in Africa. Local banks often charge high interest rates for loans and are difficult to access due to poor roads. M-PESA allows users to make deposits, withdraw money, transfer money to other people, and pay their bills by using their mobile phone. Users also get access to the competitive loan rates offered by microfinance institutions.

The Promise of Africa

As electronic signals find faster paths through the African continent and mobile phones increase in power and functionality, the people of Africa will have the opportunity to guide their own technology boom. While programs like MIT's Africa Information Technology Initiative[223] (AITI) show that institutions across the globe are rushing to invest in Africa, the success of local grassroots technology initiatives like Kenya's Malili[224] "techtropolis", Voice of Kiberia[225], and iHub[226] seem more satisfying. By empowering local Africans with the tools to chart their own future, Africa will blaze its own unique trail of innovation.

---

[222] http://www.sagentia.com/

[223] http://www.blackweb20.com/2010/09/08/mobile-apps-changing-the-face-of-africa/

[224] http://www.blackweb20.com/2010/02/05/malili-kenyas-high-tech-metropolis/

[225] http://www.blackweb20.com/2010/10/06/kibera-kenya-gains-voice-through-crowdsourcing/

[226] http://www.blackweb20.com/2010/10/21/ihub-technology-creativity-in-nairobi-kenya/

How Black People Use Twitter

01/12/2011 04:01:32 PM

I was recently quoted in an Associate Press article about the new social media digital divide that was picked up by publications like USA Today[227]. I like how the article was written, but, for space reasons, it could only contain a few lines from what was an interview over 30 minutes long.

I have quite a few thoughts about how black people use social media sites like Twitter. It is a topic that was covered quite a bit last year, and I anticipate that it will be a hot topic of discussion this year. While this discussion has been healthy, it has been tainted with negativity from time to time. This has usually been due to insensitive handling of the topic by certain members of the media.

I think the next logical step in this discussion is for serious research into how black people use Twitter. Scholarly research is the best way to address what has been for the most part rampant speculation.

Comments

AUTHOR: Tom Bardwell
URL: http://www.twitter.com/bardwellta
DATE: 01/13/2011 04:04:58 AM

Couldn't agree with you more! Thank you.

---

[227] http://www.usatoday.com/tech/news/2011-01-10-minorities-online_N.htm

Three Observations and Three Opportunities for Blacks in Technology

06/13/2011 07:14:37 AM

AUTHOR'S NOTE: This is the text of a speech I gave at the Miami conference of my friend Andrew West's NBITLO organization.

June 11, 2011
National Black Information Technology Leaders Organization
Miami Technology Thought-Leaders Symposium Keynote

As prepared for delivery.

Good morning! Thank you, Stephanie, for that generous introduction. I want to recognize all of the people who worked hard to put this conference together. I know that events like this don't create themselves, and a lot of the effort happens behind the scenes without being recognized by most of the attendees. I want to personally thank you for making all of this possible.

I am extremely grateful for the opportunity to serve as keynote speaker at this event. I'm a person who likes to know how things start, and I would like to share with you history of the word "keynote". It comes from the 1940s when groups of black singers would get together in neighborhood barbershops and sing songs acapella. These singers became known as Barbershop singers, and, before singing, they would play a note which would determine the tone in which the song should be performed and thus, the term keynote was born. It is my hope that what I share with you this morning will set the right tone for the rest of today.

This is a great time to be a black technologist. I've had the privilege of working in the technology industry for over 13 years as an information technology consultant. I've also had the privilege of observing the industry as a technology writer for various publications. I would like to share with you three observations about the state of the technology industry from my experience as a technologist and also three opportunities that we all need to take advantage of.

Observation number 1 is growth. The technology industry is rapidly expanding and will continue to do so for the foreseeable future. Even as this country struggles to shake off the effects of a steep recession, the technology sector continues to boom. The Department of Labor classifies the information technology industry as an area of high growth in our economy[228]. In a country that still struggles to create jobs, the technology industry is projected to create 1.6 million job by the year 2014[229] by growing at a rate that is much faster than other industries. Now, I know that many of you probably attended a number of college graduations over the last few weeks. While graduating from college is a significant milestone that should be celebrated, many college graduates are leaving school to enter a tough job market. But, that is not true for graduates with technical degrees, especially programmers. For those graduates, the future looks especially bright. Last month, the National Association of Colleges and Employers conducted a survey which showed that computer science graduates are receiving more job offers than any other job field. Let, me say that again, college students who graduate with degrees in programming have the best offer rate of the class of 2011. But, we don't need national surveys to understand the growth of the technology industry. We see it every day as technology becomes a more intricate part of our lives from the smartphones we carry to the cars we drive and to the air traffic control systems that allowed many of us to be here today. We also see it in the market as technology companies like Linkedin which recently had an IPO of $353 million which valued the company at $4.3 billion. The deal site Groupon is poised to have an IPO that some project to raise $1 billion and value the company at $20 billion. Even the military is equipping soldiers with iPhones and iPads with the thinking that apps are so useful that they may be effective on the battlefield. The technology industry is growing across all industries and no limit is in sight.

And that leads me to my second observation. Although the technology industry is explosively expanding, there is a lack of college graduates who have the skills needed to support this growth[230]. Dice.com, the online site for technology job postings, recently published a report called America's

---

[228] http://www.doleta.gov/brg/indprof/IT_profile.cfm

[229] http://www.bls.gov/oco/ocos305.htm

[230] http://wiredworkplace.nextgov.com/2011/05/tech_skills_in_short_supply.php

Tech Talent Crunch[231]. In that report, Dice noted that the number of computer-related bachelor's degrees fell from 60,000 in 2004 to 38,000 in 2008. While fewer students are choosing to major in technology related disciplines and computer programming, the demand for these skills have exploded in the wake of mobile applications and cloud computing. Companies want graduates who can develop software for iPhones, iPads, and Android-powered smartphones. They also want developers to work on consumer cloud services like Apple's recently introduced iCloud service as well as enterprise cloud offerings like cloud storage and virtual servers. The low number of students choosing to gain the technology skills needed to meet this demand is due to the difficulty of the courses required for graduation. This often involves college level courses in mathematics, sciences, and programming. Simply put, technology skills require hard work and dedication, and, for many students, it is much easier to simply study something else.

My third observation is that there is a critical need for diversity in the technology industry. We see this lack of diversity at work where many of us are often the only people of color on our teams. In fact, some of us go to work and don't see another brown person unless we're working late at night and the people who clean the building after hours show up. We also see this lack of diversity at technology conferences where there may be a few sprinkles of color in the audience but we're lucky if we see even one black person speaking on stage or serving on a panel. The technology industry's need for diversity is also visible on technology magazine covers which rarely show black technologists. This lack of diversity is troubling because diverse workforces allow for different and better ideas, and ideas are the lifeblood of technology. The danger of a lack of diversity was taught to us by genetics a long time ago. When close relatives marry each other, all of the small imperfections in their family tree are mixed and amplified in their offspring. When you inbreed in this manner, you don't get access to a diverse gene-pool with dominant genes that can cover up recessive traits. History has shown the devastating effects of this from the Egyptian Pharaohs to the Kings of England; from King Tut to Queen Victoria. The same principle applies to ideas. If you get a group of people who come from the same race, geographic area, gender, and socio-economic status,

---

[231] http://marketing.dice.com/pdf/Dice_TechTalentCrunch.pdf

they bring small imperfections that are derived from their common source of perceptions. They lack the ability to truly think outside of the box because they all come from the same box. I am convinced that black kids raised in Compton can out-think most of the graduates of MIT. I also believe that there are young people growing up on the south side of Chicago who can out-innovate many of the students currently attending Stanford. Why? Because many of these kids grew up like you and I did and had to be creative simply because we had limited resources. We're all wearing suits and doing well now, but I know some of you have poured water on cereal when you ran out of milk. Or, you made mayonnaise sandwiches when no ham could be found in the house. The black experience is by definition an innovative one! But, young black kids need training and job opportunities in order to bring their unique perspectives to the technology sector.

And that leads me to my three opportunities. The growing technology sector, lack of technologically skilled graduates, and need for diversity in the industry means that now is the perfect time for the emergence of black technology leadership. The old guard is ready to retire and their vacancies will have to be filled. This is the time for us to become leaders in our respective fields. But, leadership is not something that you gain simply by wanting it. It requires the display of personal excellence. Now is not the time to be the last one to arrive to work and the first one to leave. We have to lead by having a strong work ethic and displaying dedication to our craft. Leaders are chosen from those who already display leadership potential. We also have to spend time around other leaders. Leaders exude leadership and true leadership is contagious. This means that if you're the best leader in the group you hang out with, then you need to hang out with another group. Otherwise, you're just building followers instead of cultivating your own leadership. And there are small social skills that we have to master. We can't drive into the office parking garage booming Lil Wayne's song about what he wants to do to all the girls in the world. Now, I'm not saying that we have to hide who we are, but we can't do things that hide us from success. In addition to obtaining leadership positions within the walls of the companies we work for, we also have to move outside of those walls and become leaders in our industries. That means joining groups in your field of expertise (like NBITLO[232]) and becoming thought leaders. That includes

---

[232] http://www.nbitlo.org/

writing white papers about a topic your industry cares about. That also means using social media tools like Facebook and Twitter to build your personal brand and become a leader online as well as offline.

The second opportunity is that of entrepreneurship. The growth of the technology industry is due to the tremendous need that consumers have for well-engineered products. Now is the time to take that business idea, put a plan around it, and make it into a reality. Now, I know that it is not easy to make the jump into entrepreneurship. Many of us can find excuses to keep taking a paycheck from an employer instead of launching our own companies. We tell ourselves that we're in an economic recession and we'll wait until the economy improves. But, many of the best known technology companies were started during economic downturns. Texas Instruments and HP were started during the Great Depression[233]. Furthermore, the stock market crash of the early 1970s didn't stop the founding of companies like Microsoft and Apple[234]. Profits can be found in both up and down economies because there are always customer needs that need to be met by good ideas. We have to remember that Facebook was created in a Harvard dorm room on a laptop. With cheap computing and access to strong technology skills on and off shore, companies can be created with minimal capital requirements. There has never been a better time to make the move from employee to employer.

In addition to the opportunities for leadership and entrepreneurship, there is the opportunity for inspiration. Many of us grew up around peers who wanted to be athletes, singers, dancers, rappers, or some other pursuit that, honestly, the media depicts as the careers that black people should seek. But, along the way, something happened that inspired us to pursue a road less travelled. Perhaps it was a visionary parent who bought home a Commodore 64 or a Macintosh II and encouraged you to master what were then cutting edge computers. Or, perhaps there was a teacher who, though working with limited funds, invited you to join a program designed to encourage minorities to pursue degrees in math, science, and engineering.

---

[233] http://www.vcconfidential.com/2009/02/why-great-companies-get-started-in-the-downturns.html

[234] http://www.insidecrm.com/features/businesses-started-slump-111108/

Regardless of how it happened, someone made an investment in you that inspired you to become a black technologist. You now have the opportunity to pass on that inspiration to the next generation. By encouraging young people to consider a career in technology, you open the door for the profits of the technology sector to flow into our neighborhoods and households. And that cash flow is badly needed. While the news makes much of the national unemployment rate of 9.1%, unemployment among blacks is 16.2%[235]. The country is struggling to recover from the recession, but we are stuck in our own Great Depression. The only hope for blacks to emerge from this sea of unemployment is to enter fields that are growing like the technology industry. That means encouraging young black kids to pursue and complete STEM degrees. But, this won't happen without effort. In fact, recent numbers show that black representation in STEM degrees is falling. This trend must be reversed. Everyone in this room has a responsibility to represent the viability of a career in technology to every young black person you know, especially in the economically depressed areas from which many of us come. You may be the only technologist some of them may ever meet. You may be the only person who instills in them the belief that they can put in the hard work needed to master math, science, and engineering because the benefits are worth it! And inspiring young people to consider a career in technology is not hard. Simply tell your story. You never know who you will motivate to make a life changing decision.

In summary, the growing technology industry, lack of technologically skilled workers, and need for industry wide diversity represents unprecedented opportunities for black leadership, entrepreneurship, and inspiration for the next generation. I challenge all of you to take advantage of these opportunities in your own individual lives. The stakes are high, but the rewards are many. Together we can secure our dreams and lay a foundation for the future of our people. Thank you.

---

[235] http://politic365.com/2011/06/03/unemployment-rate-for-african-americans-inches-higher-in-may/

My 2012 SXSW Panel Proposal on Minorities and Technology

09/15/2011 05:13:50 PM

AUTHOR'S NOTE: This panel proposal was accepted, and I was happy to join my friends at the 2012 South by Southwest Interactive conference to talk about diversifying the technology industry. Unfortunately, Erica Mauter couldn't make it, but I'm glad that LaToya Peterson was able to step in and serve as moderator.

I thought I would share my panel proposal on minorities and technology that a group of friends and I submitted to the 2012 SXSW Interactive conference. I'm passionate about this topic, and I hope it gets picked!

Speakers

1. Adria Richards – ButYoureAGirl[236]
2. Anjuan Simmons – Infosys[237]
3. Corvida Raven – TED[238]
4. Erica Mauter – swirlspice.com[239]
5. Scott Hanselman – Microsoft[240]

Description

This panel seeks to change the conversation from "What can technology conferences do about diversity?" to "What can attendees do about diversity

---

[236] http://panelpicker.sxsw.com/ideas/http:/butyoureagirl.com

[237] http://www.anjuansimmons.com/

[238] http://shegeeks.net/

[239] http://swirlspice.com/

[240] http://hanselman.com/

at technology conferences?" The panel is composed of speakers who have each presented at multiple technology conferences on topics that did not focus on race or diversity but instead spoke on topics of sci-fi, electronic ownership of email and digital wills, the influence of mobile development via comic books, social media for youth, and business automation lessons from Amazon. While the diversity of some major tech conferences has steadily improved over the years, geek culture, which remains overwhelmingly white and male, is still the norm. This can be daunting for people who, despite being experts in technology and new media, don't see themselves reflected in the marketing materials or content. For example, there are almost no people of color on the sxsw.com home page. The panelists will share how individuals can contribute to making technology conferences more inclusive. This panel will look at some of the cultural and economic factors that shape inclusion and exclusion and generate an action list for attendees.

Questions Answered

1. How can attendees get over the feeling of exclusion at technology conferences?
2. How do I deal with feeling "invisible" in the crowds of white men that dominate technology conferences?
3. What is the best approach to get panel submissions accepted that don't focus on race and diversity issues?
4. What problems are underrepresented technology practitioners trying to solve when they create their own events?
5. How can underrepresented groups support each other to encourage attendance, speaker submissions and participation in technology conferences?

Michael Arrington, Diversity, and Silicon Valley

10/30/2011 12:53:21 PM

For those of you who don't know, CNN has created another Black in America documentary, and this time the subject is blacks in technology. It's called <u>Black in America: The New Promised Land – Silicon Valley</u>[241] and will air next month on Sunday, November 13 at 8 PM EST. As an African-American technologist, I was excited to hear that a platform as large and broad as CNN was taking time to shed light on a topic that is so near and dear to me. I should disclose that I know several of the African-American technology entrepreneurs who were filmed for the show. The people I know include <u>Angela Benton</u>[242] (who I worked for by writing for her <u>Blackweb2.0</u>[243] website), <u>Wayne Sutton</u> (who I have met at several technology conferences and also profiled me on his <u>28 Days of Diversity</u>[244] web series where he highlights blacks in technology), as well as Tiffani Ashley Bell, Hajj Flemings, and Hank Williams (who I have also met at technology conferences). So, this new Black in America series was also something that would give me a chance to see people I know and respect bring their A game to a national audience. But, then Michael Arrington got involved . . .

Arrington was interviewed for the documentary, and made some unfortunate comments. First, it's my understanding that Arrington was interviewed for three hours, but only a few minutes of what he said was included in what was printed online. I have personally been interviewed on national media outlets and saw only 10% of what I said make it into the published piece. This "editing down to the good stuff" process simply comes with the territory. Second, I don't think Arrington is a racist

---

[241] http://cnnpressroom.blogs.cnn.com/2011/10/21/soledad-o%E2%80%99brien-chronicles-journeys-of-black-tech-entrepreneurs-for-fourth-black-in-america/

[242] http://twitter.com/#!/ABenton

[243] http://www.blackweb20.com/

[244] http://28daysofdiversity.com/

(Arrington's response to this can be found here[245]). I think that Arrington is someone who says what he thinks with almost no mental filter whatsoever. In many ways, that's a good thing because our society and culture is, in general, too politically correct for honest conversations about things like race to happen. However, his statements offer a teachable moment about how race plays out in Silicon Valley.

Arrington made the following comments in the interview which set off an online debate about whether he is racist or not as well as racism in Silicon Valley (quotes taken from CNN Money[246]):

- "I don't know a single black entrepreneur".
- "There's a guy, actually, his last company just launched at our event, and he's African-American. When he asked to launch -- actually, I think it was the other way around. I think I begged him," Arrington told CNN's Soledad O'Brien. "His startup's really cool. But he could've launched a clown show on stage, and I would've put him up there, absolutely," Arrington said. "I think it's the first time we've had an African-American [be] the sole founder."

Arrington later said, continuing his response to the controversy, this on Twitter[247]:

- "There's zero race or sex bias in silicon valley."

Again, I do not believe that Michael Arrington (or even most of Silicon Valley) is racist. However, I disagree with Arrington's assertion that Silicon Valley has zero race or gender bias. Silicon Valley (and the greater

---

[245] http://uncrunched.com/2011/10/28/oh-shit-im-a-racist/

[246] http://money.cnn.com/2011/10/27/technology/silicon_valley_diversity/index.htm?iid=HP_LN

[247] http://twitter.com/#!/arrington/status/129339823675817984

technology sector) is not a meritocracy. It's a "know-ocracy" meaning that access to power is awarded based on who a person knows rather than that person's individual talent. Since the industry has historically been composed of white males, this is the demographic that has reached the upper echelons of the industry, and they tend to hire, fund, and mentor the people they know: other white males.

Some point to the late Steve Jobs as an example of the meritocracy of the technology industry. After all, Jobs was of Middle Eastern decent (through his biological father), given up for adoption, and raised by middle class people. Yet, he founded one of the most valuable companies in the world in his parent's garage. If Jobs can make it, anyone can, right? Well, let's unpack the many advantages Jobs had. First, he was raised in Mountain View, California, with easy access to the companies that make up Silicon Valley. Second, even though it was a garage, it was in a nice suburban house which presumably had access to a kitchen with food and a mortgage and utilities that were paid by someone other than Jobs. Therefore, Jobs was able to start Apple with built in savings of tens of thousands of dollars a year. Finally, Jobs had the greatest advantage of all: white skin (despite his biological father's Syrian DNA). According to his recently released biography, Jobs, after dropping out of Reed College, "talked his way" into getting hired at Atari because the chief engineer of the company "saw something in him". Maybe this "something" was a younger version of himself, or perhaps a reminder of a son or nephew. However, whatever this "something" was, I doubt that a Tyrone from Oakland or a Jenny from one of the barrios of San Francisco would have possessed it. Therefore, members of underrepresented groups the chief engineer didn't know would have been turned away where Steve Jobs was embraced.

Arrington himself benefitted from almost exactly the same privileges that Jobs enjoyed. That is why it's always amazing to me when, as Arrington has stated, people of privilege say that they don't see race or gender. Of course they don't see race or gender because neither their race nor their gender have ever hindered their access to the people who could position them for success. In the same way that people with halitosis are incapable of smelling the foulness of their own breath, people like Arrington are incapable of understanding the way they aid and abet keeping Silicon Valley a place dominated by white males.

The lack of diversity in technology, especially among entrepreneurs and the venture capitalists that fund them is bad for the industry. It limits the ability to generate innovative ideas because people from similar backgrounds often approach problems in the same way. It also limits the usefulness of products and services. We all remember the webcam that HP released a few years ago that had "face tracking" that didn't recognize the faces of dark skinned users. If HP had a diverse product testing team, then this defect would have been detected and corrected before it shipped. As minority groups continue to grow in this country and around the world (and increasingly become the majority users of technology products and services), the technology industry's diversity problems will soon have a direct impact on profits and losses.

The question is not "Is Arrington a racist?" nor is it "Is Silicon Valley racist?". The question is "Does Silicon Valley understand white privilege?" Until people in positions of power in Silicon Valley honestly answer that question, then the "know-ocracy" of the technology industry will persist in hindering the entrance of members of underrepresented groups that may have superior ideas but lack the proper skin color and genitalia.

Comments

AUTHOR: professlch
DATE: 10/30/2011 04:47:22 PM

What a measured, reasonable post on a very touchy issue. I know you'll likely suffer screeds and vitriol; however, truth is truth, no matter how unpleasant to others' ears. Thank you for this.

AUTHOR: Anjuan Simmons
DATE: 11/07/2011 04:36:47 PM

@Professlch: Thank for the support! I haven't yet received any screeds and vitriol, but I'm ready!

AUTHOR: Toni
URL: DATE: 02/17/2012 04:20:49 AM

Technology Diversification

At some point we have to stop pointing fingers At some point we have to take responsibility for self. As the other man partners and create so can a black man. Time should be spent working on unity rather than harboring on exclusivity. Maybe Tyrone should be looking to Amos instead of Bill as his partner. Maybe Amos should respect Tyrone and truly understand the value of Synergy.

Getting Minority Publications to Invest in STEM Stories

03/19/2013 02:15:43 PM

AUTHOR'S NOTE: While there is work to be done by established STEM companies to attract and hire minorities, minority publications have to take ownership of the problem as well. As legendary astronaut Sally Ride said, "You can't be what you can't see". If scientists, technologists, engineers, and mathematicians of color received half the exposure given to black celebrities and athletes, I think we would see a sharp increase in black kids who want to pursue STEM careers.

A friend of mine named Danielle Lee[248] wrote this piece [249]about the need to provide incentives for minority owned media outlets to cover STEM stories. Here is the response I sent her via Facebook:

Great piece, Danielle. I think a two pronged approach is needed. First, we should continue to use the platform provided by social media and the internet to express our opinions about STEM and support each other's projects. This platform is low cost, global, and can provide rich media options including pictures and video.

Second, while we can't be expected to go out and earn degrees in journalism, we should become as savvy as possible when it comes to traditional media. By forming relationships with traditional media gatekeepers and displaying the quality of our online content (and, hopefully, large numbers of people consuming that content), we can help them see that STEM stories are worth running, especially those that concern minorities.

I think Black Enterprise is doing the best job of all the minority media companies in doing smart reporting about STEM. Hopefully, Ebony, Jet,

---

[248] http://blogs.scientificamerican.com/urban-scientist/

[249] http://blogs.scientificamerican.com/urban-scientist/2013/03/19/science-reporting-across-cultures-diverse-audiences-evolution-other-science-topics/

Technology Diversification

Clutch, etc., will run more stories about STEM and the African-American experience.

PART 6 – Embracing "People Culture"

For most of my life, the efforts I made to make technology a more open and inclusive industry were been focused on people of color and women. However, I eventually came to realize that other groups also needed voices to advocate for them. This realization was largely caused by social media and the connections I made online.

Building and maintaining relationships is the essence of my social media engagement strategy. I have social media connections with friends who have known me for more than 30 years, but I also begin new interactions with total strangers nearly every day.

Many people use social media to connect with people who share their views. I think that is a mistake because that simply creates a social media echo chamber. While it's good to have some connections with those who see life the same way you do (to make sure you aren't insane), I think it's important to reach out and interact with people who hold views that conflict with your perceptions. The best way to test the validity of your worldview is to let others scrutinize it while you examine their worldview. When done in a respectful manner, this allows both sides to sharpen their perspectives by keeping the wisdom and discarding the foolishness that is present in every worldview.

By interacting with those who held views that were opposite to mine, I gained an appreciation for perspectives that were once foreign to me. While I am not a feminist, I grew to appreciate the efforts of my feminist friends to combat rape culture. I'm also not a homosexual, but I began to understand their positions about same sex marriage.

Social media allowed me to "get out of my head" and see the world through the eyes of other people. In doing so, I became a better person and an admirer of what my friend Scott Hanselman called "People Culture". Instead of simply loving and defending the culture and interests of people of color, I eventually embraced the wonderful diversity of all people. While I'll always have Black culture as my first love, I now see the importance of appreciating all people and the infinite variety in which they come.

Rustin, Turing, and Milk: 3 Homosexuals Everyone Should Appreciate

08/21/2012 11:37:51 PM

As an African-American man, I have always appreciated Whites who demonstrated an appreciation for Black history, particularly our accomplishments. I don't mean the accomplishments of "notable black folks" like Martin Luther King, Jr. and Rosa Parks since they are so famous that only the truly ignorant are unaware of them. When Whites understand the significance of Blacks like Martin Robinson Delany, Benjamin Bannekar, and Robert Smalls, they signal a true appreciation for Black culture and contributions.

I have often wondered if the same effect would occur if a heterosexual man (like myself) showed appreciation for the accomplishments of homosexuals in history. So, I decided to highlight three homosexuals who made amazing contributions to three areas that are dear to me: equality, technology, and politics. These men endured great opposition by those who disagreed with their sexual orientation, but they were still able to change the world in dramatic ways. They are Bayard Rustin, Alan Turing, and Harvey Milk.

Bayard Rustin

If MLK was a "Drum Major for Justice", then Bayard Rustin was the Band Director. He was born on March 17, 1912 in West Chester, Pennsylvania. Having become an activist early in life, Rustin led efforts to desegregate federal agencies and interstate travel by bus. Rustin was a student of non-violent independence movements having traveled to India in 1948 to learn from those who sought to advance Gandhi's legacy after his assassination.

Rustin began working with MLK in 1956 and convinced King (who, at the time, had armed guards and a personal handgun) to fully embrace non-violence by ending the use of guns for security. Rustin was the principal organizer of the 1963 March on Washington, and he continued lead efforts to gain equality for disenfranchised groups until his death in 1987.

Rustin deserved to be listed among the giants of the African-American Civil Rights movement like MLK, Malcolm X, and Rosa Parks.

Unfortunately, in 1953, police discovered him engaging in homosexual acts with two other men in a parked car in Pasadena, California. He eventually plead guilty to "sex perversion". While Rustin was privately open about his sexual orientation, this arrest made it a matter of public record. His homosexuality was used by his opponents both within and outside the civil rights movement, and his contributions are often diminished by historians.

Alan Turing

Unless you're reading this on paper, you're using a device that was defined by Alan Turing. Turing was an English man born a few months after Bayard Rustin on June 23, 1912 in India (when it was under British rule). He showed an advanced grasp of mathematics and science at an early age which culminated in his induction as a fellow at King's College in Cambridge at the young age of 22.

Turing presented the concept of Turing Machines in 1936 which explained the idea of a machine that could be programmed using algorithms. This became the defining concept of a modern computer, and Turing Machines are still used to this day to understand computation. Turing became involved as a code breaker during the World War II, and he was an instrumental part of the team of British scientists working to crack the German encryption code. After the war ended in 1945, Turing designed the Automatic Computing Engine (ACE) where he leveraged his time as a code breaker to bring his Turing Machine to reality. The ACE had the ability to call subroutines and could be programmed using a rudimentary programming language.

Shortly after Turing finished the design of the ACE, he became involved in the study of artificial intelligence. He proposed an idea that became known as the Turing Test which was a way of determining whether a machine had achieved intelligence. This experiment involved an observer who could read the outputs of two subjects hidden behind a curtain: one was a human and the other was a machine. If the observer could not distinguish the difference between the outputs, then the machine passed the Turing Test.

Turing's life was cut short soon after he was arrested for sexual activity with another man in January 1952. Since homosexual activity was illegal in the UK during this time, he was given a choice between prison time or probation. If he chose probation, then he would have to undergo chemical castration via injections for a year which would destroy his sexual desire and render him impotent. Turing chose to be chemically castrated. He was found dead on June 8, 1954 with a half-eaten apple near his bed. Traces of cyanide were found in his body, and cyanide poisoning was determined to be the cause of death. It is not known if Turing committed suicide or if he somehow ingested cyanide through the various chemical experiments he had in his house. Nevertheless, one of the greatest minds of computer science was lost to the world.

Harvey Milk

Harvey Milk was born on May 22, 1930 in Woodmere, New York. While Milk was aware of his homosexuality as a teenager, he kept is a secret that was only shared with a select group of friends. He went on the join the Navy during the Korean War. He was discharged from the Navy in 1955 and worked in a variety of jobs in New York City. While Milk had a variety of male lovers during this time, he avoided making his sexual orientation widely known.

After moving between California, New York, and Texas, Milk returned to San Francisco in the early 1970s. In 1973, he opened a camera shop and became increasingly aware of the growing persecution of homosexuals in San Francisco. Pro-gay groups like the Society for Individual Rights (SIR) gained attention for the fight for gay rights such as ending employment discrimination based on sexual orientation. Milk decided to enter politics and ran for city supervisor. He lost in 1973 but, after numerous failed campaigns was successful in 1977.

Milk became the first openly gay man (who was not an incumbent) to win an election for public office. Milk's energetic personality characterized his political campaigns, and it was also a trait of his identity as an elected official. Milk used the power he had over the gay voters of San Francisco which, as 25% of the population, was a powerful voting bloc, to form alliances with politicians like San Francisco Mayor George Moscone. He advocated the ending of discrimination based on sexual orientation and other infringements of gay rights.

Milk made his fair share of enemies during his political career, but his worst was a fellow supervisor named Dan White. Milk initially supported an initiative to keep a mental health hospital from being placed in White's district, but Milk changed his mind and voted against it. White considered this a betrayal and fervently opposed Milk's initiatives. Dan White became increasingly erratic, and on November 27, 1978, he shot and killed Milk as well as Mayor Moscone.

Rustin, Turing, and Milk were three homosexuals who endured extreme discrimination, but they did not let negative reactions to their sexual orientations deter them. We all have greater freedom based on the lives of Rustin and Milk and Turing brought the world closer to the amazing technology we enjoy today.

Same-Sex Marriage, Christianity, and Love

03/28/2013 01:23:04 PM

Same-sex marriage has long been a controversial topic, and the Supreme Court's hearing of two cases about same-sex marriage last month has put even more national focus on the issue. These two cases are California's Proposition 8 ruling (which legalized same-sex marriage in California but was later overturned) and the federal Defense of Marriage Act[250] (which provided a federal definition of marriage as between a man and a woman). While the exact outcome of these two cases cannot be predicted, most analysts predict that same-sex marriage will be strengthened by whatever judgment is handed down by the Supreme Court. Same-sex marriage will probably return as a right in California and DOMA will probably go the way of Don't Ask Don't Tell (DADT) and be struck down.

Regardless of the immediate legal future of same-sex marriage, it is clear that public support of the idea has dramatically changed in a short period of time. This is especially true for young people. Pew Research found in a 2012 poll that 48% of Americans support same-sex marriage while 43% oppose it[251]. A poll taken in 2001 showed 35% supported same-sex marriage while 57% opposed it. So, support for same-sex marriage has jumped from roughly one-third to almost half of the country in a little more than a decade while opposition to same-sex marriage has slowly eroded to the minority opinion. The contrast is even more stark for Millennials (those born after 1981) who have a 70% support rate for same-sex marriage[252].

Pew Research's polling of Christian groups show a general increase in support for same-sex marriage that mirrors the overall country. However, two groups have resisted the surge in support: Black Protestants and White

---

[250] http://www.gpo.gov/fdsys/pkg/PLAW-104publ199/html/PLAW-104publ199.htm

[251] http://www.pewforum.org/Gay-Marriage-and-Homosexuality/Overview-of-Same-Sex-Marriage-in-the-United-States.aspx

[252] http://features.pewforum.org/same-sex-marriage-attitudes/slide2.php

Evangelicals whose support for same-sex marriage polls at 34% and 24% respectively[253].

As a Black Evangelical who openly campaigns for equality and inclusion, particularly in the technology sector, I understand both spectrums in the polling. This piece is my attempt to document my thoughts about the Biblical definition of marriage, the weaknesses of many arguments by Christians against same-sex marriage, and where I think the church should focus its efforts if the goal really is stronger families.

Towards a Biblical Definition of Marriage

Evangelicals often use a "Biblical Definition of Marriage" to argue against same-sex marriage. However, the Biblical view of marriage is not just one of "one man and one woman". Many of the heroes of the Bible had more than one wife. Abraham was married to Sarah and had a child with Hagar, Jacob was married to Rachel and Leah, David had 300 wives, and Solomon had 300 wives and 700 concubines. Furthermore, many of the Biblical commands about marriage offend our modern sensibilities. For example, a rapist had to marry the woman he violated [254](whether she wanted the marriage or not). Also, if a man had a married brother who died, he had to marry his deceased brother's widow[255] (and name his first born child with the widow after his dead brother).

Of course, most Christians would argue that the modern world is not under the Old Testament which was "done away with" by Christ. While Christ had relatively little to say about marriage, one of the most significant

---

253 http://features.pewforum.org/same-sex-marriage-attitudes/slide3.php

254 http://www.biblegateway.com/passage/?search=Deuteronomy%2022:28-29&version=NIV

255 http://www.biblegateway.com/passage/?search=Deuteronomy%2025:5-6&version=NIV

passes is <u>Matthew 19:5-9</u>[256]. In response to a question about divorce, Christ said:

Haven't you read," he replied, "that at the beginning the Creator 'made them male and female,' and said, 'For this reason a man will leave his father and mother and be united to his wife, and the two will become one flesh'? So they are no longer two, but one flesh. Therefore what God has joined together, let no one separate.

So, Christ established the following pattern for marriage by alluding to the Creation account of Adam and Eve:

1. Man leaves Parents' house.
2. Man marries Woman.
3. Man has sex with Woman.

Notice that the Eden Example added more requirements to Christ's definition of marriage than just the gender of the two people involved. There was one man and one woman which eliminates polygamy. Also, the man and the woman had never had sex with other people or with each other which eliminates pre-marital sex. Furthermore, Adam and Eve were not previously married. So, a truly Christian definition of marriage is this:

One man and one woman who are virgins and who have never been previously married.

Would even the most zealous evangelical want this to be the legal definition of marriage? Given the high divorce rate and incidence of premarital sex among Christians, I think that would disqualify many heterosexual couples who wanted to get married. So, pushing to enshrine a Biblical definition of marriage into the legal requirements for marriage presents challenges for even heterosexual couples. This is especially true since so many marriages in the United States (even Christian ones) follow a pattern similar to this one:

---

[256] http://www.biblegateway.com/passage/?search=matthew%2019:4-6&version=NIV

1. Man has sex with Woman 1.
2. Man has sex with Woman 2.
3. Man leaves Parents' house.
4. Man has sex with Woman 3.
5. Man has sex with Woman 4.
6. Man marries Woman 4.
7. Man has sex with Woman 5.
8. Man divorces Woman 4.
9. Man marries Woman 5.

Christians often act as if proponents of same-sex marriage want to change the Biblical definition of marriage. However, this is not the case. They want the legal definition of marriage to be expanded so same-sex couples can access the same legal benefits that heterosexual couples possess.

The Weakness of the Weakens Marriage Argument

Evangelicals often argue that changing the definition of marriage weakens traditional marriage. I don't understand this argument since Christians tolerate differences in definitions of spiritual topics outside of marriage. For example, worship is a key part of Christianity. Most Christians worship on Sundays. However, some denominations like Seventh Day Adventists, Seventh Day Baptists, and The Church of God (Seventh Day) worship on Saturday in keeping with the Jewish Sabbath.

Does the definition by these denominations of worship as an event held on Saturdays weaken the worship by other denominations on Sundays? No, it does not. In fact, most Christians who worship on Sunday are probably unaware of the activities of those who worship on Saturday. In the same way, same-marriage has no effect on traditional marriage. Furthermore, most Christians who worship on Sundays would not appreciate Christians who worship on Saturdays trying to pass laws making it illegal to worship on any day other than Saturday. I'm sure the reverse is true. Christians tolerate the freedom of various denominations to have different beliefs without resorting to legal action because freedom of religious expression strengthens everyone's rights.

What Did Jesus Do?

Many of the people who initially followed Jesus later rejected him because they wanted him to be a political and military leader who would get rid of their Roman overlords. However, Jesus made it clear that he did not come to set up an earthly kingdom. Despite living in a time where slavery was routine, women were second class citizens, and children were routinely abused or killed, Jesus did not try to change the laws of His time because He was more interested in showing the love of God for humanity. Part of this included showing love for people considered sinners like tax collectors, prostitutes[257], and the diseased. Jesus welcomed these societal outcasts because He wanted to show that we are all sinners in need of the love of God.

Christians today can follow the example of Christ. Instead of trying to change laws to make people behave in line with our interpretation of the Bible, we can try to understand them and show the love of God.

Love Above All

I think Christians can do a better job promoting traditional marriage by adhering to the Biblical standard for marriage that we insist others follow. Until we dramatically reduce the divorce rate in the church and only engage in sex within the bounds of marriage we can't enter the debate from a position of moral authority. I think one reason that Christian Millennials support same-sex marriage so much is the hypocrisy they've seen in the marriages of their parents. If we claim a moral superiority for traditional marriage, then we need to stop generating so many broken heterosexual marriages and extramarital sexual relationships. Same-sex marriage won't hurt traditional families because traditional families are already broken by an extremely high divorce rate and the increase in single parent homes. Even if same-sex marriage was outlawed in all 50 states, traditional marriages have deep problems that will last for generations.

I don't think Christians should try to legislate our interpretation of the Bible into society. I think we should love everyone in keeping with the example

---

[257] http://www.biblegateway.com/passage/?search=Matthew%2021:31-32&version=NIV

of Christ. And love requires, as God gives us, the freedom to make a choice other than the one we desire. Laws can be changed based on the shifting sentiments of the day, but a heart that has been opened to the love of God is changed forever. That's where the church should place its focus. Let's lessen the focus on legal remedies and live out the life of righteousness given to us by God so we can show the world the love of God.

Comments

AUTHOR: zed power
URL: http://socyberty.com/sexuality/congratulations-on-having-sex/
DATE: 05/04/2013 02:27:10 PM

has America become incompatible with Christianity?

AUTHOR: Anjuan Simmons
DATE: 05/13/2013 02:21:54 PM

I think the better question is, "Has the Church become incompatible with Christianity?"

AUTHOR: Desilva Singleton
DATE: 06/18/2013 03:01:12 PM

Since we are on the topic of marriage, what about 1 Corinthians 7:1 - 40? I believe it's worth mentioning. This chapter starkly reminds me of 1 Samuel 8:1-22.

It seems like the word is encouraging a relationship with Him over all relationships in this world. It even warns us of earthly relationships and how those may occur at the expense of a relationship with Him.

Embracing "People Culture"

What Facebook Taught Me About Rape Prevention

DATE: 03/14/2013 08:06:36 PM

I didn't plan to write this post. I have a list of topics I plan to cover on my site, and rape was definitely not one of them. However, a few days ago I noticed posts by someone I'm connected to on Facebook about rape. Her name is Zerlina Maxwell, and I first began following her posts during the run up to the 2012 Presidential election. Zerlina actively used Twitter and appearances on cable news shows to voice the smart and well thought out political views I had come to expect from her. The posts she was making about rape stemmed from a television appearance Zerlina made on Tuesday, March 5, 2013, on The Sean Hannity Show. Zerlina was a guest on a segment about the effectiveness of teaching women to carry guns in order to prevent rape, and she made several comments including this one:

But I don't think that we should be telling women anything. I think that we should be telling men not to rape women. And start the conversation there with prevention.

Zerlina made several other statements during the segment, but I believe this one best captured her view about rape prevention. Zerlina's subsequent posts to her Facebook Timeline as well as posts made by her friends alerted me to the threats she had received following her appearance on Hannity. She received numerous death threats as well as calls for her to be raped so she could understand what she was talking about. I believe most of these threats came from Twitter.

While I couldn't understand the idiots who were threatening Zerlina, I have to admit that I struggled to fully understand her point. I have long held the belief that we should give women the same advice about rape prevention that we give to Americans who travel abroad: stay in public places, be careful what you wear, and keep your valuables close to you. However, this advice breaks down due to the fact that most women are raped by men they know and usually have a reason to trust. This includes friends, acquaintances, and relatives. I know this from experience because I have female friends who have confided in me that they have been raped, and in every case it was done by someone they know. Also, all research about rape confirms that <u>most women are raped by someone they know</u>[258]. Just like tourists can't be blamed for trusting a tour guide or host family they met overseas (who then robbed them) we need to stop blaming women for the trust they often put in the men who turn out to be their rapists. Indeed, as Zerlina stated, the best way to prevent men from raping women is for men to prevent themselves from becoming rapists.

Zerlina <u>wrote a great piece for Ebony.com</u>[259] about teaching men to not rape women. You should read it. I applaud her for taking a stand against rape, and I am happy that so many women are supporting her cause. However, we need men to also join in the effort to teach men to not rape women. Pursuant to that goal, here are four rules to help men not rape women (written in a way that I hope men can understand). Before we start, since a surprisingly large number of people seem to not know what rape is, here is a working definition: any unwanted sexual activity is rape. Ok, let's go:

Unless She Says Otherwise, Assume She Does NOT Want to Have Sex with You

Men are often taught to be over-confident. That's why men tend to negotiate for higher salaries more often than women do. An inflated ego often comes with the territory of being a man. Furthermore, men usually have high sex drives, and, therefore, often seek sexual fulfillment as often as possible. This is borne out by the fact that men think about sex more often than women. There's nothing wrong with a man thinking, "I want to have sex", but it is dangerous when this thought is combined with the assumption, "She wants to have sex with me".

---

258 http://rwu.edu/campus-life/health-counseling/counseling-center/sexual-assault/rape-myths-and-fac

259 http://www.ebony.com/news-views/5-ways-we-can-teach-men-not-to-rape-456#axzz2NebyWhX1

Embracing "People Culture"

However, the burden of proof for sexual intercourse has to be on the woman. In other words, she has to provide evidence that she wants to have sex, and that evidence cannot be imposed on her. The best way for a man to know a woman wants to have sex with him is when she says, "Yes" when he asks, "Do you want to have sex with me?"

She Can Stop the Sexual Act at Any Time

Men often assume that once sexual intercourse starts, he must continue to climax. I would venture to say that, assuming that a woman has consented to begin having sex with the man in the first place, most women have no problem with that. However, this is not always the case. Maybe she has changed her mind, maybe she is not enjoying the experience, or maybe she suddenly remembers that she left a pie baking on the oven. It doesn't matter. If a woman wants to stop having sex with a man, then that man must immediately stop having sex with her. Just because a man penetrates a woman does not mean he now possesses her. The man's heart will not stop nor will his testicles explode just because he didn't ejaculate during sex.

She Can Refuse Any Sexual Act

Just because a woman consents to one sexual act does not commit her to other sexual acts. For example, consensual oral sex does not commit her to vaginal intercourse. Similarly, consensual vaginal sex does not mean she wants to have anal sex. A woman should be allowed to always own her body and be in control over what she does with it.

She Can Remove You As a Sexual Partner Whenever She Chooses

This one is simple. Just because a man had sex with a woman in the past does not mean she is obligated to have sex with that man in the future. She can change up her roster at any time and make any additions or cuts that she sees fit. Furthermore, just because a woman has engaged in sexual activity with others in the past does not mean she wants to start having sex with you.

Teach Other Men These Principles

I am astonished by the number of women I know who have been raped. If you are a man reading this, you know someone who has been raped. I'm not talking about strangers or acquaintances. I mean wives, girlfriends, sisters, cousins, classmates, that girl who makes your caramel frap with whip and two shots at Starbucks, etc. A woman you care deeply about has been raped. An unacceptably high number of women have been raped because an unacceptably high number of men rape women. Men need to teach other men to not rape women. Older men need to teach these principles to younger men. We need to teach through actions as well. For example, when a man sees his buddies drooling over a passed out drunk girl in the corner at a party, he needs to pull them aside and school them about why sexual activity with that girl would be a bad idea. If men actively work to teach other men to not rape women, women can live free from the fear of rape.

Comments

AUTHOR: Jeanne
URL: http://FemaleSelfDefense.org
DATE: 05/21/2013 05:40:28 AM

I believe that women should get the knowledge that will allow her to make her own decision about defending herself. She does not need to depend on someone else.

AUTHOR: Anjuan Simmons
DATE: 05/22/2013 10:51:19 PM

Interesting point. Care to elaborate?

The Need to Respect Women in Tech

03/21/2013 01:56:22 PM

It's been a tough couple of weeks for women who choose to speak out about the challenges that women face in American society. Sheryl Sandberg, Chief Operating Officer of Facebook, has been making the media rounds promoting her book <u>Lean In: Women, Work, and the Will to Lead</u>[260]. While some praise the Silicon Valley executive for exposing many of the woes that women face in building their careers, many have come out against her claiming that she got to her vaulted position in life on the backs of men like Eric Schmidt and Mark Zuckerberg. Isn't that ironic? Sandberg is derided because of men who gave her a chance based on her achievements despite the fact that there were few examples of women excelling in the positions they offered her. All too often women are assumed to be "affirmative action" charity cases even before they have a chance to prove themselves.

Earlier this month, Zerlina Maxwell, a political strategist, caused controversy by appearing on The Sean Hannity Show and asserting that the key to rape prevention is teaching men to not rape women. Maxwell endured death threats, rape threats, and worse, and most of the hatred came via Twitter. I <u>wrote a post</u>[261] about the merits of Maxwell's argument because I felt it was important that a man support the need for men to be trained to not rape women.

Going back to the topic of women in technology careers, things got personal for me when my friend Adria Richards lost her job after a series of events that started when she spoke up about two men at the PyCon technology conference who made comments that made her feel uncomfortable. One of the men who made the comments was also fired from his company.

---

[260] http://www.amazon.com/Lean-In-Women-Work-Will/dp/0385349947

[261] http://www.anjuansimmons.com/blog/2013/3/14/what-facebook-taught-me-about-rape-prevention.html

Let me disclose that Adria is a friend of mine so I am not completely unbiased. However, my friendship with her is why I am writing this. Sheryl Sandberg goes home every night to a multi-million dollar house in an exclusive neighborhood and a loving family. I don't knock Sheryl for that because she has earned it. However, Adria doesn't have the same resources or support system. She shared some of her story and her struggles in this post[262]. I'm writing this because she is my fellow member of the tech community, and we need to take care of our own.

Here is Adria and I (and a friend) at Blogging While Brown.

---

[262] http://butyoureagirl.com/13871/success-against-the-odds-filling-my-technology-knapsack-from-scratch/

Here is Adria and I at South by Southwest.

The situation that led to two people being forced to look for jobs and two companies being required to find their replacements could have been handled better by everyone involved. It could have been resolved at the personal level by more open and honest conversation between Adria and the two men involved. Since that didn't happen, the situation could have been handled by SendGrid (Adria's former employer), and the company where the man worked. Since both companies are in the tech industry, this was a great opportunity to address the history of women in this country, especially when it comes to working in the technology sector. Instead, the companies chose the easy route and simply fired the people involved and tried to move past the situation.

However, this is precisely the type of crisis where communication is critical. Unless we talk about the hostile history that causes many women to feel threatened when two men share a crude joke in her presence, the technology industry will continue to be a place where too many women don't feel welcome.

Just as the hate and vitriol thrown at Sheryl Sandberg and Zerlina Maxwell underscored the validity of their arguments, the explosion of sexist and violent comments aimed at Adria justified the reason she became so upset in the first place. The world of politics has this saying about the true damage caused by political scandals: "It's not the scandal, it's the cover up". I think a variation of this applies to the true damage caused by what happened to Adria: "It's not the sexism, it's the misogyny".

When men (and women) call her crude names, threaten to kill her, and make other threats I won't mention here, they are demonstrating the hatred toward women in technology that often begins with "innocent comments" and "jokes between boys" and ends with anger and hostility. The Level Playing Field Institute published a report in late 2011 called "The Tilted Playing Field: Hidden Bias in Information Technology Workplaces". That report showed the women in technology companies often face male dominated cliques and off-color jokes. This often results in women choosing to leave tech companies for more understanding industries.

Furthermore, society overall is hostile to women. Few men in technology have ever had to deal with someone trying to rape them, but statistics show that most women will have to deal with a sexual assault at some point in their lives[263]. So, that penis joke a man says may not be a big deal to him and the guys around him, but it often stirs horrible memories in women who may be unknowingly in ear shot. Sure, we all have freedom of speech in this country, but we need to be sensitive to the reality that women are disproportionately victims of sexual violence, and many of the fears caused by those experiences affect them in the workplace.

Some may argue that if women can't cut it in technology due to a crude joke here or there, then they need to leave. However, that's a losing strategy. Women make up more than half the population in the United States. Technology companies need a strong pipeline of men AND women to fill their future employment needs. Technology companies that alienate women will soon find themselves losing the war for talent.

Furthermore, women like Sheryl Sandberg and Marissa Mayer who survive to rise to the top of elite technology companies will know about the companies that continue to be hostile environments for women. When they

---

263 http://www.thewomenscenterinc.org/sexual-assault-info/

have decision making ability to choose vendors and partners, what companies do you think they will avoid?

Women in technology fields need to be respected because they are the future of the industry. Failure to understand that fact and an unwillingness to create more welcoming environments isn't just political incorrectness. It's bad business.

Comments

AUTHOR: Shareef
URL: http://shareefjackson.com
DATE: 03/22/2013 02:20:43 AM

This is great. Excellent tie in with Zerlina and Sheryl Sandberg too. People need to realize that sometimes it doesn't matter if you were joking and didn't intend harm - it still creates an environment poisonous to the diversity that is critical to making our space the best it can be.

AUTHOR: Anjuan Simmons
DATE: 03/22/2013 09:46:56 PM

Thank you, Shareef!

AUTHOR: Ananda Leeke
URL: http://www.anandaleeke.com
DATE: 03/27/2013 03:18:23 PM

Thanks Anjuan for writing this post.

AUTHOR: Anjuan Simmons
DATE: 03/28/2013 01:22:48 PM

You're welcome, Ananda

APPENDIX A – My 100 Top Facebook Posts of 2009

The year 2009 was when my efforts to brand myself on social media began to take off. I began speaking at technology conferences and gaining more Twitter and Facebook followers. At the risk of being branded a narcissist, I compiled what I considered to be my top Facebook posts of 2009. I haven't compiled an annual list since then because I don't think I've able been able to top the content I created in 2009.

Facebook has almost become the Kleenex of the social media world. Only Twitter has as much cachet and brand identity. I joined Facebook almost as soon as it became open to more than college students because I saw the potential in the site. My early posts were very much like Twitter in that I posted whatever I was doing at that time. However, I eventually realized that Facebook provided an amazing laboratory to test my writing. I've always been a strong writer, but there were areas in which I was weak. For example, I struggled for a long time to incorporate humor into my writing. Facebook gave me the opportunity to post my attempts at humor and see how other people responded. My ability to write humor has vastly improved through this process.

I moved this to an appendix because I didn't want it to take up too much of the main part of the book. I hope you enjoy these posts. Some of you will read them for the first time, but I think many of you saw the originals.

My Top 100 Facebook Posts of 2009

12/31/2009 08:25:13 AM

First, look, I know this is a long list. When I started writing it, I thought it would contain 15 or 20 items. I advise taking it in small chunks. Drink a cup of coffee every 20 items or so. Maybe cut the yard.

I am not a big fan of New Year resolutions (after all, why wait for a new year to improve oneself?), but I do enjoy reflecting over the achievements of the past year. Here are the top posts I made to my primary online social media tool, Facebook, as selected by my panel. I thought about including my Twitter stream (http://www.twitter.com/anjuan), but no one wants to read a "My Top 1000 Facebook and Twitter Posts of 2009".

There is no significance to the order of the postings besides the fact that they are listed in chronological order. My comments on each post are in italics.

1. In 2009, I resolve to develop the perfect body, become a billionaire, heal the land, become sinless, and always tell the truth. By March. Oh, and knit. **December 31, 2008 at 10:19am**

Ok, this technically wasn't in 2009, but I thought it had to be on the list. I only achieved one of these, by the way.

2. My ideal Nanny: adores kids, Nigerian, 5' 2",350 pounds, a gourmet chef, 73 years old,30 grand kids, hump backed and a kick stand. **January 3 at 10:18am**

The nanny we actually got turned out to be decidedly not like the one described above. Well, she might have been 5' 2" . . .

3. I received a high grade for the exercise where I had to layoff someone. So, if you need to fire someone, I...guess...I'm...your guy? **January 4 at 7:18pm**

Ah, the inner revelations of the Mays MBA program never ceased . . .

4. In Omaha, Nebraska, with my fellow MBA students attending a meeting

258

with Warren Buffett.
January 9 at 10:13am

Ah, the "this is really cool!" moments of the Mays MBA program were actually high in number. I know only one other person from Omaha so I think the population of the city is something like 3 or 4 people.

5. Folks are dusting off old picture albums and getting their scan on. That's all well and fine. Just keep it 9th grade and higher, please . . . :-)
January 11 at 1:15am

The combination of the discovery of Facebook and the receipt of picture scanners from Christmas 2008 resulted in an embarrassing number of "back in the day when we were young and breaking out" photo albums on Facebook.

6. If parents curse their children by declaring, "I hope your kids are just like you!", then I must have been a pretty good child!
January 11 at 9:06am

Yes, I still believe that I have great kids!

7. I love my daughter dearly, but girls' clothing is ridiculously more complicated than boys clothing. I suspect this will worsen as she ages.
January 12 at 8:00am

Yes, yes, it does.

8. Facebook and Twitter may not last forever, but I hope the friendships (both new and old) I have formed/rekindled on these social networks do
January 13 at 7:57am

I still feel this way.

9. I need ideas for Valentine's Day and my 7th wedding anniversary. I know it's early, but I need time to plan and my wife isn't on here (yet!)
January 14 at 1:10pm

I got some great ideas! Facebook is the place to beta test things like this. And my wife is still not on Facebook . . .

10. Trying to walk in the belief that whatever light I can muster, little though it may be, may be the only light that many will ever see.
January 15 at 8:12am

Man, I was killing it last January!

11. No matter how bad things are going, a kiss from my wife or a hug from my kids makes me think, "Everything's gonna be alright."
January 16 at 8:13am

Awwwwwwwwwww

12. No ill will toward those who do, but I don't do man crushes. I don't get all glisteny and tingly over a dude. And if I did, it's probably athlete's foot.
January 18 at 5:52pm

I think this was when Tim Tebow was being worshiped on ESPN. Of course, that was before Alabama made him cry on national TV . . .

13. Often we want the storm to stop. But, sometimes it's better to find peace despite the storm. I hope America gets that stormproof peace today
January 20 at 8:30am

Well, I had my hopes . . .

14. I gave my son a haircut last night and he immediately threw a blanket over his head refusing to take it off. I didn't think I did THAT bad!
January 25 at 11:38am

I've gotten a lot better with the clippers over the past few months.

15. My youngest son had a dirty diaper. I teased him and said, "Are you a boo boo baby?" He looked offended and replied, "No, I'm a boo boo boy!"
January 26 at 8:09am

Yes, the joys of fatherhood are many.

16. 25 Random Things About Me
Once, you've been tagged, you are supposed to write a note with 25 random

things. At the end, you choose 25 people to be tagged. You have to tag the person who tagged you. If I tagged you, it's because I want to know more about you...
January 26 at 2:14pm

One of the few times I've given in to peer pressure. I just re-read my list. Not too bad, actually.

17. I drink too much caffeine-if caffeine totally left my system, I fear I would dry up and die like the guy who "chose poorly" in Indiana Jones
January 27 at 8:04am

Still true, unfortunately. Graduating from the Mays MBA program has helped tremendously, though.

18. I am touched by seeing so many people reconnect via Facebook. Indulging our essential need for friendship is rich, deep, and powerful.
January 28 at 7:38am

Awwwwwwwwwww

19. There is so much I want to do, but life is too short to not finish what I have to do.
February 2 at 7:42am

Real talk.

20. If you could live in a computer virtual world that was indistinguishable from the real world would you abide by the morality of the real world?
February 5 at 7:34am

See what too much caffeine and averaging 3 hours of sleep per night will do? You start asking questions about the future.

21. While changing my 1 year old daughter, my 4 year old son asked the inevitable question: "What happened to her penis? Did she break it off?"
February 7 at 9:21am

And that was one of the EASY questions!

22. Number of acceptable reasons for a man to hit a woman: zero. Number of acceptable reasons for a woman to take back a man who hit her: also zero.
February 9 at 2:11pm

Yeah, I came down hard on Chris Brown.

23. Sometimes, when you cannot maximize rewards, all you can do is try to minimize damages.
February 10 at 11:31am

I think this was after another fun capital budgeting exam . . .

24. Time flies when taking a finance final exam! If you gave a prisoner a really big capital budgeting problem, would it make a 20 year sentence feel like 2 days?
February 11 at 11:59am

Yep.

25. Wishing everyone a day filled with extra special love and romance on this Valentine's Day!
February 14 at 1:21pm

I think Valentine's Day 2010 will indeed be epic.

26. So, do men really wear skinny jeans? I'm having trouble with the idea of rocking a pair. I grew up in the age of baggy jeans . . .
February 15 at 6:24pm

Testing out fashion via skinny jeans. No, I have not nor ever will rock a pair.

27. Working to excel at things despite having little/no interest in them. Doing what's important so I can do what's entertaining.
February 17 at 6:36am

Real talk!

28. Channel flipping and seeing syndicated TV shows from the 80's makes

me realize I will never get back the hours I wasted watching ALF as a child.
February 18 at 5:41am

Man, if only I could . . .

29. Trying to live the authentic life where my actions are perfectly aligned with my beliefs & values. It's a difficult journey, but seeing growth makes it worth it
February 19 at 6:59am

I still aspire to do this.

30. A cashier said I look like Donnie McClurkin. New lifetime "You look like..." counts: Denzel-6,Jay Z-1,Malcolm X-3,Will Smith-4, Diddy-3,Donnie-1,"My Cousin"-28.
March 3 at 5:59am

The Jay Z one still hurts the most.

31. Open request for advice. What can I do to optimize my Daddy-Daughter relationship with my baby girl? Pick any area, but I am mostly concerned with dating.
March 4 at 7:07am

I got some good advice with this one.

32. Reminding myself that my family deserves excellent customer service and not just the people who pay me money.
March 6 at 8:24am

Thanks, Dr. Berry!

33. Springing forward - which always seemed to be an overly dramatic way to describe a government program that affects millions of people but has no scientific value
March 8 at 8:36am

I still don't like Daylight Savings Time.

34. Happy 7th Wedding Anniversary to my wonderful wife! Even the best macking wasn't enough, so I'm lucky to have her. Blame it on the EL-EL-EL-EL-EL- EL Shaddai.
March 9 at 7:00am

Wedding anniversary meets Jamie Foxx.

35. Trying to play chess in a checkers world.
March 12 at 7:59am

Hmmmm, what was that about?

36. Happy Birthday to the definition of a woman, my friend, my most ardent defender, my most loving critic, my partner, my wife - Aneika Simmons!
March 13 at 8:22am

Yes, she is my one!

37. Houston needs its own SXSWi. It could be called the Houston Technology Festival (or TechFest). Who's with me?
March 14 at 12:07pm

This was right before I discovered the vibrant technology community in Houston. In fact, Doug Ramsay's comment on this post connected me to Trel Robinson[264] who allowed me to speak at PodCamp Houston[265].

38. People seem comfortable using robots for war, but what about as police officers? How will you feel when WALL-E pulls you over and tickets you for speeding?
March 15 at 9:20am

Still too much caffeine and sleep deprivation.

---

[264] http://www.twitter.com/fave

[265] http://podcamphouston.org/wp/

39. With two young boys, I'm concerned about how wimpy male figures in kids TV shows are. Toot & Puddle, Steve, Wubbzy...really? What happened to OG's like Popeye?
March 16 at 2:22pm

I still think we need more manly cartoons.

40. Management accounting with all its weird rules reminds me of why calculus is better than accounting. Have I mentioned how much I love L'Hôpital's Rule?
March 20 at 3:45pm

Yes, I am a math nerd.

41. Can we pronounce a ban on the word 'swagger'? It's overused. By the way, I never have to turn my swag on because it's never off . . .
March 24 at 4:46pm

Hopefully, swagger will never be used in 2010. I pronounce the death of swag.

42. According to my StrengthsQuest test results, my top 5 strengths are <u>Belief, Context, Intellection, Connectedness, and Developer</u>[266]
March 25 at 8:00am

Another great outcome of the Mays MBA program.

43. As a result of an interview, I am considering changing my long term career goal from Chief Information Officer to Chief Security Officer.
March 26 at 3:35pm

I'm still struggling over whether I want to be a Geordi or a Worf.

44. Writing my strategy paper exploring Apple, Inc. from both an external and internal perspective. I am not sure if it has a sustainable competitive

---

[266] https://www.strengthsquest.com/content/111337/StrengthsQuest-Guidebook.aspx

advantage.
March 28 at 8:11pm

That turned out to be a great paper and an even better presentation. My team, Eris, advised Apple to release the Tablet before the end of the year. Too bad, Steve Jobs didn't listen.

45. Trying the 6 Things method of productivity where, at the end of each day, I list the six most important tasks to be accomplished the next day. Let's go!
March 31 at 6:46pm

I still do this to some degree.

46. The CEO of Bank of America (and his security detail) will host a town hall for my MBA class tomorrow at Texas A&M. What should I ask him?
April 1 at 5:36pm

I actually got to ask him a question. Too bad he didn't survive as CEO. I don't feel bad for him. I'm sure he sleeps in a bed made of money.

47. Putting the theory that the human mind can hold a near infinite amount of information to the test.
April 6 at 10:12pm

Yep, still more brain expansion courtesy of the Mays MBA program.

48. Yesterday, a guest speaker (an executive from Darden) furthered my interest in marketing. Maybe I can become a Chief Information-Security-Marketing Officer?
April 9 at 7:51am

And so my quest to discover what I want to be when I grow up continued.

49. People who live in glass houses should upgrade to bricks before throwing stones.
April 10 at 8:59am

People thought otherwise, but this was a totally innocent post . I just thought up the phrase, liked how it sounded, and put it on Facebook.

50. To all so inclined, Happy Easter! I love the smell of resurrection in the morning. It smells like . . . victory!
April 12 at 5:53am

Amen.

51. Trying to choose an elective. I've whittled it down to: MIS Project Management, Managing Projects, Networking & Security, eServices, and Marketing Communications.
April 14 at 5:00pm

I chose Networking & Security, by the way.

52. Celebrities will always attract tons of followers on Twitter/Facebook; the real story is the ability for regular people to mass market their personal brand.
April 20 at 8:03am

This is something I've had some success doing in 2009.

53. Amazed that my parents celebrated their 39th wedding anniversary this past Saturday. They pulled out all the stops and did it big by going to Applebees . . .
April 21 at 9:06pm

Clearly, my parents live la vida loca.

54. Foxx and Ne-Yo's lyric, "Only kinda girl I want, independent queen workin' for her throne" reminds me so much of my wife. I'm blessed to have her as my co-pilot
April 29 at 6:10pm

Nuff said!

55. One of the things I enjoy about Facebook and Twitter is the ability they provide for people to create "living autobiographies" to which we can all contribute.
May 29 at 7:27am

If you're reading this, I thank you for sharing your "autobiography" with me on Facebook, and I hope you've enjoyed reading mine!

56. The one year anniversary of my Lasik eye surgery is almost here. Getting 20/20 vision has been the best money I've ever spent. I highly recommend it.
May 30 at 8:47am

Best. Money. Ever. Spent . . . Ever. It was a lot of money, but I use it every day.

57. Our problems are mostly self-inflicted. We're volunteers rather than victims. Therefore, we must own our recovery. The self-made cage should be easiest to break
May 31 at 7:50am

Ok, now my caffeine fueled morning had me going all Socrates on Facebook.

58. I used to have beef with Kobe because of his infidelity. However, if I had my worst moment in life revealed to the world, I wouldn't want it held it against me.
June 5 at 8:03am

I will probably feel the same way about Tiger Woods someday.

59. With Microsoft's announced Oct 22nd release of Windows 7, I encourage anyone buying a new PC to wait for Windows 7! The beta version I've been using is great.
June 7 at 8:05am

I was hip to Windows 7 way before it was the new hotness.

60. It's Tech Tuesday! Are you buying a gadget, have a computer problem, or need a general technology question answered? Comment here and I'll post a solution.
June 9 at 7:45am

So began "Tech Tuesday", one of my most successful Facebook experiments. By the way, Tech Tuesday is now every day so feel free to send me your technology related questions any time!

61. I'm really enjoying the continual stream of reconnections with long lost classmates and co-workers made possible by Facebook. It's like an ongoing reunion!
June 10 at 7:59am

However, nothing beats meeting face to face.

62. I had a great time taking part in #podcamphouston as a presenter and as a listener. Thanks to @fave for putting on an outstanding event!
June 13 at 8:35pm

PodCamp Houston was a great experience. I am very thankful to have hooked up with Trel (@fave).

63. Random event invites, requests to join mafias, invitations to become fans, and other irrelevant application requests are the tax we pay to use Facebook . . .
June 14 at 8:00am

Unfortunately, this is more true than ever now.

64. My education in finance has ruined me. I can't even buy coffee from Starbucks without worrying about NPV, opportunity cost, ROI, breakeven point, IRR . . .
June 17 at 7:52am

Getting an MBA can be hazardous to your consumerism.

65. When I first heard Lil Wayne's "A Milli" song, I thought it was about a girl named Emily. "Emily, Emily, Emily..." What happened to enunciation in the rap game?
June 19 at 8:00am

Actually, this has gotten better. Thanks, Drake.

66. I look at my kids, and I see the child I once was. I wonder if they will look at me one day and see the adults they will become?
June 21 at 7:29am

Mirror, mirror, on the wall . . .

67. The number of Facebook friends or Twitter followers you have means nothing if you are not willing to connect with all of them and serve them in some way.
June 24 at 8:23am

This is still a core part of my philosophy about online social media.

68. I know a lot of people spent last night remembering wanting to be/date Michael Jackson. I'm focusing on the message of my favorite MJ song: "Man in the Mirror"
June 26 at 8:13am

This event, though tragic, showed the ability of online social media to bring people, old friends and total strangers alike, together.

69. Life is too short to waste time arguing about minor issues. Eventually, you will be invited to their funeral or they will be invited to yours. Let's enjoy life.
June 29 at 8:13am

Let's keep short accounts with each other and enjoy the brief time we have in this life.

70. I'm moved by the Michael Jackson Memorial. His flaws in light of his great talent made him a tragic hero. Yet, he was the People's Prince.
July 7 at 1:22pm

A lot of people didn't understand why he meant so much, but I hope even they were moved by the outpour of grief.

71. Updating my career management plan and getting my interview suits cleaned. My goal is find the best company I can serve after I graduate with my MBA in December
July 8 at 7:55am

In this economy, I was very fortunate to get a job offer from Deloitte. I start on January 4th!

72. Facebook and Twitter show me that people who are COMPLETELY different often do and think the same things. People usually have more in common than they realize.
July 12 at 6:10pm

You'll be surprised how many people take Sunday afternoon naps, enjoy the same types of holiday food, and have the same morning rituals despite being totally different.

73. I wish the IRS would let citizens decide exactly what projects they want their tax dollars to support. That would make it a bit easier to pay federal taxes.
July 22 at 9:02am

I still wish this was the case.

74. Conferences I want to attend one day: SXSWi, E3, ComicCon, WWDC, The Up Experience, and TED. Are any of you avid conference attendees?
July 24 at 7:53am

This was unknown to me when I wrote this, but I'll achieve the first one in March!

75. 4 Things a grown man should never wear: 1. Crocs 2. Capri Pants 3. Skinny jeans 4. Shirts with ruffles #youmightaswellputonadress
July 25 at 9:08am

Yeah, I'm old school . . .

76. I submitted two panel proposals to South by Southwest Interactive 2010, and you can support my ideas (and others) when voting begins on August 10th.
July 27 at 9:04am

And this was the beginning of how I got a free Gold Badge to attend South by Southwest Interactive 2010. One of my proposals was accepted. I thank everyone who voted for me!

77. Facebook and Twitter are helping people see the amazing lives of

people they already know instead of stalking celebrities they will never meet.
July 30 at 8:03am

Real talk.

78. Instead of thinking of people who position themselves against me as enemies, I try to think of them as friends I haven't converted yet.
July 31 at 9:00am

I would like to think that I converted a few friends in 2009.

79. I prefer to have people discover my religious beliefs by how I live my life instead of by telling them how to live theirs.
August 2 at 9:27am

Not that I'm shy about sharing my beliefs when appropriate . . .

80. I'm honored to be speaking at Houston's Caroline Collective this Wednesday about making Houston one of the country's hubs of technological growth and innovation
August 3 at 6:13pm

This was another great public speaking opportunity for me this year. Thanks, Grace Rodriguez[267], for inviting me to speak at Caroline Collective[268]!

81. You're not truly "hood" unless you've: 1-Poured water on cereal,2-Had a mayonnaise sandwich,3-Fed 5 people with 99 cents,4-Jumped a fence to escape a rabid dog
August 6 at 8:01am

I had to let 'em know.

---

[267] http://www.twitter.com/gracerodriguez

[268] http://carolinecollective.cc/2009/08/03/c2-creative-presents-anjuan-simmons/

82. My wife and I enjoyed meeting a friend at the only "Obama Favorite Restaurant" that wasn't booked up: RJ Grunts. Thanks, Lalapalooza!
August 9 at 8:59am

It wasn't my first choice, but the food was pretty good.

83. I'm looking forward to a family portrait, "Beauty and the Beast" at the Wichita Falls Theatre, and a nice dinner this evening.
August 15 at 8:31am

My August trip to Wichita Falls was surprisingly enjoyable.

84. I really liked the movie "District 9". It was an interesting allegory of the Cross Racial Identity Scale (CRIS) and how people move along it
August 21 at 8:11am

Come to think of it, "Avatar" was another allegory of <u>CRIS</u>[269]:

85. I'm a bit amused by people who won't join Facebook because "affairs happen there". 70% of affairs happen at work so, to "affair proof" yourself, quit your job!
August 24 at 8:02am

I still find this amusing.

86. Jesus walks, huh Kanye? Such actions further the perception that Christianity is a bankrupt religion with no impact on actual behavior. We have to do better.
September 14 at 7:48am

In hindsight, I was too harsh here. However, I do think that Christians need to do a better job of living Christianity.

87. I'm actually enjoying being interviewed. It's like having a conversation with a colleague. Of course, it's a very one sided conversation that's being

---

[269]
http://en.wikipedia.org/w/index.php?title=William_E._Cross,_Jr.&oldid=292803356

recorded.
September 16 at 7:24am

While I still enjoyed a lot of the interviews I went through, after 60 or 70 of them, some did start to get old.

88. My rough Facebook friend distribution: Birth (.1%), Kindergarten to High School (10%), UT (5%), Accenture (10%), TAMU (5%), Unknown (69.9%).
September 23 at 7:14am

This distribution still holds true.

89. Sometimes, instead of parting a Red Sea, God simply provides a row boat.
September 28 at 7:32am

I've had to paddle my share of row boats in 2009. But, I made it to the other side!

90. I'll be serving as a panelist at the National Black Pre-MBA Conference this Saturday, November 7th, at the University of Houston Downtown. My fellow panelists and I will cover the topic "The Business School Experience" and share our perspectives with prospective and current entrepreneurs and professionals.
November 4 at 2:17pm

This was another great public speaking opportunity in 2009! I thank Evangeline Mitchell for the opportunity to speak at her <u>conference</u>[270]!

91. In many ways, I live a life far better than I deserve. So, I am thankful for my awesome wife and three amazing kids, for friends both long lost and newly discovered, and for adventures both well documented and yet to be experienced!
November 18 at 6:56am

---

[270] http://www.blackpremba.com/

I think this will always be true for me!

92. I am happy to announce that my panel idea, "How Social Media Can Destroy Your Business Model" was accepted to be presented at the South by Southwest Interactive Festival! I am very excited to get the opportunity to speak before a great group of technologists!
December 1 at 11:35am

It's on like Donkey Kong. Thanks again for your votes!

93. My fellow husbands, we need to be 100% faithful to our wives. It's really not that hard. Even if you don't get caught (and that's very unlikely), cheating does irreversible damage to your marriage that can't be hidden. Man up and honor your commitment.
December 2 at 2:04pm

I'll go easy on celebrities next year no matter how many of them mess up. My flaws remind me that it's hard being an unknown imperfect person. It must be almost impossible to be a famous one.

94. Today is my 35th birthday. While far from perfect, I am extremely happy with my life, especially regarding my wife and kids. If I have achieved any level of success, it is only because of God. I can only take credit for the mistakes.
December 4 at 8:09am

Thanks again for the mountain of birthday wishes I received!

95. The Gators are who we thought they were.
December 5 at 6:27pm

Yep, no man crushes here.

96. Longhorns, some may question the challenge level of your path to this point. Ignore them. Summon the will to win and fight your way to victory. Hook 'em!
December 5 at 8:20pm

The Longhorns are who we thought they were!

97. As a graduate of The University of Texas at Austin (BS Electrical Engineering, 1997) and a soon-to-be graduate of Texas A&M (MBA, Dec 19, 2009), I feel strangely compelled to reconcile the rivalry between these two great institutions. Maybe we can combine the school yells? Ghook 'em or Hig 'em?
December 8 at 9:34am

This did not go over very well . . .

98. I'll take the last final exam in my MBA degree plan today. It will probably be the last final exam I'll ever take, but I've learned to never say never!
December 15 at 7:24am

I will say that a lot of time will probably pass before I step foot on a college campus as a student again . . .

99. To all to whom these presents may come, Greeting. Be it known that Anjuan Simmons, having completed the studies and satisfied the requirements for the Degree of Master of Business Administration, has accordingly been admitted to that Degree with all the honors, rights and privileges belonging thereto.

Or, for some of my people back home, "I got 99 problems but an MBA ain't one!"
December 16 at 7:13am

This was probably my greatest accomplishment of 2009!

100. This morning I had the honor of giving my Student Speaker speech to my fellow MBA students at our private graduation ceremony. I hope they were encouraged by my words and know the deep respect and affection I have for all of them. It has been a privilege to be counted as one of them!
December 17 at 6:04pm

And this was my greatest honor.

That's my year in review. I have to say that 2009 has been a mix of challenges and triumphs. However, overall, it has been a great year for me. I hope that 2010 can top it!

APPENDIX B – Tech Tuesdays

As I received more and more questions on my blog and other social media outlets from people about their technology problems, I decided to start what I called "Tech Tuesdays". Every Tuesday I received questions from my social graph and gave free tech advice. It was often a very time consuming experiment, but I enjoyed the process of helping people. Tech Tuesdays also solidified my brand as a technologist which has proved to be beneficial to me professionally as well as personally.

Here's the disclaimer I put at the end of each Tech Tuesday. Use my advice at your own risk!

Disclaimer: The information Anjuan Simmons provides during Tech Tuesdays is for educational purposes only and does not guarantee verified or factual information. Anjuan Simmons tries to provide content that is true and accurate as of the date of writing; however, he gives no assurance or warranty regarding the accuracy, timeliness, or applicability of any of the content.

All content and information Anjuan Simmons provides might be changed or updated without notice.

This information is provided "as is" and Anjuan Simmons expressly disclaims any and all warranties, express or implied, to the extent permitted by law.

Anjuan Simmons hereby excludes liability for any claims, losses, demands, or damages of any kind whatsoever with regard to any information or content provided by him, including but not limited to direct, indirect, incidental, or consequential loss or damages, compensatory damages, loss of profits, or data, or otherwise.

Tech Tuesday #1 - Archive - June 9th, 2009 (Keys, Old PC, HD's, Dead Dell, Media Center, FAT32, Sound, Erase HD, Tablet PC)

DATE: 09/19/2011 06:57:15 PM

Q. I have a hardware tech support question. My son flickd the v,n, and the spacebar keys off of my laptop keyboard, is that an easy thing to fix and should I expect paying and arm and 2 toes for it?
Christina Bernard

A. As the father to a 4, 3, and 18 month old, I have also had to deal with missing keys on a laptop. You have a few options. First, the keys are relatively easy to put back on if you have them. You'll have to slide them on at the right angle and then lightly press them until they click in place. It takes patience and good hand/eye coordination, but I know you can do it. Alternatively, if you have a spare desktop computer keyboard, you can plug it into the laptop if it has a spare USB port (or PS/2 if it's an older laptop). This will work if you don't move the laptop very often and it usually sits in one place. Finally, you can pay someone to do it, and I don't think it will cost that much to fix (I'm thinking about $50). You may want to go by your local Best Buy and ask a Geek Squad employee for a quote.

Q: I have a custom built desktop that is about 4-5 years old. I have Vista running on it and I use it to manage documents, upload photos, surf the net and the ilk. I don't do multimedia stuff or watch video on it. It's been running reaaaallly slow to the point that it inhibits my productivity. I have run the defrag, assorted defender utilities, pop-up removers and they do nothing to increase the speed. How do I know when I have a dinosaur on my hands and should go out an buy a new computer? Are there free programs online that can determine whether there are hidden viruses that I can remove myself? Basically, I'd like some sort of computer maintenance checklist that I can make sure that my computer is running the right programs and if necessary run extra ones to support continuous efficiency.
Heather Green

A: Your computer may be slowing down for a variety of reasons. First, computers accumulate all kinds of files as they run. Some of them are put there by the operation system and others are added by applications (those that came with the computer and those you install yourself). It's often called "bit rot" and it tends to get worse over time. I find that the best way to fix this is to reinstall the operating system (AFTER you make sure you BACK UP your data). That way, you get a fresh OS and you can also reinstall the applications you really use instead of having a lot of programs that just sit in the background. I find that doing a clean install is better than any utility, popup blocker, defrag, etc. Also, since you don't do any multimedia on the machine, you may want to give Ubuntu a try. It's a free Linux distribution that does all the things you said you do with the computer and should run faster than Vista.

Second, you may have spyware, adware, and a virus on your machine. This is hard to know for sure until you run an application designed to search your system for infections. You have a lot of options you can buy (like the Norton suite), but I think AVG 8.5 Free (which is, as the name suggests, free) is a good solution to try first. It is lightweight and easy to use.

As for a maintenance checklist, I would say doing a fresh OS install once a year, running AVG 8.5 daily (making sure the virus definitions are regularly updated), and maybe doing a defrag once a month is fine. I believe that good computing is mostly behavioral. That is, don't open email attachments, don't go to questionable sites (e.g., porn, gambling, etc), only install applications you use and trust, and make sure you have a router between your computer and your internet connection will protect you from most viruses.

Heather later provided this update:

This is great. Reading the other inquiries, I was able to get two questions answered for the price of one. AVG Free has already been running on my computer so I guess the spyware, adware and viruses are at bay. I also have Windows Defender running on the computer but I wonder if both running simultaneously may be also contributing to the slowdown.

Once I find a reasonably priced external drive (I will look into the ones you have listed above) I will back up my system and do a OS reinstall as suggested. I recently purchased a netbook for my daughter but I haven't set it up yet. I may try Ubuntu for that. I went to their website and they have a page on how to install as well as any issues that my particular netbook may have running the platform.

I will inform you of my advances. THANKS!

I'm glad that you were helped. Running AVG Free and Windows Defender at the same time may be part of the problem, but they are supposed to be relatively lightweight. In any case, I think you will immediately see a performance improvement once you reinstall the operating system (especially if you use Ubuntu).

Speaking of Ubuntu, I highly recommend it for netbooks. It has a much smaller footprint than Windows XP and definitely smaller than Windows Vista.

Q. well i'm looking to buy a small 500gb drive to put all my music on. i'm looking at iomega, seagate and toshiba. which is best? i'm going to buy a big ipod once i migratemy music over.
Stacy Lindley

A. I can't recommend Toshiba (because I have never used their drives), but Iomega and Seagate (who bought Maxtor in 2006) are great drive makers. You'll also find a lot of drives by a company called Western Digital. However, I would recommend Seagate since I've had the fewest problems with their hard drives.

I'm not sure if you plan to use this hard drive as a backup drive, but I highly recommend you have some place to back up your data. Every hard drive will eventually fail; it's just a question of when it will happen and it could happen at any time even if the drive is brand new! So, since hard drives are so cheap these days, I would recommend getting two 500 GB drives and using one as a backup (again, if you don't already have a place to back up your data). You can probably even buy two 1 terabyte (TB) drives for about $200 if you shop around.

Q. I am trying to figure out if there is no hope for my sorry Dell computer. It will not boot up all the way..I have tried to restart from a previous date and complete a system restore but nothing has worked. :-(Is my computer dead, is there anyway I can get to my saved files..
LaTonya Holman

A. There could be a variety of issues with your Dell ranging from a bad memory card, a defective power supply, to inefficient cooling due to dust build up in the case. However, one quick way to see if your computer can be resurrected is to try Ubuntu. However, this requires a bit of hackery, and I assume you have another computer to use since you're on Facebook!. So, to use Ubuntu go to http://www.ubuntu.com/ and follow the instructions to download the latest version (ubuntu-9.04-desktop-i386.iso). Burn the ISO file to a CD. Turn on the Dell, and, immediately after it turn on, hit the F12 key (or it may be the Escape key) to go to the boot order menu. Before you do anything, open the CD-ROM drive and put the Ubuntu CD in it and then close the drive. On the boot order menu, select the CD-ROM drive as the first drive to boot from and hit OK. You'll soon see an Ubuntu menu with the option to run Ubuntu without installing it.

Basically, you'll use Ubuntu as a "Live CD" where it runs from the CD-ROM drive using everything in your Dell except for the physical hard drive. If you get to the Ubuntu desktop, try browsing through the hard drive. If you can do so, immediately copy everything to another hard drive. If Ubuntu fails, then you probably have so other hard ware issue.

If Ubuntu sounds too tough, you can also remove the physical hard drive from the Dell and put it into another computer. If your working computer does not have space for another drive, then you can buy a hard drive enclosure and put the Dell hard drive in it and connect via USB.

Q. I recently purchased a PC desktop for my folks (i'm a Mac man so this was a tough purchase). Windows Media Center will not let them play regular DVDs (get some standard windows error). I googled the error message and everyone that has had this issue said you had to download "codecs" to enable the windows media player to play regular dvds. I downloaded 2 codecs...no joy. Can you help me?? (in the meantime I downloaded a free dvd player but I just think it inefficient that you cant use all the functions of that media center because it is actually kinda cool).
Marcus Cole

A. Unfortunately, Windows Media Player is notorious for having trouble with the playback of DVD's. This is because DVD's have copy protection on them, and Microsoft usually restricts playing DVD in order to honor this copy protection. I would be careful with downloading codecs to circumvent this since many of them have viruses and spyware hidden in them. However, I can recommend an open source application called VLC that will almost definitely play DVD's and not have any malware in it. You can find it at http://www.videolan.org/vlc/ . Download the Windows version and install it on your parent's computer. Believe me, VLC has never failed to play anything I've thrown at it including divx, avi, mpg, etc.

Q. I'm looking for a terabyte external hard drive that can be accessble by the playststion 3 and the xbox 360. I know they are only supposed to read fat32 formatted drives but I have heard of exceptions where larger drives do in fact work. How can I know which drives or brands will work?
Josh Coleman

A. Unfortunately, Microsoft and Sony made the decision to use the ancient Fat32 file format instead of NTFS. This is strange because any recent version of Windows uses NTFS, and Fat 32 has limitations like the inability to recognize files greater than 4 GB in size and a maximum volume limit of 32 GB. So, if you want to use a large terabyte drive, you'll have to hook it up to another computer and stream the media from it to your XBOX/PS3. This is not an optimal solution because it means that the XBOX/PS3 AND the computer has to be on in order for you to watch movies, listen to music, view pictures, etc., on the 1 TB drive.

Another solution I have seen in my research is to use a program called FAT32FORMAT to format large 500 GB drives in FAT32. This may work on your 1 TB drive, but I'm pretty skeptical about this solution. However, if it works, then you'll be able to play your media straight from the hard drive.

As I think about this some more, the partition solution may be the best solution. Similar to what I suggested to LaTonya above, you can download the live CD version of gparted from http://tinyurl.com/5mq9su. Gparted is a Linux based partition editor. Put the gparted live CD into the CD-ROM drive of a computer with the 1 TB drive attached and boot from the CD. You'll see the gparted interface, and you can use it to format the hard drive in Fat32 format. From my research, it looks like people have gotten this to work on 500 GB hard drives so it may work on your 1 TB hard drive. If this works, then you will be able to allow your XBOX/PS3 to directly access the media on the external hard drive. Of course, I would back up everything on the hard drive first before trying this.

I forgot to mention that even if you can format the 1 TB drive in FAT32 format, you'll still be limited to file sizes under 4 GB. That may be a problem because some high definition video files can easily exceed that file size.

Q. My personal laptop will no longer charge. When it's plugged in a little blue light comes on to show that it's charging. The blue light no longer comes on. Where do I get a new charger & if it's not the charger causing the issue, what else could it be?
Sarah Morgan

A. I'll assume that the blue light is on the laptop and not on the power cord. I'll also assume that the laptop works when it is plugged in and that you just have a problem when you want to use the battery. The problem is probably the battery or the power cord. If you know someone with the same laptop try swapping with them to use their power cord to see if it works. If it does, you need a new power cord. If that does not work, using your original power cord, swap with them to use their battery. If your laptop charges, you need a new battery. If that does not work either, then the problem is probably inside the laptop somewhere, and the laptop probably needs to be serviced (hopefully it's still under warranty).

By the way, if you don't have someone to swap parts with, try taking it to an electronics store like Best Buy and ask a salesperson if you can test using their display machines. I've had success with this in that past.

You can usually buy replacement cords or batteries from the manufacturer. Or, you can buy third party products that work with a variety of laptops.

I hope that helps!

Also, my friend Leo Yamato offered this advice:

I've had the same problem on my own laptop and it turns out that the battery was not properly seated. One quick thing you can try is to disconnect the battery and then reattach it.

Q. Hi Anjuan, I cannot hear any sound on my laptop. I have looked under the control panel/sounds and most everything is grayed out. We

recently had to do a system restore...any suggestions?
Canditha Davis

A. I assume that the sound worked before the system restore, right? To rule out a hardware problem, if you have a set of external speakers (or even a set of headphones), try plugging them into the laptop. If you can hear sound, then the laptop speakers themselves have stopped working and will need to be repaired (or, you can just use the external speakers).

If you still can't hear sound, then maybe the driver for your internal sound card were somehow affected by the system restore. If you right click on "My Computer" and select properties, you should be able to get to Device Manger. From there, look for your sound card and see if it has a yellow exclamation point over the icon. If so, you can go the sound card manufacturer's website, download the latest driver, and reinstall it.

Q. I installed Norton 360 version 3.0 (all-in-one security) six days ago. Whenever a search engine is used, this version is suppose to identify unsafe websites and suspicious sellers so that I can surf and shop with confidence. It is suppose to show the safety level with red and green symbols. I went to Webcrawler and Dogpile. Norton did not identify the results with the red and green symbols. This feature was one of the reasons I bought Norton and it is not working. Can you offer a solution?
Marilyn Simmons

A. Norton and other security packages can only identify sites that are in its list of potentially bad vendors. It may be that the sites on the first page of results returned by Webcrawler and Dogpile were not questionable. Try scrolling through several pages of search results and see if you can find any that are being flagged. Also, are you sure that the software works with all search engines? Some may be more compatible with Google since it is the most popular search site.

My mother later provided this update:

Anjuan, your advice saved me some frustration. I used Google as a search engine and the alerts worked. Thank you!! Thank you!!!

I'm glad I saved you some frustration!

Q. This is great! I have two laptops which I need to dispose (the right way). I have already copied all my data on to cds. I want to destroy any ounce of data that remains so that when it is shipped to another country to be thrown in the trash there (instead of here) that no one takes the opportunity to try to grab any of my personal information. What is the best way to completely destroy the information on the laptop. I have heard software (but cds may not work and connecting to the internet takes energy and time that I don't want to expend). I have heard magnets. But is there really a way to tell it is all gone? Thanks. Maybe you should start a group and we can post questions there.
Karen Ramsey Davis

A. The only way to guarantee that information cannot be retrieved from a computer is to destroy it. That means incinerating it or taking out the hard drive and smashing each platter to smithereens. Some people even dip hard drives in liquid nitrogen and then shatter them. Even the RAM sticks have been shown to hold data after a power down so they should be destroyed as well.

Of course, it's hard to donate a destroyed computer.

So, a reasonably safe alternative is to use a free utility called Darik's Boot and Duke (http://www.dban.org/). It uses the same hard drive erasing routines that government agencies use to wipe machines that held classified data. This basically consists of writing meaningless data over the drive multiple times. You burn Darik's Boot and Duke to a CD, put it into your CD-ROM drive, restart the computer and run it. I would chose the highest wipe level, but it will take a long time to complete. However, you can feel almost 100% safe.

I'll think about setting up a group. That would make it easier to maintain a history of the questions and my answers. Thanks for the suggestion!

Q. hey Anjuan, is there a way to log multiple users on a Vista Professionial tablet pc? everytime a guest user tries to log on while i'm still logged on, the damn computer would freeze.....
Selene Cong

A. Are you doing screen sharing (i.e., more than one person working on a file at once) or are do you just want more than one person to log into the tablet pc in separate sessions? If it's the former, it should not be a problem. If it's the latter, the tablet pc may not have enough memory to support multiple logins. If possible, I would recommend 4 GM of RAM to do this.

By the way, if you want to do screen sharing, then you can try a VNC client. My favorite is the free TightVNC (http://www.tightvnc.com/). You install the VNC server on the tablet pc and the VNC client on the guest pc. The guest pc will then log into the tablet pc and see the screen. You can even give it control over the mouse.

A more expensive solution would be GoToMyPC or GoToMeeting which also provide remote access and more robust collaboration tools.

Tech Tuesday #2 - Archive - June 16th, 2009 (Buy MS Office, Anti-Spyware, Sticky Keys, Frozen Blackberry, Netbooks, Outlook)

09/20/2011 11:08:18 PM

Q. I need a copy of Microsoft office and some good spyware...
Rico Williams

A. I assume you want Microsoft Office Professional 2007 (the latest edition of the application). You can find it at a store like Best Buy for around $500. If you're upgrading from a previous version of Office, it will cost a little bit less. As for spyware, Norton AntiVirus 2009 costs about $40 and will provide protection against viruses as well as spyware.

If you're a registered developer with Microsoft's developer network (MSDN), you can download a free version of Office. You may be able to get an MSDN subscription through your job.

If you don't mind working with open source software, OpenOffice provides many of the capabilities of Microsoft Office for free. It runs on both Macintosh and Linux. Also, AVG Free is a good free antivirus and antispyware tool.

I understand the desire to save some money! Software can be expensive. You can download OpenOffice from http://www.openoffice.org/ to give it a try. You may also want to see if your workplace offers a download of office. Many employers strike deals with Microsoft to offer free or low cost downloads since Office is pretty ubiquitous in the workplace.

My friend Matt Nikolaiev added this great suggestion:

I recently went deal hunting for office for some family members. if you want Office 2007 Pro, it is cheaper at places like www.newegg.com than at Best Buy.... About $350 at newegg...

Also, if you have a .edu email address, you can get office 2007 for $59.99 direct from Microsoft:

Tech Tuesdays

http://www.microsoft.com/student/discounts/theultimatesteal-
us/default.aspx

**Q. How do I clean the keyboard of my laptop which had orange juice
spilled on it? It's working ok, but the keys stick.**
Sarah Minnis

A. Laptop keyboards are much harder to clean than desktop keyboards
because they are integrated into the machine itself. I have seen tutorials on
how to remove each key and clean the area beneath them with Q-Tips and
liquid cleaners. In fact, here is one: http://tinyurl.com/anjuan

However, you have to be very handy when doing this and very careful
when replacing the keys. If you do this, it helps to draw a keymap so you
can know where each key goes.

Since the keyboard is working, it may be safer to just get a can of
compressed air and blow between the keys.

I would also suggest keeping liquids far away from the keyboard, but I also
frequently eat around computers myself!

**Q. I have my emails coming to my Blackberry Pearl. If it get to over
100...then comes the houglass. I have to remove the battery everytime
before I can come out of the hourglass freeze. I delete the emails, but I
have to do it before it gets to the 100 mark.**
Gloria A. Smith

A. My research suggests that your Blackberry Pearl has a memory problem.
Try Menu->Options->Status and see how much free space you have. If
you're running low, then it may help to delete unnecessary or unused files
or applications. Another suggestion I saw was to back up your data and
then do a complete wipe of the phone. This will reset it to the state it was in
when you received the phone

Q. I almost forgot!!! OK here it is.
I have Acer Aspire One netbook (my daughter's).
I'm about to buy a HP laptop (to replace the desktop)
I'm upgrading to the Palm Pre.
My iPod Classic is busted, so I'm going for the iTouch.... Read More

288

I'm thinking about a 40" Samsung LCD flat panel.

How do you economically insure them all and make sure you're covered for everything that could happen (maintenance, accidental stuff, lost or stolen, etc.). Thanks!
Heather R Green

A. I think you have a couple of options. You can probably contact Acer and see if you can get an extended warranty for the Acer. However, this will only cover you if some manufacturing error caused the device to fail. More coverage can be provided by a service plan from wherever you purchased the Acer. Since you already have it in your possession, they probably would want to inspect it before providing coverage for you.

It looks like you're about to buy everything else so you can also purchase a service plan or insurance at the time of purchase from the retailer. I will say that this will probably be expensive since a lot of retail stores make their money by selling such plans. I have only purchased insurance for my cell phone since I know I bang it up a lot . Even my 50 inch plasma TV is not covered because I am reasonably confident that it will last for a while, doesn't move, and is mounted on the wall out of reach (for now) from my kids!

The bottom line is you have to do what you can afford and what will help you sleep well at night. I tend to think that most electronics made by major manufacturers are subjected to intense amounts of quality control and rarely fail under most conditions. If you are rough with your technology or are buying it for someone who... Read More is, then it probably makes sense to get some coverage. However, I think that most service/insurance plans are revenue generating tools for retailers and are rarely used in practice. But, that is pretty much the definition of insurance.

Heather later added this update:

Thanks. So far I have the full coverage insurance from Staples for the netbook. 2 years worked out to 6.80 a month. Same with the phone. 7 bucks a month with Sprint.

You're right about the TV. It would be out of the way and the only way it would be touched would be if I misplaced the remote.

Sounds like you're pretty well covered. I would be interested to know how often you use the insurance and your experience with Staples and Sprint.

Q. Up until yesterday, my Microsoft Outlook 2007 had been working fine. Now, it gives a message about failing to open properly and asks if i want to open in 'Safe Mode'. When I select yes, it stalls and does not open.

Just so you know... there were 4 automatic Outlook updates to my computer in the last week.

Thanks in advance for your help!
Sherri Miles

Sherri did some research and posted this update:

I did a little tech support for myself and removed one of the Outlook updates. That seems to have resolved the problem. I can now access my Outlook.

Now I have a new question... I have my Outlook e-mails forwarded to my GMail account, but notice that not all of my Outlook e-mails get forwarded to my GMail account. What could be happening?

I'm glad you were able to answer your initial question! However, it's odd that you had to remove an updated to get Outlook working. What was the update you removed?

Regarding Outlook not forwarding to GMail, it depends on how you're doing the forward. Are you forwarding every single email that hits your Outlook Exchange account to GMail? Or, do you have a rule in Outlook that selectively forwards certain emails but not others? If it's the latter, then the logic of the rule may result in emails not meeting the criteria you specified. Check how the rule is defined and which emails are not being forwarded and see if you can see a link.

I assume that you want Outlook forwarded to your GMail because you want to read your email on a mobile device that doesn't support Exchange? Is that the case? If so, let me know what mobile device you're using because I may be able to help you with that.

Sherri provided this update:

The update was KB969907.

As far as the Outlook, yes, I am forwarding every single e-mail to GMail. I am forwarding from Outlook to GMail because the Outlook account is my grad school e-mail that want to have forwarded to GMail now that I've graduated.

I think it may have something to do with the update that I had installed.

That update seems to have been geared to fix issues with Outlook meeting requests so it's odd that it affected anything else. Do you access the grad school Outlook account via Outlook Web Access (i.e., a web site) or using the outlook client? If you're not using the client, you can set it up to get your grad school email.

Tech Tuesday #3 - Archive - June 23rd, 2009 (Slow Laptop, CPU's, Load Sharepoint, Vista Windows, iTunes Sync, DOS, Google Voice)

09/21/2011 12:35:27 PM

Q. My laptop is running REALLY slowly! What can I do?
Zainab Ntaamah

Laptops run slow for a number of reasons. A few easy to do things you can do include:

1. Make sure you use it on a flat hard surface (like a desk). Many people like to use laptops on, well, their laps or other soft surfaces like beds or pillows. While comfortable, this can actually restrict airflow through the laptop which can cause heat to build up inside the machine. Since laptops produce a lot of heat, this can lead to a gradual slowdown in performance. You probably have a heat problem if the machine works fine once you turn it on but eventually slows down.

2. Uninstall unnecessary/unused applications. I often download software just to try it but eventually end up not using it. These programs often run in the background taking up valuable computer resources. By removing them, you free up these resources for tasks you are actually doing.

3. Defragment the hard drive. While I've seen mixed reviews about the usefulness of this process, some swear that it works wonders for performance. Basically, as you use a computer, it writes data (called fragments) all over the hard drive. As this data spreads over the disc, it takes more and more time for the drive head... Read More to seek out the data you need. This slows things down. Defragmenting the hard drive moves this data closer together to make it easier to find. Windows has a built in defragmentation program that you can run.

4. Backup and Reinstall Windows. This is probably the best solution, but it also takes the most time. Backup your hard drive to another computer or to an external hard drive and reinstall Windows. First, make sure you have the Windows installation disc that should have come with your computer (sometimes called a recovery disc). Once you reinstall Windows, you'll see a noticeable increase in speed. Then reinstall your applications.

292

Q. Good morning!!! Question: When a processor processes what is it ACTUALLY processing?
Michael Dickens II

A. A CPU (central processing unit) is in many ways the "brains" of a computer. It processes instructions given to it by the operating system (e.g., Windows, Mac OS, Linux, Unix, etc.). These instructions include things like requests to fetch data, execute commands, and write the data back. Just like your brain still works even when you're asleep, the CPU still processes even when you're not doing anything with the computer. It runs a number of housekeeping background processes and waits for you to do something requiring work.

I can get fairly detailed and technical if you want more information, but that is the basic idea behind what a CPU processes.

Q. Is there a way in SharePoint to load multiple files without checking them in individually?
Misty Shannon

A. I'll assume you're using the latest version of Sharepoint and that you're uploading data into a document library. Sharepoint usually provides an option to upload multiple files when you try to upload one file. You should see a link on the upload screen. Another trick I have used is to directly upload the data to the shared folder. Whenever you upload a file to Sharepoint, your Windows machine will map a drive to the Sharepoint server. You'll usually find it under your Network Places in Windows Explorer. This works just like a folder on your hard drive, and you can copy and paste documents directly into it. Once you're done, you should see them in the Sharepoint front end.

Q. all of a sudden my windows open up smaller instead in full screen mode...how do i get them to go back? btw i am running vista
Tiffany Clepper Uelner

Tech Tuesdays

A. I've read about this happening to Vista users, and it seems that a patch was pushed by Microsoft that caused the problem. Have you installed a patch recently? One suggested solution was to right click the white "X" on the upper right corner of every window and deselect "autohide". Another suggestion was to hit the F11 key which should make the program go full screen. Unfortunately, I'm not on a Vista computer right now, but try those suggestions and let me know how it goes. If it doesn't work, I'll install Vista on a test machine and continue to look for a solution.

Q. How can I sync an ipod to two itunes libraries on two different computers? Plus, when I sync, I don't want to erase either the apps (stored on a library on computer A) or the music/photos (stored on a library on computer B)?

Hope this qualifies for Tech Tuesday :) Thanks Anjuan!
Carrie Belsito

A. This definitely qualifies for Tech Tuesday! I watch a lot of "how to" technology podcasts (which is one reason I love doing Tech Tuesday so I can share what I learn with my friends), and I JUST heard CNET discuss this in a video. I normally don't like just sharing links when I provide solutions, but I think that Molly Wood (a CNET editor) does a great job of explaining how to sync iTunes to two computers in this video:

http://cnettv.cnet.com/sync-your-ipod-two-computers/9742-1_53-50004835.html

Let me know if this helps!

Q. How do I load DOS into high memory?
Johnny Wood

A. Load *,8,1. Oh, sorry, that's for something else!

So, I assume you're running Windows 3.1 or straight DOS. In my research, I saw two ways to do this by editing either the AUTOEXEC.BAT or the CONFIG.SYS file in the root directory (which I'll also assume is C:\). The CONFIG.SYS option seemed more sound to me so here is the solution (of course, you're changing key OS files so be careful):

1. Use a text editor (NOT MS Word) like Notepad to edit the file.... Read More
2. Locate the CONFIG.SYS file in the root of the C drive and open it. Make sure the top of the file has these two lines:

DEVICE=C:\WINDOWS\HIMEM.SYS
DEVICE=C:\WINDOWS\EMM386.EXE NOEMS

3. Look for a "DOS=" line in CONFIG.SYS. If it's there replace it with:

DOS=HIGH,UMB

If not, add it to the end of CONFIG.SYS.

4. Save the file and reboot. DOS will be loaded into high memory getting past the 640 kb low memory limit.

Let me know if this works (and what DOS app or game you're trying to run)!

Q. I didn't know there was a such thing as Google Voice, so I've benefited already!
Robin Murphy

Yes, Google Voice is very cool! You have to be a Grand Central user (purchased by Google not too long ago) to qualify for an existing account. It's basically a VOIP service like Skype that allows people to call your Google Voice number which you can then use to forward the call to multiple devices. I use it as an online answering machine, but I plan to use it more in the future.

Tech Tuesday #4 - Archive - June 30th, 2009 (CMS, Mobile Flash, FB Logo, Splunk/ArcSight, FB Highlights, PC Specs, PC Speed)

09/22/2011 11:28:53 AM

Q. What do you consider the best open source enterprise CMS and why? It must be of the GPL software license type. (I thought I would give you an interesting challenge to start your Tuesday).
-Mark Slater

A. My friend Leo added this comment:

I've had good success with Alfresco. It has a powerful type definition system, strong access controls, and is highly extensible through JavaScript or Java. It's more of an enterprise product, so it's less "fun" than alternatives, such as Joomla! or Drupal, but some people like to use it for the back-end and Drupal, Django, or Liferay on the front-end for the widget support.
-Leo Yamamoto

This is my fourth weekly Tech Tuesday, and they are usually quite challenging. One reason I do them is to share my expertise and help the community of people who are networked with me on Facebook. That being said, you've provided my first enterprise level question!

First, I need to get some definitions out of the way since I don't think everyone will understand the acronyms. Bear with me because I know this is obvious to you. CMS stands for Content Management System, and they are used to store, share, and manage data. This includes the usual work files like documents, spreadsheets, presentations, etc. Most also provide some form of version control and workflow. The most common enterprise class CMS software titles are Microsoft Sharepoint and Oracle Content Management. However, you want software with a GPL license. GPL stands for GNU Public License which, for simplicity's sake, means that the software can be distributed and used for non-commercial purposes and the source code for the software must be publicly available. Applications with a GPL license are often referred to as free software (the most well-known example being Linux).

Ok, now that I have gotten a foundation laid, let me make a few assumptions. I assume you have a well-trained a capable IT department that is familiar with both commercial and open source CMS systems. Also, I assume you want a cross-platform (i.e., Windows, Linux, and Unix) solution that supports common productivity formats (like MS Office). Finally, I'll assume that you want out of the box functionality and do not plan to do a lot of custom development. If any of these assumptions are false, then my answer may not completely fit your needs.

Now I can directly answer your question. Leo (who is a friend of mine and has a lot of IT expertise) has already recommended Alfresco. Since you wanted a GPL software solution, I assume he's referring to Alfresco LABS which is the open source version. I'm glad Leo has had good luck with it, and I think it's a good recommendation. Leo rightly called them "fun alternatives", but my direct experience with open source CMS solutions include Joomla! and Drupal. I think Drupal is more powerful from an implementation perspective, but I strongly dislike its usage paradigm and the interface. I personally like Joomla! better because it is much easier to use and relatively feature rich.

Other alternatives I found in my research include Sensenet (which requires the .NET framework), Jumper, and the open source version of Knowledge Tree. However, my official list of recommendations (in order from most recommended to least), would include Joomla!, Drupal, and Alfresco LABS.

I do want to add some of the issues with using GPL software in the enterprise. First, support can be difficult to find since many vendors don't officially support their products or charge for support. So, you're usually dependent on your own IT support team or a broad community of enthusiasts. Second, security vulnerabilities can be a problem since penetration testing may not be a priority for the vendor. So, I would devote a considerable amount of your testing budget to security testing. Finally, performance and scalability can also be a concern so I would also spend more time in testing that aspect of whatever solution you chose.

Mark later responded with this comment:

Hi Leo and Anjuan, I think it is really great that you are doing this Anjuan! It is great you are willing to help others and share your knowledge with your FB firends. I imagine it is also a wonderful process for learning about new technologies and solving real world problems. I am in the process for rolling out Typo3 as my company's enterprise Content Management System solution. We were a publishing company with books and articles that dealt with wellness and eldercare issues prior to my employment. I have taken them to an online version of the product that is sold to companies and through insurance brokers. Our current CVS is home grown and has some limitations. I am moving to a more modular system and hope Typo3 will meet my needs. Leo I would be interested in hearing about your success with Alfresco.

Thank you

Mark Slater

And I responded:

I host Tech Tuesday, but, working in the technology industry (and enjoying tech), I have built relationships with quite a few technologists like Leo. I appreciate the time they take to add their perspective to the conversation. In my opinion, serving others is the heart of online social networking (or networking of any kind for that manner), so Tech Tuesday is one way I can give back to the community.

I hope you keep us posted on how things go with Typo3 or Alfresco.

**Q. Which cell phones can support Flash... legitimately or not?
-Micco Phey**

A. If you mean "play YouTube videos" when you say support Flash, then a wide variety of cell phones can do that. Even the Samsung Propel that I use can play YouTube videos as well as the iPhone. However, if you mean full flash support with the ability to play a wide variety of Flash video (not just YouTube) and run Flash applications in a browser (like games) then very few do. This requires adoption of Adobe's Flash Lite application which has not been widely done by US carriers. A few of the Nokia E-series and N-series phones do, and the upcoming Android based HTC Hero is rumored to do so as well. A few carriers like Verizon, Sony Ericsson, and LG has also announced plan to incorporate Flash Lite. So, again, if you want full Flash support, then there are slim pickings for now. However, you can watch YouTube videos on a wide variety of handsets.

Q. How does one paste the facebook logo in an email signature (and link it back to my fan page)? My current workaround is to place the entire (long) link in my email signature for now.

Let me know if this question doesn't meet the Tech Tuesday criteria. Thanks!
-Jenifer Price

A. Yes, this is a perfect question for Tech Tuesday! I'm not sure what email client you're using, but I have successfully copied and pasted graphics straight into emails using Microsoft Outlook. This is harder to do if you use online email services like Hotmail, Yahoo Mail, or GMail.

The best way to link to a Facebook profile or a Facebook fan page is to sign up for a vanity URL. Facebook made this available to all profiles last week (e.g., my vanity URL is facebook.com/anjuan). You have to have a certain number of users (I think 1000 or more) signed up for you fan page to have a vanity URL for it, however.

Q. Friend is asking how to get Twitter to update her FB status. Did mine so long ago, I can't remember how, and can't seem to figure it out either. Thanks.
-Jennifer Lesseraux Collins

A. Facebook has a Twitter application that allows you to have your Twitter update also update your Facebook status. I also recommend ping.fm which allows you to send one update to several services (including Facebook, Twitter, WordPress, Linkedin, Plurk, etc.)

Tech Tuesdays

Q. Whichis a better tool enterprise wide...Splunk or ArcSight?
-Maria Andrews

A. While similar, I see Splunk and ArcSight as similar products that serve two different purposes. Splunk is geared more toward enterprise system monitoring. It primarily gathers data from sources like log files, servers, and storage devices in order to diagnose and solve system problems. ArcSight serves a similar function, but it is more focused on security and intrusion detection. Both are enterprise class solutions, but I am more familiar with the respective solutions provided by IBM's Tivoli Framework.

I will say that a good open source monitoring solution is Nagios, but you have to run Linux (or other supported version of Unix) to use it.

Q. I don't expect an answer before the end of this day since I am so late. However, how do I close the "highlights" section of my Facebook page that appears on the right hand side? Also, is it possible to "hide" a comment from FB without hiding every post that an individual made?
-Dee McKinney

A. One limitation of Facebook is the inability to customize the user interface. So, you won't be able to move the highlights section that appears on your Facebook Homepage. You can, however, simply click on the "Profile" link at the top of the page and bookmark it. The highlights section does not appear on your Profile page.

If you hover your mouse over the right side of a comment on your Profile page, you'll see a "Remove" button. If you click it, you'll have the option to remove that comment, thereby hiding it.

Q. What's a good desktop pc these days? What are good mid to high end specs I should
be looking for?
-Patrick Long

A. This is a good time to buy a desktop due to relatively low prices caused by the slow economy. I'll cover the major features. Of course, opinions

300

vary, but hopefully, this will provide you ballpark figures:

Mid-range specs: Dual Core Processor (AMD or Intel), 4 GB RAM, 250 GB Storage, DVD Burner, integrated graphics and sound card, 19" LCD monitor

High-end specs: Quad Core Processor (Intel's Core i7 is very nice), 8 GM Ram, 1 TB Storage, Blu-Ray burner, discrete graphics (e.g., nvidia or ATi) and sound card, 24" LCD monitor

By the way, when it comes to storage, get as much as possible. In fact, for a high-end setup, I would consider a NAS device that you plug into a router that other devices can use. The same principle applies to RAM. Buy as much as you can afford.

Q. Where can I find info about removing processes, & unecessary programs for a new laptop purchase 2 heighten performance? -SuprStarr

A. I highly recommend Black Viper's site (http://www.blackviper.com/) as a great place to find tweaks to improve system performance.

Tech Tuesday #5 - Archive - July 7th, 2009 (Movie Maker, What is RSS, Improve Browser Speed, Laptop and Zune Charge Problems)

09/27/2011 05:31:47 AM

Q. This is great! On Movie Maker, how can I extend the time of a clip transition i.e. Fade in/out, etc.?
Altrivice Revis

A. I assume you're referring to Windows Movie Maker which is the built in video editing software that comes with Windows (at least XP and up). I'll also assume you're using Windows Vista. Yes, you can extend a clip by adding a transition. I prefer the Timeline view to the default Storyboard view so try using that. You can drag video... Read More clips to the Timeline, split them, and (if you right click on them), add Effects, Fade In, and Fade Out.

Windows Movie Maker is often criticized for being under powered, but it works well for making simple videos. However, if you want more powerful video editing features, you can try Adobe Premiere Elements (or the full Adobe Premiere).

Q. What is an RSS feed and why would I want to subscribe to it? Is it the same as a newsletter?
Heather R Green

A. Leo provided a great link (http://www.youtube.com/watch?v=0klgLsSxGsU) to a video that explains it well. I think that a simple way to understand RSS is in terms of magazines. Before RSS, people used the internet like browsing the magazine rack at a book store. You would have to look for the particular issues you liked while overlooking the ones in which you were not interested... Read More. RSS is like having a subscription to your favorite magazines. So, you get your favorite web sites delivered to you instead of browsing the internet.

Many web sites offer RSS feeds of their content. There are many RSS readers, but my favorite is Google Reader (which is free).

302

Q. Can you share a more effective way/steps to to clean your browser's memory to enable better performance? Should I just empty the Temp folder?
Ron Eldridge

A. Poor browser performance can be caused by a variety of factors. One quick thing you can try is to clear the browser's cache. Web browsers often store parts of a web page as you browse the web so that they load faster when you return to pages you have visited before. However, the accumulation of these files can, in aggregate, slow the browser. How you clear the cache varies by browser, but I found instructions for several browsers here:

http://kb.iu.edu/data/ahic.html

Furthermore, some browsers are simply faster than others so you may gain speed by switching to a faster browser. Different browsers perform in different ways depending on what you're doing with it, but the fastest browsers are usually Opera, Google Chrome, and Firefox. Internet Explorer is usually the slowest.

Finally, if your computer is running slow, then your browser will, too. So, you can speed up your computer by doing things like removing unused programs, defragmenting the hard drive, and adding RAM.

Q. I have a laptop that cuts off on me when it wants to. It's charging (I think) , what could possibly be wrong with it?
Talia Clemons

A. I'll assume this happens whether the laptop is plugged into an AC outlet or running off the battery. It sounds like your battery may be undergoing what is called a "memory effect". This often happens to older batteries, but it can also happen to new ones. Basically, after several partial charges, the battery thinks it's fully charged when it actually is not . You can recondition it, but unplugging the laptop, run the battery until the laptop shuts off, plug in the laptop (with it turned off), charge the battery to full capacity. Repeat this three or four times. If it works, then your battery will last much longer.

You could also have a defective battery or power cord. If possible, try using a compatible battery or power cord and see if you still have the problem. If the problem goes away, then permanently replace whichever one was not working.

Q. Ok AnJ - my Zune doesn't stay charged long....what's REALLY going on.......it's my only salvation when traveling. HELP a sista out. Tks.
Dukes Hazard

A. Regarding your Zune, it may have the same memory effect I described to Talia. Try doing what I suggested to her (discharge and then fully charge a few times) and see if it works. If that doesn't work, then the nice thing about the Zune (as opposed to an iPod or iPhone) is that you can purchase a replacement battery.

Q. This is great! On Movie Maker, how can I extend the time of a clip transition i.e. Fade in/out, etc.?
Altrivice Revis

A. I assume you're referring to Windows Movie Maker which is the built in video editing software that comes with Windows (at least XP and up). I'll also assume you're using Windows Vista. Yes, you can extend a clip by adding a transition. I prefer the Timeline view to the default Storyboard view so try using that. You can drag video clips to the Timeline, split them, and (if you right click on them), add Effects, Fade In, and Fade Out.

Tech Tuesday #6 - Archive - July 14th, 2009 (EHR in a Recession, Best Gadgets of 2009, URI too Large, Virus, 3G or 3GS)

09/28/2011 11:26:26 PM

Q. How can one capitalize an EHR system and meet federal compliance standards for a healthcare organization when the capital markets are frozen, reimbursements are declining, operating costs are expanding due to energy and labor costs and it is current policy bears both civil and criminal penalties as well as covenants to reduce revenues from government payers who fail to comply in a timely fashion? Just like planes are falling apart in the sky due to lack of capital for maintenance.. your healthcare is compromised due to lack of adequate funding. Your thoughts?
Shawn Fry

A. Thanks for posing a question with such interesting challenges! I enjoy seeing more enterprise level Tech Tuesday questions to complement the consumer technology questions I usually receive. I also want to admit upfront that you're raising an issue with many complications.

From a technology point of view, capitalizing an EHR (Electronic Health Record) system in a time of high visibility, high costs, and intense government scrutiny is similar to past IT compliance projects like the Y2K problem and SOX (Sarbanes Oxley). These IT projects were extremely costly and had the additional complexity of high media coverage (which will eventually come to Health IT). I think a variety of techniques were useful then and will be helpful now.

I firmly believe that technology is usually the least important aspect of the decisions a CIO should make. Usually, the number of realistic options are small and software selection (while nontrivial) is often a mature process.

The challenge for working as an effective CIO lies with relationships instead of simply being a master of technology. Difficult economic times coupled with the threat of federal penalties reiterate the importance of partnering with your compliance officer as well the project management office. The case you can present to them will be based on long term view of the problems facing healthcare providers. A key selling point of

implementing EHR system is the cost savings they provide. While I believe this is true, I don't think that the cost savings will justify the cost of implementation for most companies. A better justification is the likely increase of government regulation of healthcare including stricter privacy rules. Large fines will be imposed for non-compliance and future government funds to support healthcare IT initiatives will probably favor organizations that are already compliant.
July 15 at 12:14am · Delete

In my opinion, the threat of government penalties and the loss of government funding are two defensible reasons you can get compliance/audit and PMO on your side. They can work with you to flesh out your argument (and add empirical support to the NPV, ROI, and other financial analysis I'm sure you've already done) and present it to the decision makers in your organization.

Of course, many companies are short-sighted and prone to not look much farther than the next annual budgeting cycle so presenting a long term view to defend capitalizing your EHR system may have limited effect. Hopefully, your organization has leaders that are as reasonable as you are!

I hope that helps! I'll think about this further and add more detail if anything comes to mind.

Q. If you have $500 to spend on new gadgets for the rest of 2009, what do you buy?
Scott Davis

A. It depends (Big Answer # . . . . 3?) on your areas of interest (music, video, gaming, etc) and if you would rather get one big item or several small ones. I'll list a few items that I know will cost under $500, and, hopefully, you'll find a few of them compelling.

- External Hard Drive: I'm a big believer in backing up computer data because every hard drive has an unknown expiration date. You should buy as much as possible so I would go with a 1 TB model. I like Seagate drives the best. ($175)

- Netbook: Although not as powerful as full notebooks, netbooks provide access to web sites and applications like office. the Asus, Acer, HP, and

Dell models are seem nice. ($300)

- Verizon Mifi: This device gives you a portable personal hotspot so you can get online anywhere there's a Verizon signal. Up to five devices can be connected to this mobile Wifi connection.
($40 - $60 per month)

- Flip UltraHD: This is a nice compact camera that records in HD. It has a flip out USB port that makes it easy to connect to a computer and upload high quality video.
$200

- GPS: I'm not sure how often you travel, but a GPS device is a nice gadget for your car. Your iPhone will have GPS capability, but even a cheap dedicated GPS will have a few features the iPhone will lack. I like the Garmin Nuvi and the TomTom ONE.
($100 - $300)

- Amazon Kindle 2: While I'm sure that Apple will release a tablet computer that will also be a killer electronic reader, the best on the market is the Kindle 2. It recently dropped in price so now is a good time to buy because it probably won't get any cheaper. I like the Whispernet feature which allows you to browser Amazon, buy books, and have them wirelessly sent to the Kindle 2 over the air.
($359)

Hopefully, something on this list works for you. I know it includes stuff I would buy!

Shawn Fry added this great insight:

As for you Scott.. I would get a HTC TouchPro 2. I have an HTC Kaiser (older version) and it is my cell phone, 32 GB storage, Satellite TV with Tivo, GPS, Media Center, VoIP phone so I can receive my office calls anywhere in the world or for cheap international dialing, one button turns it into a Wifi Router for my laptop or any computer to give access to my 3G network (1MB/sec speed) and basically my "everything device". I also use it to RDP to my servers if needed and it manages all my email not only securely, but meet federal compliance standards. That is just the start. It is worth every bit of the cost and should be even less than $500 if you have a contract.

**Q. I just tried to play Scrabble on Facebook and the page won"t load.
It keeps saying that the "URI is too large" What does that mean?
Heather R Green**

A. URI stands for Uniform Resource Identifier and is just a way to identify
something on the web. Your particular error indicates that the web page
you're on is sending a URL that has too many characters (or bytes) in it.
This is often caused by programs that pass variables (or pieces of code) to
the server in the URL. You'll often see this is you look in the address bar of
a page you're visiting and you see a question marks (like "?ref=profile"). If
a program passes too many variables, then you get the error. This also
happens if the program passes cookies in the URL.

You may have better luck switching to a different browser that better
manages long URL's or you can try clearing out your cookies in your
current browser. These were two common suggestions I found in my
research into the "URI is too large" error.

**Q. Hey Anjuan. A friend of mine got a virus on here yesterday and has
been having a hard time getting rid of it. She's run a couple of
antivirus' but her system is still crashing. Any suggestions? (I know it's
not Tech Tuesday but it's an emergency - she works from home!)
Thanks!
Zainab Ntaamah**

A. Sure, I hope I can help! Is she sure she has a virus? Is an antirvirus
program giving her a warning that she is infected? I'll assume that's the
case, but people sometimes think they have virus when it could be another
issue.

I'll assume she's running Windows Vista. She should try booting into Safe
Mode. She can do this by rebooting the computer and holding the F8 key
while it's starting up. She'll get a window called "Windows Advanced
Options Menu" where she can select Safe Mode. This is a very minimalistic
mode where Windows will run just basic operations. If she can successfully
use Safe Mode, I recommend she immediately copy the data off of the
computer onto an external hard drive.

Once her data is safe, have her try running the anti-virus while in Safe Mode. Hopefully, that will clear up the infection.

Zainab later provided this update:

Thanks! It was a link that she saw as a friend's status telling her to watch a home video. When she clicked it it set it as her status and then kicked her off facebook and started showing porn, then shut her system down. She ran Norton, and then another one she found online on a forum about that virus, but it's still giving her a hard time.

I'll forward this to her.

Q. I am buying an iPhone. Is the 3GS worth the extra $100 over the 3G? Should I get the Apple Care warranty or roll with the standard? Will you tell me the must-have apps so I don't limit myself to Maps and Urbanspoon?
Scott Davis

A. I assume you don't already have an iPhone and you're already using AT&T as your carrier. If those are both true, then I would recommend getting the iPhone 3GS. This is primarily due two key features that were introduced with the 3GS: the ability to capture and playback video and the better hardware (processor, memory, and graphics chip) that was introduced in the 3GS. There are a few other cool features of the 3GS (like the anti-oil screen, compass, and voice control), but for me the key improvements are video capability and hardware.

Regarding the warranty question, you get one year of hardware repair coverage and 90 days of technical support (both calculated from the date of purchase) when you buy an iPhone. Apple Care just extends those to two years. I'm not a big fan of buying additional coverage simply because I rarely use them. If you think you'll call Apple's support a lot or if you just want peace of mind, then I say go with Apple Care.

I have to admit I'm not very familiar with iPhone applications beyond the big ones. It also depends on what services you use and if they have an iPhone interface. For example, I have a Slingbox at home so the iPhone Slingplayer would be key. However, that wouldn't be the case for someone without a Slingbox.

Some of the top apps I've read about are Beejive (multi-protocol instant messaging), Fandango (local movie listings), Pandora/Last.FM (streaming music), and Yelp (similar to Urbanspoon, but it can't hurt to try it out to compare). Some good games a podcast I listen to just recommended are Mass Effect Galaxy and Hero of Sparta.

Keep in mind that games that take advantage of the improved hardware specs of the 3GS haven't appeared yet, but you should see them soon.

I hope that helps!

Scott later provided this update:

Thanks, Anjuan. I went with the 3GS and should get it next week. I am skipping the warranty because Amex doubles the length of factory warranties anyway.

Tech Tuesday #7 - Archive - July 21st, 2009 (Blue Screen of Death, Google Voice, Netbooks, Virtual Memory Low, Audio, CMS)

10/07/2011 03:37:43 PM

Q. What is the quickest way to recover from the blue screen of death at start up that shows C:/Windows/System32/Config/System showing that the file is either corrupted or missing?
Thanx ;)
Maria Andrews

A. That error indicates that something is wrong with your hard drive. The C:/Windows/System32/Config/System folder contains critical files that Windows loads at start up, and, since it can't find those files, it cannot load the operating system. You have a few options.

First, you can try to repair your computer using the installation disk. I assume you're using Windows Vista so insert the Windows Vista installation disk into your CD-ROM and reboot the computer (you may have to change your BIOS settings to boot from the CD-ROM drive instead of the hard drive). Once it loads, you'll see an option to repair your computer. Try running that.

Second, you can remove the hard drive from the computer and place it as a secondary slave drive in a working computer. Boot up the working computer and it will see the secondary drive. Run check disk (chkdisk) on the secondary drive.

Third, you can load a live Linux distribution like Knoppix from the CD-ROM drive of your computer. This will launch a Linux based operating system that runs from your CD-ROM drive (and available RAM memory) instead of from your hard drive. This will at least let you see if you can access that hard drive.

Whatever option you choose, it's important that you immediately back up the data on your computer. You can get a 500 GB external drive for about $80. The error you're getting suggests that the hard drive is failing so I suggest you pull the data off soon.

Q. What is google voice?
Karen Ramsey Davis

A. Google Voice is a free online service that lets you have a telephone number that people can call. When people call, Google Voice will send the call to one or more telephony devices (e.g., home phone, cell phone, work phone, etc.) You can take the call on whatever device you want to use. It also provides voice mail capability and transcribes voice mail to text (although it does so imperfectly).

For those who have supported phones, Google Voice can also be used to place and receive phone calls using a data plan instead of cell phone minutes.

Google Voice was made available to GrandCentral (the original company Google bought) initially, but Google has been sending out numbers by invite only. You can sign up for an invite at voice.google.com.

Q. Also, looking at buying a cheap laptop (remember my post from several weeks ago, trying to find one to rent for the weekend). I am thinking $399, just to travel with, internet (both wireless and wired), standard office apps, maybe even playing dvds for plane or road trips. I saw a couple at office depot at this price but they had a strangely named processor, not Intel but ATOM? Should I care for such a cheap laptop? Are there processors that I should stay away from? Battery life is also a big concern. The one I looked at said 9 hours life, 8 cell (or something). Does that really mean 9 hours or is there something else I should be looking at. Thanks!
Karen Ramsey Davis

A.
Scott Davis provided this perspective:

You want to make sure there's enough processing power to run DVDs without skipping. For this reason, I'd be wary of something like a NetBook or low-end laptop for DVD playback. You might consider a dedicated portable DVD player for this purpose (in addition to your laptop). They are fairly inexpensive.

Those low powered cheap computers you're talking about are called netbooks. They are meant to cover the gap between smart phones and full laptops. The netbook name is based on the fact that people are increasingly using internet applications instead of the traditional hard drive installed applications. For example, people use GMail instead of Outlook, Google Docs instead of MS Office, Youtube instead of Movie Player, etc.

The Atom processor is the CPU created by Intel to be used in low power devices like netbooks. Almost of them use the Intel Atom so you won't have to worry about other options.

Scott, is right in that a dedicated DVD player would be a better option if you only wanted to use it to watch DVD's. First, most netbooks don't have an optical drive so you would have to rip the DVD to the hard drive first. Second, even if you did rip the DVD, the playback would probably not be as crisp as on a dedicated DVD player.

One big benefit of netbooks is the long battery life. While you probably won't get the battery life advertised, many of them last six hours or more. This is because the Intel Atom processor consumes less electricity than the one used in laptops. Also, netbooks are designed to be used as portable computing devices that have to run for a long time before charges.

I think a netbook is a good option is you want something that is cheap (under $500), small, portable, has great battery life, and will be used for light computing. So, web surfing and creating MS Office documents would work. However, if you want to edit video, play video games, watch HD video, or work on spreadsheets with a lot of columns, then a full notebook (or desktop) would be a much better option. Netbooks are good choices for college students to take from class to class or maybe a professional to take to meetings. However, I see them as a compliment to a full powered computer; not a replacement.

One more point about netbooks. I would stay away from anything under $299. Good models are the ones offered by Asus, Acer, Dell, HP, and IBM.

Q. Why is my computer so slow? And why do I get the "virtual memory too low" warning? How do I fix it?

Tech Tuesdays

Danielle Ochoa Brown

A. Danielle: The "virtual memory too low" message means that your page file is too small. A page file is a physical file on your computer's hard drive that Windows uses to supplement low physical RAM. You can either increase the size of the page file (a good Microsoft Knowledge Base article about this is here: http://support.microsoft.com/kb/826513) or add more physical RAM to your computer. Adding more physical RAM will probably also speed up your computer. Consult the documentation that came with your computer for instructions on the kind of RAM it uses and how much it can take.

I've gotten a question about a slow computer before so I hope you don't mind if I paste in my original solutions:

1. Uninstall unnecessary/unused applications. I often download software just to try it but eventually end up not using it. These programs often run in the background taking up valuable computer resources. By removing them, you free up these resources for tasks you are actually doing.

2. Defragment the hard drive. While I've seen mixed reviews about the usefulness of this process, some swear that it works wonders for performance. Basically, as you use a computer, it writes data (called fragments) all over the hard drive. As this data spreads over the disc, it takes more and more time for the drive head... Read More to seek out the data you need. This slows things down. Defragmenting the hard drive moves this data closer together to make it easier to find. Windows has a built in defragmentation program that you can run.

3. Backup and Reinstall Windows. This is probably the best solution, but it also takes the most time. Backup your hard drive to another computer or to an external hard drive and reinstall Windows. First, make sure you have the Windows installation disc that should have come with your computer (sometimes called a recovery disc). Once you reinstall Windows, you'll see a noticeable increase in speed. Then reinstall your applications

Q. When I click on the icon to adjust pc volume, I get a warning that says Windows-Corrupt File The file or directory \WINDOWS\Prefetch\SNDVOL32.EXE-0EC6FD20.pf is corrupt and unreadable. Please run the Chkdsk utility.

Tamieka Jackson Tavares

A. It looks like either the audio driver for your computer has been damaged or some other system file related to audio playback is not working. You can try a few things:

1. If you have Windows XP, you can use the XP installation disk to repair your computer. Restart your computer with the install disk in your hard drive, press any key when prompted, and choose the "repair computer option". You can do the same thing with the Windows Vista install disk.

2. Test your Direct X drivers by using the Direct X Diagnostic utility. Press the Start button and then select Run. In the Run box, type dxdiag and press Enter. It will scan and test your drivers as well as allow you to perform other tests.

3. Go the web site of the manufacturer who made your computer (e.g., Dell, HP, Gateway, IBM, etc.) and search for your computer's model number. Download and install the audio driver that matches your computer.

Q. I'm setting up a site for potentially many, many users to share text, photos, and videos related to a specific topic. I want to be able to customize everything. PHP is my language of choice and AJAX interfaces are a plus. Users will be able to join content teams and do all kinds of madness. I don't feel like reinventing the wheel, so what should I use? WordPress maybe? I want the solution to be scalable so if I had millions of users and I could support the bandwidth, my web app of choice wouldn't be problematic. The site may be commercial at some point. Thoughts?
Scott Davis

A. It sounds like you want a CMS (Content Management System), and the good news is there are a lot of open source choices available. Most of them use the LAMP (Linux Apache MySQL, PHP/Python/Perl/other-languages-starting-with-P) stack so you should be able to use your language of choice with most of them. I'll assume that you will provide your own web hosting since it may be difficult to go commercial if you use a third party hosted solution. Also, you'll have far more flexibility if you host it yourself.

You have a ton of choices. There is a website that lets you "test drive"

315

several open source CMS solutions (http://www.opensourcecms.com/). It nicely splits them into those that use PHP and those that use aspx. Years ago, I used a previous version of the site, and it is even more useful than back then.

Despite the many choices, I think it's going to come down to WordPress, Joomla!, or Drupal. I would add Movable Type (which became free in 2007), but it uses Perl.

I like WordPress, and it's the CMS I use for my blogs. While there are many templates and plugins available for WordPress, I think it can be challenging to extend it beyond anything but a blog. I tried my own installations of Drupal and Joomla! (let me disclose that this was a couple of years ago) on my own web server, and I can say that Joomla! provides a better out of the box experience, a wide array of features, and a much easier learning curve. I also believe that Joomla! performs and scales better than Drupal (assuming, as you said, that bandwidth is not a problem) I have heard that Drupal can be very powerful, but I personally hate the administration panels and doing even basic tasks seem to take 10 more steps than necessary.

So, I would go with Joomla! (or the CMS from which it forked, Mambo). Of course, these are free open source solutions. I can provide commercial CMS recommendations if you would like.

Q. What is the quickest way to recover from the blue screen of death at start up that shows C:/Windows/System32/Config/System showing that the file is either corrupted or missing?
Thanx ;)
Maria Andrews

A. That error indicates that something is wrong with your hard drive. The C:/Windows/System32/Config/System folder contains critical files that Windows loads at start up, and, since it can't find those files, it cannot load the operating system. You have a few options.

Tech Tuesday #8 - Archive - July 28th, 2009 (Web 2.0, Extended Warranties, IP, Google Voice, Treo to Blackberry, Tagged Picts)

10/11/2011 01:35:43 PM

Q. How will Web 2.0 transform the public sector?
Brandy Hays

A. First, let me define Web 2.0. While "2.0" would suggest that new features or capabilities have been added to a product, Web 2.0 is no different from Web 1.0 in terms of the technology that underlies the internet. However, it does describe the change from the internet as a one way publishing system (similar to brochures) to an interactive experience that allows anyone to contribute content. So, Web 2.0 does not really describe new technology but is more a way of describing the new design and programming principles applied to web sites. I personally don't care for the term, but I'll use it for the sake of discussion.

To specifically answer your question, I think "transform" may be too strong of a word. However, I do think that Web 2.0 will enhance and expand the public sector as it has other industries. By allowing government entities to directly interact with those who use their products and services, a better alignment between those entities and those customers can be created. Furthermore, customers will have a voice (via Twitter, Facebook, blogs, etc.) for voicing their praise or disgust with offerings from the public sector. Public sector companies who are smart will even apply the information they gather from use of Web 2.0 to how they design products and services. So, I think Web 2.0 will impact public relations, marketing, customer service, and operations for the public sector. However, I don't think it will necessarily be different from how Web 2.0 will change other industries, although the details will be different.

Q. Extended warranties on high-priced electronics. Yes or no?
Willie Jefferson

A. I am not a fan of extended warranties. First, most high end electronics have been designed and built with enough quality management to not fail within the free warranty you get with the product. If you buy an expensive

317

high definition television, it probably will fail in the first few months of use if it has a manufacturing defect. Of course, we have all owned products that failed on day 366 of a 365 day warranty, but I think that is a very rare occurrence. Second, because retailers know this, they usually use extended warranties for nothing more than additional revenue. Often, you have to jump through hoops to prove that the problem was caused by the manufacturer and not through user error. I have heard that some vendors (specifically Apple and their Apple Care service) are better at this than others, but I personally don't see a justification of the cost.

Despite my dislike of extended warranties, I would say that, if you have a track record of breaking high end electronics and you'll sleep better at night knowing you're covered, then go ahead and buy an extended warranty. Insurance industries exist because people fear disaster, no matter how small the statistical probability, so peace of mind is a very real benefit. For me, I usually am comfortable rolling the dice when it comes to high end electronics.

I will add the caveat that this does not apply to expensive products outside of the consumer electronics category. For example, I believe in buying extended warranties for cars simply because problems often take a while to appear and cars are usually used more rigorously than consumer electronic products. The purchase of an extended warranty on my vehicles has saved me hundreds of dollars on more than one occasion.

My colleague, Scott Davis added this bit of insight:

On the subject of warranties, I've found that there are rare purchases where a warranty is justified. I purchased an extended warranty for my last television and it covered bulb replacements. I ended up getting 3 bulbs and the light engine replaced, saving about $1000 overall by getting the warranty. Since I knew the bulb would need to be replaced at least twice during the warranty period, it just made sense to pay the extra $300. Also, a lot of credit cards (AMEX Gold and Plat come to mind) will extend the life of the manufacturer's warranty automatically. I know AMEX doubles the manuf. warranty period.

Q. Should a website with user-created content be held liable for intellectual property infringement?

318

Anthony Verna

A. I'm probably speaking to a Supreme Court Justice about the Constitution (given your expertise!), but I do not think that a web site with user-generated content should be held liable for infringements of intellectual property by its users. However, this is based on the assumption that the web site has a strict and well communicated policy forbidding the addition of content that is not owned by the users and that good faith actions are taken to remove infringing content once discovered or reported.

My position on this topic is that based on the fact that we don't hold telephone companies liable for crimes that are committed over the lines they own. If I read the text of "1984" to someone over the telephone, I could technically be charged with violating intellectual property laws. However, it would be ridiculous for someone to hold Comcast (the provider of my telephone service) liable for my actions. I think this applies to web sites.

Scott Davis again added an interesting perspective:

Websites need to respond properly when intellectual property owners make a claim on content. If the website owners ignore such claims and fail to take action, they may be found liable. A lot of this is covered in the 1998 Digital Millennium Copyright Act. Of course, your question started with "Should" and my opinion is... it depends!

Scott, thanks for weighing in about extended warranties and IP infringement. I was typing while you were posting so I just saw them.

Anthony, as an intellectual property attorney, I would be very interested in hearing your point of view about the points raised by Scott and I.

Q. I have a Google Voice account now. Why should I care or ever need such a thing?
Scott Davis

A. Regarding Google Voice, I think it's a nice service to have if you want to consolidate all of your voice communication devices. Instead of having a cell, home, and work number, you can publish one number (the Google Voice number) and it will ring all of those devices. Also, I like the way it can transcribe voice mails (of course, as an AT&T iPhone owner, you already have that capability). Also, I think that Google is working to make applications for the iPhone and Blackberry that will allow you to place calls using a data plan (or WiFi connection) instead of using talk time. So, it will bring VOIP to mobile devices. This is the most exciting potential of Google Voice, but I'm sure that telecommunication companies like AT&T will try to block it in the same way they tried to stop Vonage.

I thought about this some more and added this point:

I want to clarify something about Google Voice. Apple recently removed the Google Voice app from the App Store so it may not be available for the iPhone. However, it looks like there will be application support for Blackberry and Android based phones. Other phones can access Google Voice via a browser by going to

Q. Any advice for a trio user switching to a blackberry to enjoy the blackberry experience because right now it is not a good switch? Jackie Carpenter

A. I assume you're using one of the later Treo models (maybe the Treo Pro or the Treo 800w) and a current Blackberry (like the Storm or the Pearl). If that's the case, then they are fairly similar when it comes to form factor, WiFi, Bluetooth, call quality, etc. However, the Treo line has a far greater number of third party applications than the Blackberry line. So, I think you won't have many problems switching.

I would also add that the Apple iPhone and the Palm Pre are a step above anything you'll find from the Palm Treo or any of RIM's Blackberry devices. If you can get one of those, then I think you'll have a much richer experience in terms of web browsing, music, camera, etc.

Jackie later added a few more details:

It's a Curve 8330. I'm asking for an officemate. I have an iPhone, of course it is better than all of that! (Uh-oh, that's not going to spark a debate from the blackberry users, is it?)

Jackie, thanks for the clarification. I think your officemate will find the Blackberry Curve to be a fairly solid device and will have little trouble converting from the Palm platform.

Q. I am familiar with your posts' for Tech Tuesday. I was wondering if you could assist me with a technical on fb? How would I remove a photo from my wall? The photo does not appear in one of my albums, but when I'm on my wall and click the tab photos, there is a photo that I would like removed. Also when using mobile fb the phot is listed under photos. My issue is that when this tab is selected, I do not get the option to edit photos as I have with other photos. The photo was posted to my page by someone else and seems to be included in my profile photos. So how would one remove this photo?

Your help will be greatly appreciated.
Thanks,:)
Name Withheld

A. I'd be happy to help! I assume this picture is in the "Photos of You" section and not in the "Your Albums" section of your Photos tab. "Photos of You" include pictures that anyone (including yourself) have tagged with your name. There are two ways to remove this from your profile. You can use the "remove tag" option (which you should see beneath the picture) which will untag you. This should cause the picture to disappear, but, if someone tags you in the picture again, it will show back up. A more permanent solution can be found if you go to Settings -> Privacy -> Manage -> Profile -> Photos Tagged of You. If you click the drop down, you'll see several options. You can restrict the viewing of tagged pictures of you to "Everyone", "My Network and Friends", "Friends of Friends", "Only Friends", or "Customize" (there may be one or two other options as well). If you select "Customize", you can select "Only Me" which will allow only you to see tagged pictures.

It can be tough to test privacy settings without another account. So, you can try changing the settings and having someone you trust use their Facebook account to see if they are being properly applied. Also, you can create a dummy Facebook account for testing purposes, but I'm sure the people behind Facebook would discourage this.

Q. Can you invite me to join google voice? I hear that it's only available by invite.

321

Tech Tuesdays

Name Withheld

A. I checked my Google Voice account and did a Google search, and it appears that, unfortunately, only Google can send an invitation to join Google Voice. This is odd because I remember that Google used to let GMail users invite people to the service before they opened it up to everyone. So, I think your best bet is to sign up for an invite and then hope that Google sends it to you soon!

Tech Tuesday #9 - Archive - August 4th, 2009 (Outlook, Google Voice, Intel CPU's, AT&T U-Verse, Biz Growth, Buying a Computer)

10/12/2011 12:23:54 PM

Q. Question about Microsoft Outlook. Is it possible to make someone a delegated author of emails, but not a reader. I need to have someone send emails on my behalf, but not be able to read any of my emails.

Let me know if you come up with something.
Kasandra Blyden Maender

A. I assume that you're using Outlook 2007 and that you're already set up to access a properly configured Exchange Server. There are four delegate permission levels: None, Reviewer, Author, and Editor. To allow someone to send emails on your behalf, you have to make them an Author or Editor. I would suggest making them an Author.

Outlook doesn't have a delegate permission level for allowing someone to send emails on your behalf without giving them read access to your inbox. However, you can get around this by making sure that the "Delegate can see my private items" is NOT checked. You can then set up a rule on the Exchange server to automatically mark any email sent to you with the private flag. You'll also have to select any existing email in your inbox and set them with the private flag.

Note, this is a workaround and an enterprising delegate could use a third party email program and some hackery to get around this. However, it should work for most people.

Q. How do you like Google Voice? I'm not sure I understand the draw.
Kyle Keys

A. I like Google Voice because it gives me one number I can publish on, say a business card, that can forward calls to my work phone, home phone, or any other telephone. I also like the online voice mailbox and transcription of voice mails to text. Google Voice also allows me to make free calls in the United States and to make cheap international calls. It's like a free telephone line and voice mailbox.

However, the true potential of Google Voice is the reason telecommunication companies are trying to cripple it. When used on a mobile phone, Google Voice uses the data plan instead of the voice plan to make calls and send SMS text messages. So, it's possible to get a data and voice plan from a carrier (e.g., AT&T) and only use the data plan to make calls and send texts. That is probably the reason that Apple pulled the Google Voice application from the App Store. It gives Google Voice users the ability to reduce their voice plan usage to zero.

Q. OK, I am trying to understand if Intel's Core 2 Solo processor is a good deal or complete crap. I am under the impression that the processor has a dual core platform; however, it is only capable of using one of those cores-not one at a time-but one core period end of story. Can you clarify this for me?
Michael Dickens

A. The "Core 2" is really a brand instead of a distinct processor. So, a "Core 2" could refer to a single core (the Solo) or a dual-core (the Duo) processor. Note, the Solo is just a dual-core processor with one disabled core. So, if you're looking at a "Core 2 Solo", then you only have one core working on your computer. I think you want a "Core 2 Duo" from the context of your question. A "Core 2 Duo" does indeed give Windows Vista two cores to use when processing instructions. You can even go into Task Manager and assign a process to a particular core (by using the "Affinity") setting.

That being said, a true dual-core processor does give a performance increase for certain applications. Windows Vista does a fair job of allocating work to each core when needed. However, for a lot of tasks, one core will just be idle. So, I think it's worth the investment to get a "Core 2 Duo" or even the "Core 2 Quad" (with four cores) if you do processor intensive activities.

Examples of such activities include high end gaming, video editing, and using CAD tools.

Also, if this is for a desktop, you may want to look at the "Core i7" processors which are the successors to the Intel Core 2 brand. You'll pay more, but the Core i7's all come with four cores and offer the latest technology.

Q. Question: does google voice phone calls VoIP, i.e. Using ur data plan or is it using ur voice plan?
Selene Cong

A. Yes, Google Voice does use the data plan when accessed via a mobile application. However, the only devices that currently have supported Google Voice apps are Android and Blackberry phones. The FCC is looking into Apple's pull of the Google Voice application from the App Store so it's possible that Apple may be forced to restore it for download on iPhones.

However, I did some more research and posted this update:

I did some more digging and it looks like AT&T does indeed charge voice plan minutes for calls made over Google Voice. Here's a link that provides more info:

http://gigaom.com/2009/07/28/google-voice-iphone/

However, I have seen other sources on the web that state only the data plan is used. I'll do some more investigating and look for a definitive answer.

I then posted this update:

Regarding Google Voice, making calls using the service does indeed use voice plan minutes. However, sending SMS through Google Voice uses the data plan. To place true VOIP calls an application like Skype or Fring would have to be running on the cell phone.

I hope that clears that up!

Q. Good morning. I recently switched to AT&T Uverse complete home package. I have had always had their internet service since Southwestern Bell first introduced it. Now that there is no longer a direct telephone line into my pc that initially served as my network hub, I experience frequent loss of connection. AT&T has provided a wireless 2wire usb, external adapter. This is all baffling because

another pc that has a wireless internal adapter hardly ever looses connection. I haven't experienced this issue with neither laptop. I've contacted AT&T's level two tier support and their response was remove the usb and reinsert it to establish connection. This hardly appears to be the most optimal solution as it has become a nuisance to continually repeat such a process. In addition, there is no guarantee that a connection will be immediately established.
In short, I'm seeking any viable solution that can at least decrease the number of times connection is lost.
Lisa Carter

A. For those who don't use the service, U-Verse is AT&T's service that bundles phone, internet, and television access into one package. So, it is similar to Comcast's "Triple Play" package.

It sounds like AT&T needs to either replace the USB adaptor or the wireless router that sends the signal to the USB adaptor. You may also want to go into the router settings and select a different WiFi channel since you may be experiencing interference from other wireless users around you. Consult the documentation that came with the router for instructions on how to do this.

Q. How can I use technology to grow my Life Coaching Business?
Stephanie Walkes

A. I think that any company from a small business to a Fortune 500 company will have to use technology to grow and survive. This is especially true with the emergence of social media services like Facebook and Twitter. That being said, I can suggest the following:

Blog: Set up a blog branded with your name (I checked and stephaniewalkes.com is currently available). You can use WordPress as the backend and Go Daddy to register the domain name. Create posts about the areas of your expertise. Comment on other blogs that cater to your market and, if you leave interesting comments, people will come to visit your blog. By regularly posting compelling content, you'll make connections with people who can help you or buy your services.

Facebook: You already have an account so use it to become friends with other Life Coaches. Follow their updates to see how they run their business. Again, make interesting posts on their walls and you'll see them (or their friends) begin to post on your wall. A large number of my 2000+ Facebook friends became connected with me by saying "I saw what you said on so-and-so's wall and just had to friend you". Create interesting Facebook notes and tag people who are Life Coaches in order to share your expertise. Tech Tuesdays have worked well for me so you may want to have a Coach Wednesday (or whatever day works best for you) where you offer free advice to anyone who posts a question. By doing that, you expand your brand as an expert and help people who may want to pay for full service.

Twitter: Twitter has a much smaller audience than Facebook, but you'll find a lot of Life Coaches use it. Seek them out and follow them on Twitter. Again, send interesting comments and they will usually reply to you. You can tweet about how you go about serving your clients and providing your services. Eventually, you'll have people following you in order to benefit from your expertise.

Q. How can I get a computer made to fit my school requirements but make sure it's the best bargain I can find?
Kim Maryland

A. Well, Dell pioneered the direct model where you give the exact requirements for your computer and they build it for you. However, the other major manufacturer's (HP, IBM, et al.) soon copied this so it's no longer the innovation it once was. However, I would suggest you go to each of the manufacturer websites and put in your specifications. Compare the prices they quote and then go with the cheapest option. You can also use this information if you when comparing prices of the options provided by brick and mortar retail outlets like Best Buy.

Netbooks are currently very popular, and you should probably consider them in your search. They are not good for intensive tasks like playing games or editing video. However, they are fine for taking notes in class or writing papers and are cheap.

On the other end of the price spectrum are Tablet PC's. They are usually quite expensive, but you can write on the screen which I think is ideal for students if you can afford them.

Afterword

Thanks for reading my book. This is the first book I ever published, and I never thought that I could produce a manuscript that turned out to be over 300 pages. However, it turns out that I was producing one every day simply through posting regular blog entries.

Being a minority in technology has allowed me to understand the fear that many people of color and women feel about entering the technology sector. Not only do you have to master hard disciplines like science, engineering, or math, but you will probably encounter people who think you don't deserve a place in the technology industry. They will think that you're some affirmative action charity case or that you used your feminine wiles to seduce your way into the field. You'll hear insensitive jokes or be asked to conform to racial stereotypes. Some may even be sexually assaulted or verbally abused.

It's still worth it.

Most people of color and women choose technology careers because they truly love technology. Perhaps they dream of writing elegant code, or data mining huge databases, designing a killer app, or leading a successful startup. There are few professions that offer high salaries with such a minimal investment. Most jobs in the technology industry simply require an undergraduate degree. Sure, you can become a doctor, but that requires years of medical school, residency, and the accumulation of massive levels of debt. Or, you can become an attorney, but you'll need to go to law school and pass a state bar. The technology industry is one of the few sectors of the economy that have such a low barrier to entry and a large return on your investment.

Also, the technology sectors needs diversity. Diverse teams lead to innovative ideas, and the world, especially the United States, is becoming browner every year. If technology companies want to make products and services that appeal to the people most likely to buy them, then they need to hire more women and people of color.